SR1507·12 TH1 27/6/06 YHB

Thinking
Through
SCIENCE

Arthur Cheney
Howard Flavell
Chris Harrison
George Hurst
Carolyn Yates

Series editor: Chris Harrison

3
BLUE

C

JOHN
MURRAY

The cover image shows a flower reflected in a dew drop.

Although every effort has been made to ensure that website addresses are correct at the time of going to press, John Murray (Publishers) Ltd cannot be held responsible for the content of any website mentioned in this book.

Papers used in this book are natural, renewable and recyclable products. They are made from wood grown in sustainable forests. The logging and manufacturing processes conform to the environmental regulations of the country of origin.

Orders: please contact Bookpoint Ltd, 130 Milton Park, Abingdon, Oxon OX14 4SB. Tel (44) 01235 827720. Fax (44) 01235 400454. Lines are open 9.00a.m.–6.00p.m., Monday to Saturday, with a 24-hour message answering service. You can also visit our website www.hodderheadline.co.uk and www.hoddersamplepages.co.uk

First published in 2004
by John Murray Publishers Ltd, a member of the Hodder Headline Group
338 Euston Road
London NW1 3BH

Impression number	10 9 8 7 6 5 4 3 2 1
Year	2007 2006 2005 2004

Layouts by Stephen Rowling/springworks
Artwork by Oxford Designers and Illustrators Ltd

Typeset in 11/13pt Lucida by Fakenham Phototypesetting

Printed and bound in Italy

A CIP catalogue record for this book is available from the British Library

ISBN 0 7195 7860 4
Teacher's Book Blue 3 0 7195 8058 7
CD-ROM 3 0 7195 7859 0

Contents

Acknowledgements

Source acknowledgements
The following are sources from which artwork and text have been taken:

p.1 'I keep six honest serving men...' from *The Elephant's Child*, by Rudyard Kipling. Voyager Books; **p.82** Which? Ltd; **p.156** NETCEN on behalf of DEFRA; **p.206** BBC News Online.

Photo credits
Thanks are due to the following for permission to reproduce copyright photographs:

Cover, p.i © Steve Terrill/CORBIS; **p.2** M.I. Walker/Science Photo Library; **p.9** *all* Andrew Lambert Photography/Science Photo Library; **p.10** *all* John townson/Creation; **p.21** *all* John Townson/Creation; **p.37** Action Plus/Chris Cole; **p.38** Lunagrafix/Science Photo Library; **p.43** Susumu Nishinaga/Science Photo Library; **p.48** *far l* Rex Features/Sipa Press, *c, r* John townson/Creation; **p.55** *tl* Jason Timson, *top r* Jeremy Horner/CORBIS, *bl, r* Mark de Fraeye/Science Photo Library; **p.59** John Townson/Creation; **p.71** Rex Features/David Hartley; **p.73** Alan Sirulnikoff/Science Photo Library; **p.76** *t* Alamy Images, *b* © Robin Adshead; **p.77** John Townson/Creation; **p.78** Martyn F. Chillmaid/Science Photo Library; **p.79** *tl* Victor de Schwanberg/Science Photo Library, *tr* John Townson/Creation, *b* Andrew Lambert Photography/Science Photo Library; **p.81** Sheila Terry/Science Photo Library; **p.83** *t* John Townson/Creation, *b* BDI Images; **p.84** © Chris Davies; **p.85** *tl, r* Alamy Images, *bl* © Woman Magazine/Rex Features; **p.95** *l* © Photography by Chris Davies, *r* Alan Schein Photography/CORBIS; **p.98** *l* Alex Bartel/Science Photo Library, *r* Joseph Sohm; ChromoSohm Inc./CORBIS; **p.101** *all* John Townson/Creation *except br* Cristina Pedrazzini; **p.105** *l* Photodisk; **p.112** NASA/Science Photo Library; *l* Sanford Roth/Science Photo Library, *r* © NASA/STScI/Corbis; **p.115** David A. Hardy/Science Photo Library; **p.116** *tl* US Air Force/Science Photo Library, *tr* Cinzano, Falchi, Eldvidge 2000/Blackwell, Science/Science Photo Library, *bl* NASA/Goddard Space Flight Center/Science Photo Library; **p.118** NASA/CORBIS; **p.125** Martin Dohrn/Science Photo Library, *bl, r* John Townson/Creation; **p.129** *all* John Townson/Creation *except cr* Rex Features; **p.130** *all* John Townson/Creation *except second row l* Grant Smith/CORBIS, *second row r* Carl & Ann Purcell/CORBIS; **p.131** *l* Andrew Lambert Photography/Science Photo Library, *r* John Townson/Creation; **p.132** *r* © Andrew Lambert; **p.135** John Townson/Creation; **p.138** NASA; **p.139** *all* John Townson/Creation; **p.141** Colin Garratt; Milepost 92 1/2/CORBIS; **p.143** David Butow/CORBIS SABA; **p.144** Roger Wood/CORBIS; **p.145** *t* Mary Evans Picture Library, *b* Archivo Iconografico, S.A./CORBIS; **p.146** *l* Robert Harding Picture Library, *r* © V&A Images; **p.150** *all* John Townson/Creation; **p.152** *tl* Dallas and John Heaton/CORBIS, *tr* Michael St. Maur Sheil/CORBIS, *b* Hans Georg Roth/CORBIS; **p.157** *t* Photodisk, *bl* Bob Krist/CORBIS, *br* Arte & Immagini srl/CORBIS; **p.162** Sheila Terry/Science Photo Library; **p.166** *both* © Andrew Lambert; **p.168** Joseph Sohm; ChromoSohm Inc./CORBIS; **p.169** Alamy Images; **p.172** *all* Bruce Coleman; **p.176** *tl* Jacqui Hurst/Corbis, *tc* Paul A. Souders/CORBIS, *tr, bl* John Townson/Creation, *br* Maximilian Stock Ltd/Science Photo Library, **p.178** *l* David Cole/Rex Features, *r* Stock Connection, Inc/Alamy, **p.179** *tl* Isopress Senepart/Rex Features, *tr* Astrid & Hanns-Frieder Michler/Science Photo Library, *b* Jeremy Walker/Science Photo Library; **p.180** *l* Bettmann/CORBIS, *r* Archivo Iconagrafico, S.A./CORBIS; **p.186** Dr Jeremy Burgess/Science Photo Library; **p.191** © CORBIS; **p.192** *l* Mary Evans Picture Library, *bc* © Bettmann/CORBIS; **p.194** *all* Lester V. Bergman/CORBIS; **p.198** *bl* Dr Jeremy Burgess/Science Photo Library, *br* Claude Nuridsany & Marie Perennou/Science Photo Library; **p.210** *l* © Rex Features, *r* © James Fraser/Rex Features; **p.205** Saturn Stills/Science Photo Library; **p.212** *from l to r* The Garden Picture Library/Alamy, © A C Searle/Rex Features, Neil Hardwick/Alamy, © Eric and David Hosking/CORBIS; **p.214** *t* Science Photo Library, *bl, c* © Bettmann/CORBIS, *br* Science Photo Library; **p.216** Alfred Pasieka/Science Photo Library; **p.218** *l* Sipa Press/Rex Features, *r* © Kim Kulish/CORBIS; **p.220** *both* © Bettmann/CORBIS; **p.222** *lt* © NHPA/Joe Blossom, *lc* Reuters/CORBIS, *lb* Dewitt Jones/CORBIS, *ct* © Tim Zurowski/CORBIS, *b* Tom Brakefield/CORBIS, *rt* © NHPA/Joe Blossom, *rc* Nils Jorgensen/Rex Features, *rb* Reuteurs/CORBIS; **p.223** *tl, c* Yann Arthus-Bertrand/CORBIS, *tr* Photolibrary/OSF/Mark Hamblin, *b all* John Townson/Creation; **p.224** *all* John Townson/Creation; **p.225** *all* John Townson/Creation; **p.226** CNRI/Science Photo Library; **p.232** Science Photo Library; **p.233** Sheila Terry/Science Photo Library; **p.235** *t* Elizabeth Lippmann/Rex Features, *b* Theo Allofs/CORBIS; **p.239** *both* © Andrew Lambert; **p.241** © Bettmann/CORBIS; **p.242** © Gabe Palmer/CORBIS; **p.243** Barry Batchelor/PA Photos; **p.246** *c* Getty Images/Stone, *bl* Science Photo Library; **p.249** *t* Bettmann/CORBIS, *b* John Townson/Creation; **p.251** Sam Ogden/Science Photo Library, *b* John Townson/Creation; **p.252** John Townson/Creation; **p.253** Topham Picturepoint; **p.258** Charles O'Rear/CORBIS; **p.261** Andrew Drysdale/Rex Features; **p.264** *l to r* Guy Motil/CORBIS, Picimpact/CORBIS, Klaus Guldbrandsen/Science Photo Library, Otto Rogge/CORBIS; **p.267** Mary Evans Picture Library; **p.270** TopFoto/Science Museum/HIP; **p.273** *l* Bojan Brecelj/CORBIS, *r* Firefly Productions/CORBIS; **p.274** Stefano Bianchett/CORBIS; **p.278** *tl* © Alamy Images, *r* BDI images, *c* © Alamy Images, *b* TopFoto/National Pictures; **p.285** Francoise Sauze/Science Photo Library.

l = left, *r* = right, *t* = top, *b* = bottom, *c* = centre

Introduction

→ Science audit sheet

An audit sheet is a checklist. Draw up a science audit sheet that shows the many skills that you already have.

SAFETY		SKILLS	
Know lab rules	✔	Read a 0–100°C thermometer	✔
Light a Bunsen burner	✔	Use a measuring cylinder	✔
Know when to wear safety specs	✔		
SET-UP		TESTS	
A mat, tripod and Bunsen burner	✔	Know how to test for oxygen	✔
A series circuit with 2 bulbs	✔	Know how to test for water	✔

→ Asking questions

Key words
* observations
* evidence
* inference
* disproof

Science helps us find out more about the world around us and how it works. An important skill in science is the ability to ask questions. The types of question that are important in science are not just the 'What?' questions, but also the 'How?' and 'Why?' questions. It is finding answers to the 'How?' and 'Why?' questions that drives forward ideas in science.

> I keep six honest serving men
> (They taught me all I knew);
> Their names are What and Why and When
> And How and Where and Who
>
> Rudyard Kipling

Let's look at an example. Here is an enlarged photograph of a small animal in a sample of pondwater.

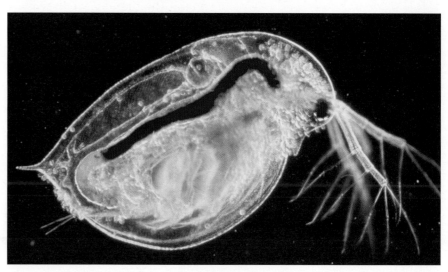

Here are some questions you might ask:

What is it?

How is it similar to other water animals I know?

How is it different from other water animals I know?

Does it have legs or fins? How does it move?

What does it feed on?

How does it manage to find and get that type of food?

What feeds on it?

How does it avoid or escape predators?

The answers to some of these questions can be worked out from careful **observations** which can become **evidence** to support ideas. This is strong evidence. Sometimes the evidence is rather weak and we make an educated guess as to what is happening. This is called **inference**.

In science we make many observations and inferences. In looking for more data we might strengthen our evidence for a particular idea. Sometimes more data makes us realise that our initial idea was wrong. This is called **disproof**, and it is a very important part of how scientists work.

We can answer some questions from our observations and experiments. The answers to other questions require research in books or on the internet, or finding an expert who can tell you what you need to know. While we have various ways of finding the answers, it's the framing of the questions that is the important first step.

Reasoning ## Sycamore

Look at the drawings and think about what questions you might ask. Here are a few to start with:

Why does the sycamore fruit have a wing?
Where do the sycamore fruits land when they drop from the tree?

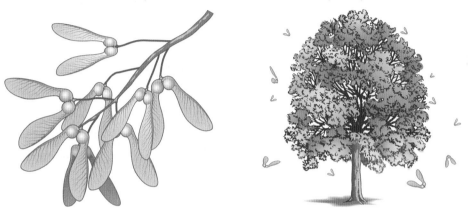

1 Compare your questions with others in your group.

2 Decide on a group list of good questions. Good questions will help you find out more about what is going on with this tree and its fruit.

3 As a group decide which questions you can answer.

4 Will research help you?

5 Would trying things out help you to find out more?

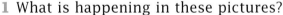

1 What is happening in these pictures?

2 Make a two-column table and fill in your observations and inferences. Remember – observations are what you can see, and inferences are what you think is happening.

3 Look at other pupils' tables and see if they have written down the same observations and inferences as you.

4 Why do you think you have made the inferences that you have?

5 Could the explanations for what you observe happening be different? Would it help to expand the picture that you are looking at? Would it help to look at the scene later?

6 Turn to page 4 and find a later scene of each picture.

Has more evidence changed your ideas?

→ Answering questions

Sometimes it is easy to see the answer to a question but difficult to find the words to answer it. Making key word and ideas cards for that topic helps you select the best ones to use in your answer.

Let's look at an example:

Why is glucose an example of a compound?

Key words in this topic area might be:

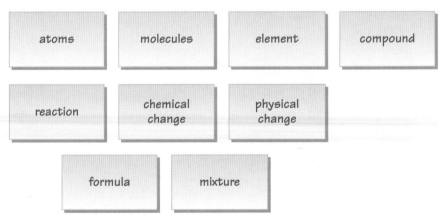

The answer might be:

Because **compounds** are made from two or more **elements** and glucose has carbon, hydrogen and oxygen **atoms** in it.

Reasoning ## Good answers

Try to work out good answers to some of the questions below. For each question first list the key words and ideas to help you word your answer.

1 Why is seawater an example of a mixture?

2 Why is copper used in electrical wiring?

3 How do the cells in heart muscle get their supply of oxygen?

Sometimes questions want us to look at an answer from two different viewpoints. Looking for what is the same between two things is sometimes harder than recognising the differences. Let's look at an example:

What is the same and what is different about tap water and seawater?

Listing 'What is the same?' and then listing 'What is different?' provides us with the information that we need to answer the whole question.

What is the same?	What is different?
both are liquids	seawater tastes salty
both have other chemicals dissolved in them	seawater contains a lot more salt
both are solutions	boats float more easily in seawater
	tap water has been treated to make it safe to drink

An answer might be:

Both tap water and seawater are solutions, that is liquids that have other chemicals dissolved in them. Seawater is salty because it contains more salt than tap water. This means that it helps boats float more easily than fresh water. Tap water is fresh water that has been made safe to drink in a purification plant.

Reasoning ## Same and different

Work out answers to some of the questions below. Each time make two lists of key words and ideas and use these to help you.

1 What is the same and what is different about birds and mammals?

2 Why are saucepans made of metal but their handles made of wood or plastic?

3 Why do both stirring and heating increase the rate at which sugar dissolves?

EXTENSION **4** What is similar and what is different about burning coal and solar heating?

→ *Answering in steps*

To explain an answer clearly we sometimes need to find steps in which to answer it. Often we need to select evidence and pick particular examples to explain our answer.

Let's look at an example. If we were asked:

Is it always true that green organisms photosynthesise?

we would need to ask ourselves:

What happens in photosynthesis?
Why is it important to organisms?
Which types of organisms photosynthesise?
Why has green been selected rather than blue or red?
What part has the 'greenness' to play in this answer?
Which green organisms do I know that do photosynthesise?
Which green organisms don't photosynthesise?

In answering these questions we are provided with the various parts that we need to answer the big question – Is it always true that green organisms photosynthesise?

The answer might be:

Photosynthesis is the way that plants trap the energy from sunlight to make glucose from carbon dioxide and water. Plants are able to photosynthesise because they contain the green pigment chlorophyll. Some animals are green, such as frogs and parrots, but this is not because they contain chlorophyll. Animals do not photosynthesise, and if they are green it is for some reason other than photosynthesis. So it is NOT always true that green organisms photosynthesise.

Reasoning Is it true?

Try to work out clear answers to some of the questions below. Each time make a list of smaller questions to help you find parts of the answer for the big question.

1 Is it true that metals conduct electricity?

2 Is it always true that water is a liquid?

EXTENSION **3** Is it always true that mammals give birth to live young?

You also need to look at questions carefully to check what they are really asking. Look at these questions. Do they mean the same as Question 1 above?

Is it true that only metals conduct electricity?
Is it always true that metals conduct electricity?

Try writing some 'Is it true?' and 'Is it always true?' questions for one of the topics that you have recently studied. Swap your questions with another pupil to answer, and try to answer their questions. Check that the answers you give are what they expected, and whether you have fully answered the question asked.

→ *Analysing data*

The data in the table below gives some information about public health in the nineteenth century. To make sense of the data we need to look at them very carefully.

Average ages of death in 1842

Type of people	Wiltshire	Liverpool
gentry, professional people and their families	49	45
farmers, tradesmen and their families	40	39
labourers and their families	37	32

7 What does the title of the table tell you about the data?
8 Look at the first column – Type of people.
  a) Which of these three groups is rich and which are poor?
  b) What would the lifestyles of gentry and professional people have been like?
  c) What would the lifestyles of farmers and tradesmen have been like?
  d) What would the lifestyle of labourers have been like?
  e) Which of these groups would have had the hardest lifestyle?
  f) Which of these groups is likely to have had a good diet?
  g) Which of these groups is likely to have come into contact with disease organisms?
9 The first row of the table tells us that the data are about people living in two different places. What is similar and what is different about Wiltshire and Liverpool?
10 Which parts of the table tell us that rich people live longer than poor people?
11 a) Does the data tell us that people lived longer in the towns than the countryside in 1842, or that those who lived in the countryside lived longer than those in towns?
  b) Which parts of the table tells us this?
12 In your opinion, which is the best way to present this data – a line graph or bar chart? Why?

EXTENSION 13 Use your answers to Questions 7–12 to write a summary that would explain what the table of data shows.

1 Salts of the Earth

In this chapter you will learn:

➡ about the properties of metals and non-metals
➡ that different acids react in similar ways with metals
➡ that different acids react in similar ways with metal oxides
➡ that different acids react in similar ways with metal carbonates
➡ to describe how metal salts are made and explain some of their uses
➡ how to recognise that a chemical reaction has taken place
➡ how to represent elements by symbols and compounds by formulae
➡ how to use word equations to describe the above reactions

You will also develop your skills in:

➡ describing patterns in qualitative data about reactions
➡ using patterns in reactions to make predictions about other reactions
➡ devising and evaluating a method for preparing a sample of a salt
➡ using models to recognise what happens in a reaction

➡➡➡ WHAT DO YOU KNOW?

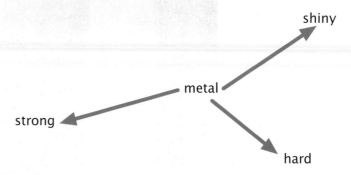

Key words
* elements
* symbols

1 Look at the concept map about metals. It has not been completed. Copy it onto a large sheet of paper and let each member of your group add in one link until you have included all the ones that you can think of. Compare your concept map with that of another group. Look for similarities and differences.

Magnesium reacting with
dilute hydrochloric acid.

Limestone (calcium carbonate)
reacting with dilute hydrochloric acid.

2 Both of the above chemical reactions produce a gas. Which gas is
produced in the reaction between:
  a) hydrochloric acid and magnesium
  b) hydrochloric acid and limestone (calcium carbonate)?

These are some of the tests that scientists use to identify
different gases:

Test	Method
1	bubble the gas through Universal Indicator solution
2	bubble the gas through limewater
3	place a burning splint at the top of a test tube of a mixture of the gas and air
4	place a burning splint into a test tube full of the gas
5	place a glowing splint into a test tube full of the gas

3 In which of these test tubes do you think a chemical reaction is
taking place. Why?

4 Name ten **elements**. Can you remember their **symbols**? Divide
them into groups. You could divide them into solids, liquids and
gases, or into metals and non-metals.

What are salts?

Key words
* salts
* minerals
* substances

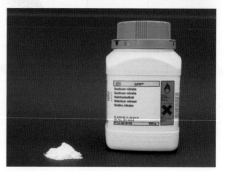

In *Thinking Through Science 1* (Book 1) and *Thinking Through Science 2* (Book 2) you will have come across **salts** such as common salt (sodium chloride), Glauber's salt (sodium sulphate) and plaster of Paris (calcium sulphate).

1 Pick two of these salts and write a sentence about each one.

Some salts, such as calcium sulphate, are found as **minerals** in the Earth's crust, and there is a plentiful supply of them. Others, such as sodium nitrate, can be found as minerals but they are in very short supply. Some salts, such as copper chloride, are not found naturally.

Scientists have found ways of making these salts by chemical reactions between other **substances**. This is what you will be looking at in this chapter.

Common salt is just one example of a metal salt. Many of these salts have important uses:

Salt	Use
copper chloride	cures fish fungus
sodium chloride	preserving food
copper sulphate	cures plant fungus
calcium sulphate	plaster casts
sodium nitrate	plant fertiliser

The simplest way to make a salt is to react an acid with either a <u>metal</u>, a <u>metal carbonate</u> or a <u>metal oxide</u>.

acid + metal → salt

acid + metal carbonate → salt

acid + metal oxide → salt

The pair of reacting substances must be chosen carefully because some may react explosively, and others may react too slowly or not react at all.

2 a) Which metal oxide and which acid react together to make copper chloride?

b) Which metal carbonate and which acid react together to make copper nitrate?

The salt sodium nitrate (Chile saltpetre) is only found in the desert regions of Chile in South America. In this part of Chile it hardly ever rains. Sodium nitrate is very soluble in water, and scientists think that this is why it is only found in this region – it would be washed away by the rain in wetter areas.

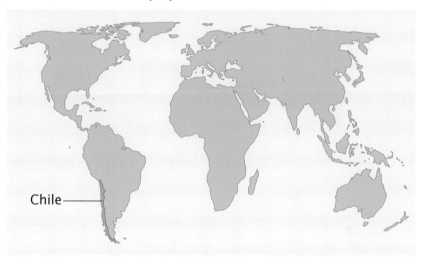

Chile

→ *Reacting acids with metals*

Key words
* metals
* non-metals
* periodic table

In Book 2 we saw that all materials are made up of just a few elements. The elements can be divided into **metals** and **non-metals**.

3 Which of these are properties of metals but are not properties of non-metals? Compare your answers with others in your group. Make a group list of the differences between metals and non-metals. Can you think of any differences that aren't listed?
* conduct electricity
* always shiny
* always solids
* sometimes solids
* magnetic
* sometimes soluble
* never soluble

4 Look at the following diagram. Is it always true that metals are listed in the shaded part of the **periodic table**?

8

group: 1 2

																	2 He
3 Li	4 Be											5 B	6 C	7 N	8 O	9 F	10 Ne
11 Na	12 Mg											13 Al	14 Si	15 P	16 S	17 Cl	18 Ar
19 K	20 Ca	21 Sc	22 Ti	23 V	24 Cr	25 Mn	26 Fe	27 Co	28 Ni	29 Cu	30 Zn	31 Ga	32 Ge	33 As	34 Se	35 Br	36 Kr
37 Rb	38 Sr	39 Y	40 Zr	41 Nb	42 Mo	43 Tc	44 Ru	45 Rh	46 Pd	47 Ag	48 Cd	49 In	50 Sn	51 Sb	52 Te	53 I	54 Xe
55 Cs	56 Ba	57 La	72 Hf	73 Ta	74 W	75 Re	76 Os	77 Ir	78 Pt	79 Au	80 Hg	81 Tl	82 Pb	83 Bi	84 Po	85 At	86 Rn

1 H

key: ▢ metal

▢ metalloid (have some of the properties of metals)

Research — Make a card game to help you learn the names and symbols of elements in the periodic table.

In Book 1 we saw that the metal magnesium reacts with dilute hydrochloric acid to produce bubbles of the gas hydrogen.

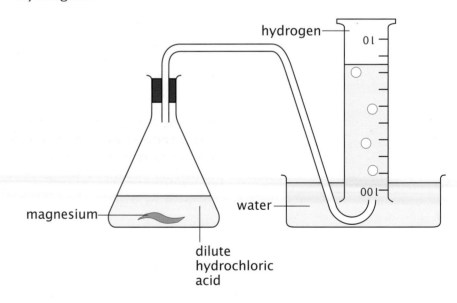

When the reaction is complete, the measuring cylinder contains hydrogen gas. All of the magnesium has reacted.

5 Where do you think the hydrogen came from?

Key words

* scientific method
* evidence
* hypothesis
* prediction

A scientific way of experimenting

One scientific way of experimenting is by the **scientific method**, which is used by many scientists throughout the world. This is how it works:

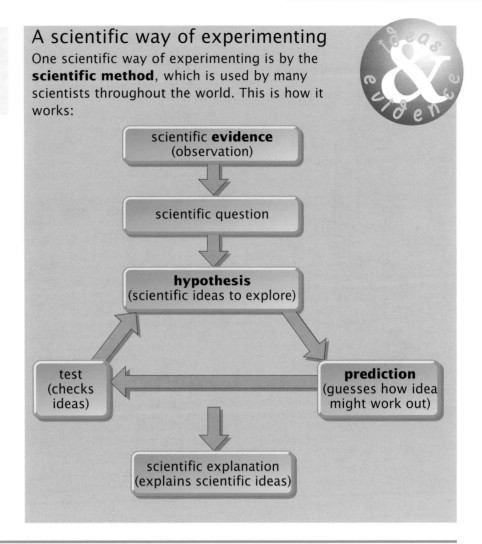

Enquiry *Do other acids react with metals to produce hydrogen?*

The scientific method can be used to answer scientific questions about the reaction of magnesium with dilute hydrochloric acid.

This cartoon strip shows how we might answer the question 'Do other acids react with metals to produce hydrogen?'.

What do you think will happen?

Scientific evidence   **Scientific question**

I wonder if other acids react with magnesium to produce hydrogen...

Maybe it is just **hydro**chloric acid that reacts because it is the only acid with **hydro** in its name, which means that it contains **hydro**gen.

Hypothesis

When sulphuric acid is added to magnesium, hydrogen will **not** be formed because the acid does not have **hydro** in its name.

Prediction

I will add a piece of magnesium ribbon to some dilute sulphuric acid. No gas should be given off, but if it is I will test it to see if it is hydrogen.

Test

Result

1 Draw a similar cartoon strip to show how we might answer a different question such as 'Where has the magnesium gone?' or 'Do other metals react with hydrochloric acid to produce hydrogen?'. Compare your cartoon strip with at least two others in your class.

Formulae

Key words
* atom
* compounds
* formulae

Elements are pure substances containing only one type of **atom**. **Compounds** contain two or more types of atom. The **formulae** of chemicals tell us which type of atoms (elements) a substance contains, and how many of each atom there are in each molecule.

6 Copy and complete the table below:

Substance	Type and number of atoms	Element or compound
Mg	1 Mg	element
H_2O	2 H 1 O	compound
HCl		
H_2		
$MgCl_2$		
H_2SO_4		

7 Can you match each substance with its correct formula?

carbon dioxide O_2
hydrochloric acid   NaOH
oxygen CO_2
sodium hydroxide   HCl

→ Equations

Key words
* word equations
* symbol equation

In Books 1 and 2 you were introduced to **word equations**. They are used to summarise chemical reactions. These are the word equations for three reactions:

$$\text{sodium hydroxide} + \text{hydrochloric acid} \rightarrow \text{sodium chloride} + \text{water}$$

$$\text{magnesium} + \text{hydrochloric acid} \rightarrow \text{magnesium chloride} + \text{hydrogen}$$

$$\text{magnesium} + \text{sulphuric acid} \rightarrow \text{magnesium sulphate} + \text{hydrogen}$$

Word equations are useful for making predictions about reactions by looking for patterns. For example:

Pattern	Prediction
hydrogen is formed when magnesium (a metal) reacts with two different acids	all metals react with acids to form hydrogen

If the names of the substances in a word equation are replaced by chemical symbols, we get a **symbol equation**. This type of equation tells us the ratio of the number of atoms of each element involved in the reaction. It also shows us the ratio of the particles of each substance in the reaction. For example, the reaction of sodium hydroxide with hydrochloric acid is shown below as both a symbol equation and particle picture:

$$NaOH + HCl \rightarrow NaCl + H_2O$$

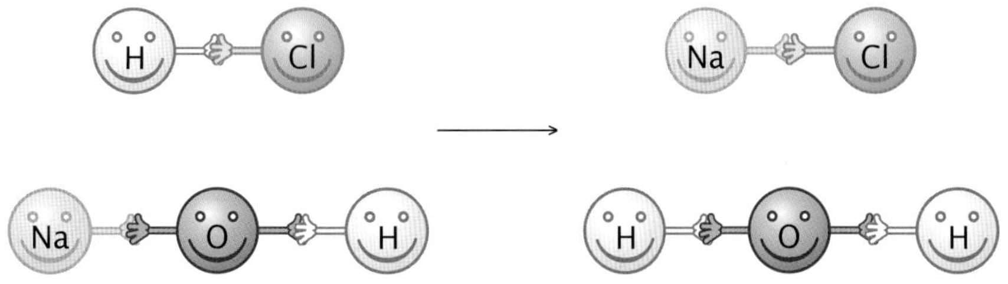

From the particle picture we can see that when a chemical reaction occurs the atoms of the elements involved do not change into other elements. They change their 'partners'.

For example in hydrochloric acid the chlorine atom is bonded to the hydrogen atom, but after the chemical reaction it is bonded to the sodium atom.

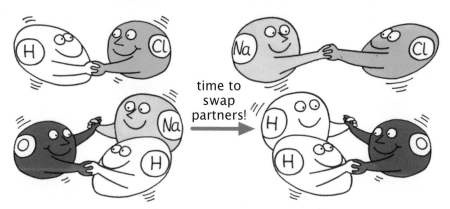

Word play | What is a symbol? Think of some of the symbols that you see every day.

→ # Balancing equations

Key words
* balance
* ratios

To understand how equations **balance** in chemistry we need to think about **ratios**. If you have 12 sweets and divide them equally between two people, each person will get six sweets.

Susie

6
1 share

James

6
1 share

The ratio is 1:1.

If you decide to give Susie twice as many sweets as James, the share is different.

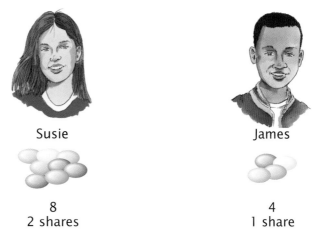

Susie	James
8	4
2 shares	1 share

The ratio is 2:1.

If you decide to give James twice as many sweets as Susie then the share is different again.

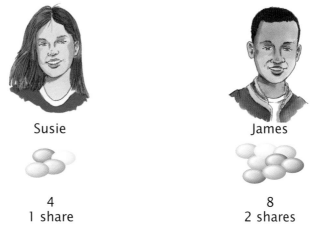

Susie	James
4	8
1 share	2 shares

The ratio is 1:2.

Ratio of atoms on each side of the equation

The information in the table comes from the symbol equation for the reaction of sodium hydroxide with hydrochloric acid given on page 15.

Element	Number of atoms on the left	Number of atoms on the right
Na	1	1
O	1	1
H	2	2
Cl	1	1

From the table we can see that there are the same number of atoms of each element on both sides of the equation.

This shows that a symbol equation must always balance.

Element	Number of atoms
Na	1
O	1
H	2
Cl	1

Element	Number of atoms
Na	1
O	1
H	2
Cl	1

Word play

The word 'balanced' can have different meanings in science compared with everyday use. Discuss the meaning of 'balanced' in the following sentences:

1 The circus performer balanced a chair on her head.
2 Peter gave a balanced viewpoint on using animals for testing drugs.
3 Paul is very careful to follow a balanced diet.
4 Molly has balanced the symbol equation to give the right answer.

In which of these sentences is 'balanced' used scientifically?
Make up one more scientific sentence using the word 'balanced'.

Reasoning   ## Making predictions

The word equation for the reaction of magnesium with hydrochloric acid is:

magnesium + hydrochloric acid → magnesium chloride + hydrogen

In one class pupils gave three different predictions to explain what would happen to the magnesium if it reacted with hydrochloric acid.

1 a) What is a prediction?

b) Which of the three predictions do you agree with? Why?

c) What test would you carry out to test the prediction that you have selected?

2 Would you expect the metals zinc, iron and copper to react with hydrochloric acid in a way similar to how magnesium reacts with hydrochloric acid? Write a word equation for each reaction.

Information processing   ## Recognising patterns

The results from some experiments involving metals and acids are shown in the table below.

Metal	Acid	Observations	Hydrogen formed?
aluminium	sulphuric	fizzing after a while	✓
calcium	hydrochloric	fizzing, solid made which dissolves	✓
lead	sulphuric	no bubbles	✗
calcium	sulphuric	fizzing, but stops after a while	✓
lead	hydrochloric	no bubbles	✗
aluminium	hydrochloric	fizzing after a while	✓

1 Copy the table, reorganising it so that it shows the order of reactivity.

2 Is it true to say that all metals react with dilute acids?

The word equations for two of the reactions in the table are:

calcium + hydrochloric acid → calcium chloride + hydrogen

aluminium + sulphuric acid → aluminium sulphate + hydrogen

3 Is it true that all metal and acid reactions produce the same gas?

➡ # Reacting metal oxides and acids

We have seen that some metals react with some acids to make metal salts, but not all salts are made this way. This reaction cannot be used to make salts such as copper sulphate, which is used as a cure for plant fungus, and sodium nitrate, which is used as a fertiliser.

8 a) Think of a reason why the 'metal + acid' reaction cannot be used to make the salt copper sulphate.

b) Think of a reason why the 'metal + acid' reaction cannot be used to make the salt sodium nitrate.

To make salts such as copper sulphate and sodium nitrate the metal *oxide* can be used instead of the metal.

For example, copper oxide and sulphuric acid will react together to produce copper sulphate. When they react together water is also produced.

9 To make the salt sodium nitrate:
  a) Which metal compound might you use?
  b) Which dilute acid would you use?
  c) What might you expect to see if a reaction occurs?
  d) The metal salt that is produced in the reaction will be in solution. How would you separate the metal salt from the water?

Enquiry ## Obtaining evidence

We know that metal oxides can be used to make metal salts. The following experimental write-up is taken from a pupil's exercise book.

Making a metal salt

We measured 20 cm³ of dilute hydrochloric acid into a 25 cm³ measuring cylinder and then poured it into a 100 cm³ beaker.

We gently warmed the acid until it was about 60°C.

We added one spatula-end of black copper oxide and stirred it.

The black powder dissolved in the acid to form a blue/green solution.

We kept adding copper oxide until some remained undissolved.

We filtered the mixture using a funnel and filter paper.

The liquid in the beaker went a deep blue.

We then slowly evaporated the mixture by heating it with a Bunsen burner.

We saw some blue crystals in the bottom of the evaporating dish.

Beakers are available in many sizes.

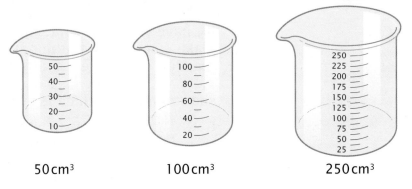

50 cm³   100 cm³   250 cm³

1 Why was the 100 cm³ beaker best for this experiment?

2 Why is it dangerous to boil an acid?

3 What is the evidence that a chemical reaction has occurred in this experiment?

4 Why did further copper oxide eventually no longer react?

5 What substance caused the blue colour?

6 Why was the blue solution heated?

7 What would be a good conclusion for this experiment? Get another group to check your answer.

Reasoning ## Metal oxide equations

The general word equation for the reaction of a metal oxide with a dilute acid is:

metal oxide + acid $\longrightarrow$ metal salt + water

1 Write out word equations for the following reactions:

    a) zinc oxide + sulphuric acid $\longrightarrow$

    b) calcium oxide + nitric acid $\longrightarrow$

    c) magnesium oxide + hydrochloric acid $\longrightarrow$

Reaction of metal carbonates with dilute acids

Information processing ## Recognising patterns for metal carbonates

iron carbonate

magnesium carbonate

The results from an experiment using the three common acids (sulphuric, nitric and hydrochloric) are shown in the table below.

Metal carbonate	Dilute acid	Observations	CO_2 formed?
iron carbonate	hydrochloric	fizzing, green solid produced which dissolves	✓
potassium carbonate	hydrochloric	fizzing, white solid produced which dissolves	✓
iron carbonate	sulphuric	fizzing, green solid produced which dissolves	✓
magnesium carbonate	hydrochloric	fizzing, white solid produced which dissolves	✓
iron carbonate	nitric	fizzing, green solid produced which dissolves	✓
magnesium carbonate	sulphuric	fizzing, white solid produced which dissolves	✓
potassium carbonate	sulphuric	fizzing, white solid produced which dissolves	✓
magnesium carbonate	nitric	fizzing, white solid produced which dissolves	✓
potassium carbonate	nitric	fizzing, white solid produced which dissolves	✓

Use the data to answer the following questions:

1 Do all metal carbonates react with dilute acids?

2 Name one substance that is formed in all of the reactions. How would you test for this?

3 Name two differences between the reaction of metals with acids and the reaction of metal carbonates with acids.

The word equations for three of the reactions in the above table are:

iron carbonate + hydrochloric acid → iron chloride + carbon dioxide + water

magnesium carbonate + nitric acid → magnesium nitrate + carbon dioxide + water

potassium carbonate + sulphuric acid → potassium sulphate + carbon dioxide + water

4 Use the pattern in the above three equations to write word equations for the following reactions from the table:
a) iron carbonate + sulphuric acid →
b) potassium carbonate + nitric acid →
c) magnesium carbonate + hydrochloric acid →

5 Write a general word equation for the reaction of a metal carbonate with an acid:

metal carbonate + acid →

6 Which question or questions did you find easy and which ones were hard? Do others in your group agree with you?

Time to think

Here are three incomplete word equations that describe how to make metal salts.

metal + acid ⟶

metal carbonate + acid ⟶

metal oxide + acid ⟶

1 Working in groups, use individual pieces of card to make:

- seven plus sign cards
- three arrow cards
- three metal salt cards
- three acid cards
- one hydrogen card
- one metal card
- one metal oxide card
- one metal carbonate card
- one carbon dioxide card
- two water cards

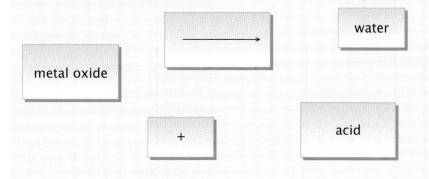

2 Use the cards to complete the word equations.

DID YOU KNOW?

Algal blooms make ponds turn green and kill off pond life. This happens when excess sodium nitrate fertiliser gets washed out of the soil and into the pond. The fertiliser causes algae to reproduce very rapidly, using up all the available oxygen.

➡ *Purity*

Key words
* pure
* impurities
* fungicide
* soluble
* titration
* neutralise
* burette

When we make a metal salt for a particular use, it must be **pure**. Any **impurities** from the reaction must be removed during the process. For example, copper sulphate is a **fungicide** – it reduces fungal infections in plants. Copper sulphate is made from copper oxide and sulphuric acid. If the copper sulphate that is produced has some copper oxide mixed with it, it is not such an effective fungicide. The excess copper oxide is removed by filtering.

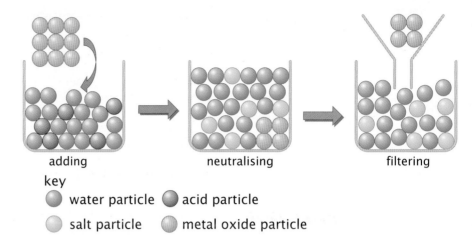

adding — neutralising — filtering

key
- water particle
- acid particle
- salt particle
- metal oxide particle

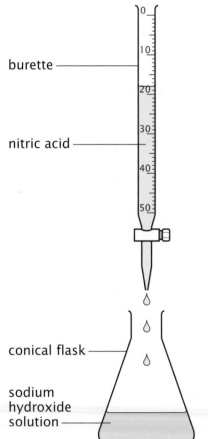

burette

nitric acid

conical flask

sodium hydroxide solution

Sodium oxide and sodium carbonate are both **soluble** in water. They are used to make sodium nitrate fertiliser. If the wrong amount of sodium oxide or sodium carbonate is used in the reaction, it makes the fertiliser impure. This can harm the plants when it is used as a fertiliser. If not enough oxide or carbonate is used there will be some acid left over. This acid will mix with the sodium nitrate and damage the plants.

To measure out the correct amounts of reactants a special method is used. This is called the **titration** method. It uses a precise amount of a solution of the metal carbonate or metal hydroxide to **neutralise** the acid.

$$\text{sodium hydroxide} + \text{nitric acid} \rightarrow \text{sodium nitrate} + \text{water}$$

$$\text{NaOH} + \text{HNO}_3 \rightarrow \text{NaNO}_3 + \text{H}_2\text{O}$$

10 How does a **burette** work? Why is it better to use a burette than a measuring cylinder for carrying out titrations?

11 How could you check that all of the sodium hydroxide had reacted with the nitric acid?

12 What safety precautions would you take when doing this experiment?

Reasoning *Making potassium chloride*

The titration method is also used to make salts such as potassium chloride.

1 Give the main steps in the method, and the names of the metal hydroxide and acid needed to make potassium chloride. Include a word equation.

Research

For each of the salts listed below, name the two substances that are used to make it, and find out an everyday use of the salt. Use the internet, CD-ROMs, library books or other sources to help you.

- potassium nitrate
- iron sulphate
- magnesium sulphate
- sodium stearate

Make a leaflet or poster to explain the use of the salts to others.

Time to think

These are some of the things that you should know, having worked through this chapter.
You should be able to:

- recognise when a chemical reaction is occurring, for example, 'the test tube got hotter'
- write word equations for some reactions
- describe the pattern in some similar word equations and produce a general equation
- work out the number of atoms of each element present in a formula.

Working in groups, write five questions that could assess some of the above outcomes. Swap your questions with another group and see if you can answer their questions. Swap answers and see how many each group got correct. Make a note of what you need to study to get any wrong answers correct in the future.

2 Fit and healthy

In this chapter you will learn:

➜ how the human respiratory, digestive and circulatory systems interact to maintain activity
➜ the functions of the human skeleton
➜ how diet, drugs, exercise and smoking affect health
➜ the difference between fitness and health
➜ the role of vitamins and minerals in staying healthy
➜ about the effects of stress

You will also develop your skills in:

➜ collecting sufficient, reliable data to form conclusions
➜ plotting, drawing and interpreting graphs
➜ evaluating conflicting evidence
➜ working collaboratively to carry out a scientific investigation

➡ ➡ ➡ WHAT DO YOU KNOW?

Fitness means different things to different people.

What does it mean to you? What does it mean to other people in your group?

How do you stay fit?

Can you be fit but not healthy?

Can you be healthy but not fit?

Working with your group, on a large sheet of paper draw two boxes like this:

In the first box list the five most important things that you must do to stay healthy.

In the second box write the five things you think are the biggest dangers to health.

Compare your lists with other groups in your class. Which ideas are similar and which are different?

As a class, decide on the top three factors necessary for good health, and the top three dangers to health.

Do you think other classes would agree with you?

Research The internet can help you find the answers to lots of questions about personal health. Use a search engine like Google or Yahoo! and type in some key words, for example, 'kids' health'. Look at some of the websites that you find.

→ *Fitness*

Key words
* fitness
* rate

Fitness can be measured by how quickly the heart recovers to its normal resting **rate** of beating after vigorous exercise. An average adult healthy heart beats 65 to 75 times a minute. During a race the heart rate will increase to about 180 beats per minute. A fit person's heart rate will return to normal within 3 minutes of the end of the race; it may take up to 10 minutes for an unfit person's heart rate to return to normal.

Enquiry *Fitness test*

Form a team of four people. Design and carry out an investigation to compare your team members' fitness.

1 First decide which of these activities you will use as a suitable test of fitness:

Running up and down a short flight of stairs five times.
Running round the playing field once.
Sitting at a desk for 5 minutes.
Touching your toes and stretching up above your head 20 times.

2 Will each person do the same activity, or will you let each person choose his or her own activity? Explain your decisions.

3 What are the **independent** (input) **variables** and the **dependent** (outcome) **variables** in your investigation?

4 When you carry out the investigation, what health and safety measures will you think about? Your teacher will help you with this.

5 Record each person's pulse rate straight after the exercise and then 3 minutes later. Why does the pulse rate indicate how fit your heart is?

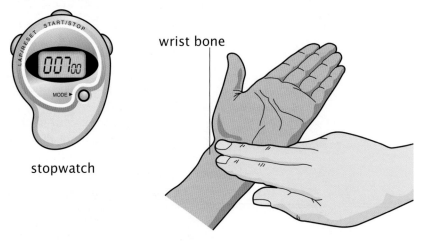

stopwatch

wrist bone

How to measure pulse rates.

6 Draw a suitable table to record your results in. Your table needs to include the name of each person doing the exercise, and their two pulse rate readings.

7 Whose heart rate returns to their normal resting rate after exercise most quickly? What does this indicate?

8 To make your investigation more **reliable**, which of these will you do?

Repeat the whole investigation at least once more, having given everyone time for his or her pulse rate to return to normal.

Include another groups' results with yours so that your sample of people is bigger.

Measure the pulse rate at more frequent intervals, for example immediately before the exercise, immediately after, 1 minute after, 2 minutes after, 3 minutes after, etc.

Explain your groups' thinking.

9 To decide who is the fittest in your team, which of the following would you do?

Repeat the investigation and compare the average results for each person.

Only compare the pulse rate after 3 minutes, ignoring the first reading when the activity stops.

Plot a graph of the resting pulse rate and the final pulse rate for everybody.

Explain your group's thinking.

Word play

The *Oxford Dictionary* definition of 'reliable' is:
an adjective; to be certain, conscientious, consistent, constant, dependable, devoted, efficient, faithful, honest, loyal, predictable, proven, regular, safe, solid, sound, stable, steady, sure, trusted, unchanging, unfailing.

With a partner, look at each word and list the definitions that you think a scientist would use to describe how an experiment is reliable.

Two definitions of **reliability** are:
1 a noun meaning the quality or state of being reliable
2 the extent to which an experiment, test or measuring procedure gives the same results in repeated trials.

Make up two sentences using the word 'reliability', one for each of its meanings.

→ # *The human body as a system*

Key words
* system
* digestive system
* respiratory system
* circulatory system
* interrelate

A **system** is made up of sets of things or parts that operate together to function as a whole.

1 What parts make up these systems:
  a) a railway system
  b) an education system
  c) the heating system in your house?

Here is a diagram showing how the body systems interact to keep operating effectively.

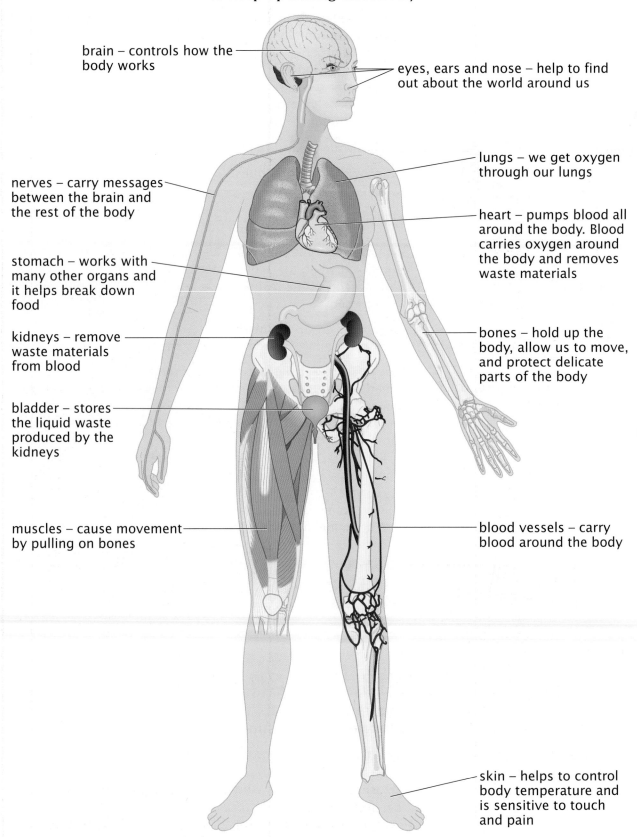

brain – controls how the body works

eyes, ears and nose – help to find out about the world around us

nerves – carry messages between the brain and the rest of the body

lungs – we get oxygen through our lungs

heart – pumps blood all around the body. Blood carries oxygen around the body and removes waste materials

stomach – works with many other organs and it helps break down food

kidneys – remove waste materials from blood

bones – hold up the body, allow us to move, and protect delicate parts of the body

bladder – stores the liquid waste produced by the kidneys

muscles – cause movement by pulling on bones

blood vessels – carry blood around the body

skin – helps to control body temperature and is sensitive to touch and pain

The human body is complex and made up of lots of interacting systems.

The **digestive**, **respiratory** and **circulatory systems** all **interrelate** (connect with each other) to keep us healthy.

2 Which set of organs make up these systems in the human body:
a) the circulatory system
b) the digestive system
c) the respiratory system?

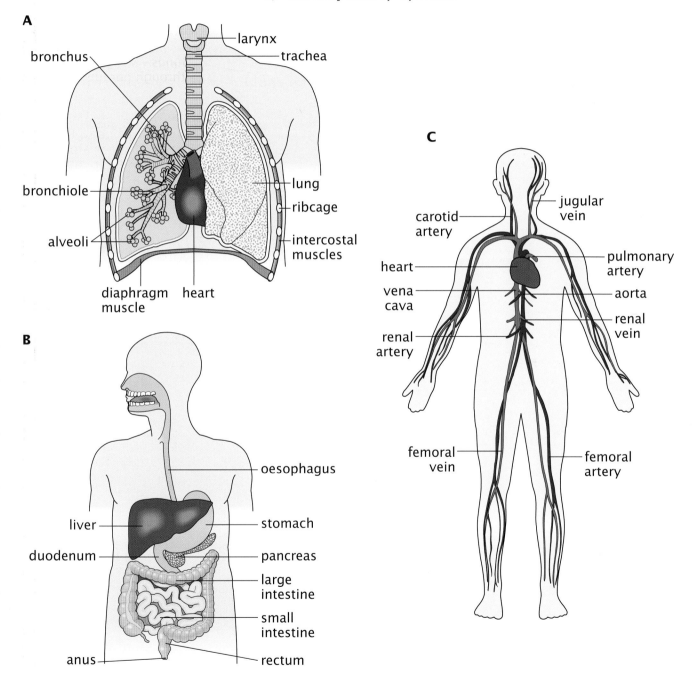

3 Which organs help you take in oxygen and give out carbon dioxide?
4 Which organ pumps blood around the body? Why is blood important to our health?
5 Where is food digested?

→ *The support and movement system*

Key words
* muscles
* skeleton
* bone
* cartilage
* connective tissue
* ligaments
* tendons
* contract
* mitochondria
* contracting
* relaxed

The skeleton

Fitness depends on how well the **muscles** and **skeleton** function together as a system.

6 Sketch a rough copy of this skeleton in your notebook. Without looking at the diagram here, label the parts of the skeleton that you know the names for. Look at your partner's labels. Who could remember the most names?

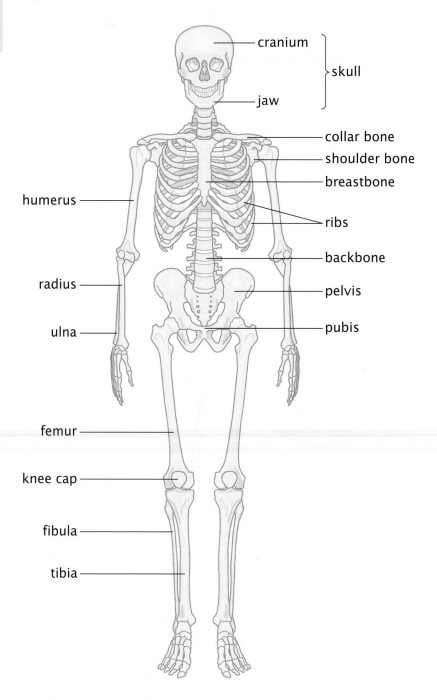

- cranium
- skull
- jaw
- collar bone
- shoulder bone
- breastbone
- humerus
- ribs
- backbone
- radius
- pelvis
- ulna
- pubis
- femur
- knee cap
- fibula
- tibia

7 Fill in those that you did not know by looking at the labelled diagram opposite.

8 Decide what grade you and your partner deserve:

A – excellent memory
B – good memory
C – need to improve memory

The skeleton is part of the system that moves and supports your body. This system is made up of **bone**, **cartilage**, **connective tissue** (**ligaments** and **tendons**) and muscle. Ligaments hold the bones together. Tendons attach the muscles to the bone.

A nerve impulse to the muscles causes them to **contract**. This requires energy. Muscle cells get their energy from **mitochondria**. Mitochondria release energy from sugar during cell respiration. Muscles need a good supply of blood so that the cells get lots of oxygen for cell respiration. As muscle fibres contract they get shorter and pull on the bones. This causes movement. Muscles work in pairs because they can pull but cannot push.

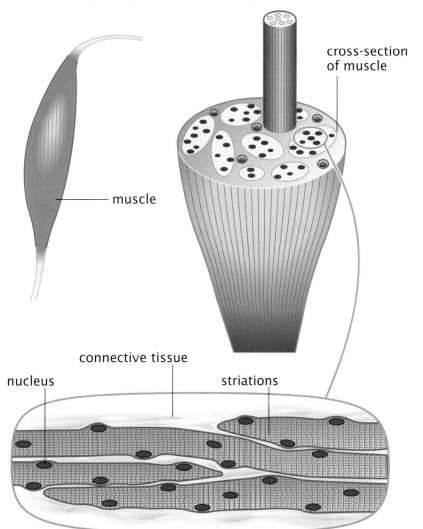

cross-section of muscle

muscle

connective tissue

nucleus

striations

Time to think

1 Copy this drawing of a leg and add labels (at 1, 2, 3 and 4) to explain how it moves. The arrow on the drawing shows which way that part of the limb is moving. Indicate which muscles are getting shorter (**contracting**) and which are being stretched (**relaxed**).

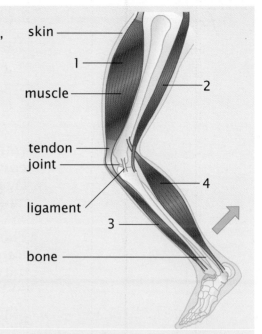

skin

1

muscle

2

tendon

joint

ligament

4

3

bone

2 One of the jobs of bones is to protect delicate parts of the body. Which parts of the body do these bones protect:
   a) ribs
   b) skull
   c) pelvis?
3 Why do muscle cells need a good blood supply?
4 What part of the cell releases energy from sugar?
5 What is this energy used for in muscle cells?
6 Which type of cell do you think will contain the most mitochondria – a muscle cell or a bone cell? Why?

Creative thinking No skeleton

Imagine what your body would be like without a skeleton. Think about a jellyfish – it does not have a skeleton. Think about how we move. How does a jellyfish move? If you lived in the sea, what features would you want to be added to your skeleton?

Research

When people play sport and train seriously they may put a lot of strain on parts of their bodies.
   Have you or anyone in your group ever had a sports-related injury? If so, what happened and how did it get better?

Information processing *Sports injuries*

Look at this bar chart:

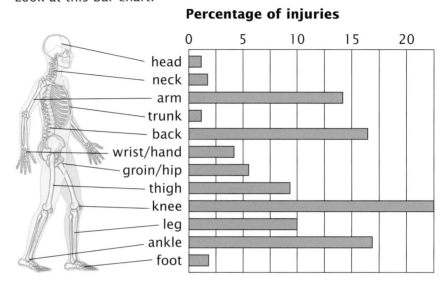

Percentage of injuries

1 What data does the bar chart show?

2 Which parts of the body are most likely to be damaged during sports?

3 What type of sports do you think cause these frequent injuries? Why?

4 Which area of the body is most likely to get damaged if you play:
   ▪ squash
   ▪ football
   ▪ netball?

5 Match the definitions to the parts of the support and locomotion system:

attaches muscle to bones	cartilage
work in pairs to move limbs	mitochondria
part of a cell that releases energy from sugar	tendon
place where two bones move relative to each other	joint
joins bones to each other at the joints	muscle

DID YOU KNOW? Old bone is constantly broken down and replaced by new bone cells. In childhood this happens very rapidly, but by their mid-20s most people have reached their full bone mass and after that bone cells do not replace themselves as fast as they die, so bone mass starts to decrease.

Research

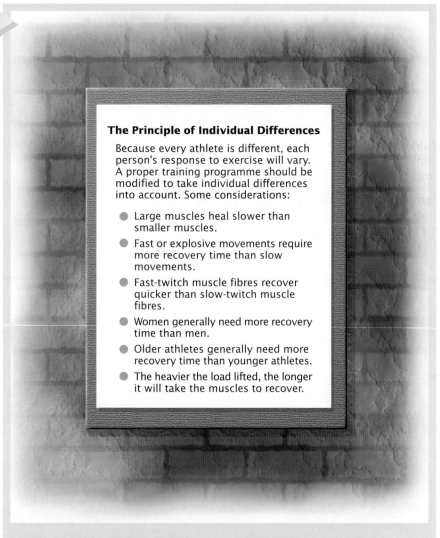

The Principle of Individual Differences

Because every athlete is different, each person's response to exercise will vary. A proper training programme should be modified to take individual differences into account. Some considerations:

● Large muscles heal slower than smaller muscles.

● Fast or explosive movements require more recovery time than slow movements.

● Fast-twitch muscle fibres recover quicker than slow-twitch muscle fibres.

● Women generally need more recovery time than men.

● Older athletes generally need more recovery time than younger athletes.

● The heavier the load lifted, the longer it will take the muscles to recover.

These are just some of the many things that have to be considered when deciding an athlete's training routine.

Information processing ## Safe training

Interview your PE teachers to find out how they decide what training each school team needs. Record what you find out – you could use a tape recorder or make notes. Check back with your PE teachers that you have recorded their responses to your questions correctly.

You could use your interview to write a short article for the school newspaper or prospectus.

→ *Knee joint*

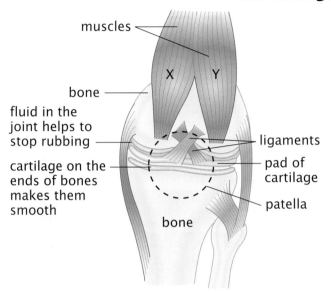

muscles

bone

fluid in the joint helps to stop rubbing

cartilage on the ends of bones makes them smooth

bone

X   Y

ligaments

pad of cartilage

patella

One of the strongest and most complex joints in your body is the knee joint. Normally, both the muscles labelled X and Y in the diagram pull with equal force on the knee bones. In 'runner's knee' one of these muscles is weaker and a knee bone slips to one side, causing pain and inflammation as the knee bones rub the connective tissues together.

9 Why does the knee joint need to be so strong?
10 What do you think is the function of the two pads of cartilage between the long bones?
11 Suggest two other ways the knee could be injured.
12 When a joint is injured it becomes stiff and hard to move. What is the advantage of this happening?

Creative thinking   *Ideal footwear*

The diagrams below show some injuries caused by wearing incorrect footwear when exercising. Look at the parts of the body that are affected.

Ankle pain if shoes don't give ankle support.

Heel pain caused by pounding on the ball of the foot or shoes having thin material at the heel.

Instep soreness caused by shoes that rub across the top of the foot.

Achilles tendon injury is very painful and is caused by stiff shoes or lack of support at back and top of heel.

Shin splints caused by soft shoes or running on the toes instead of using the whole foot.

1 Look at the shoe on the left and discuss what features you would add or modify to make it a better shoe for protecting someone from injury.

2 What type of shoe do you wear for running in PE?

3 You probably have a pair of trainers – what features made you choose them?

4 Ask three people in your class what criteria they use to decide which trainers to buy. Do you think these are good criteria for preventing sports injuries?

Information processing Trainers

Work as a group to design and carry out a survey to find out how much people in your school know about trainers and their relationship to sports injures. Think about how many people you want to survey in each class, and how to present your data. You could write a short report for your school's PE department.

➡ *Arm bones*

This is Shona having an X-ray of her arm.

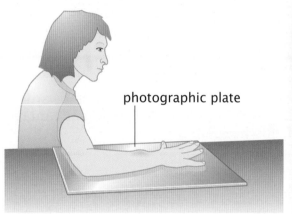

photographic plate

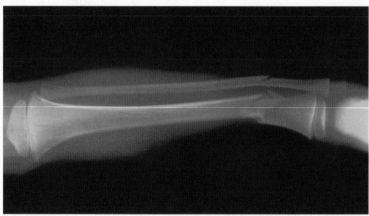

Key words
* radius
* ulna
* humerus
* hinge joint
* slipping joint
* rotating
* biceps
* triceps

This photograph shows the X-ray that was taken.

The two long bones shown in the X-ray are the **radius** and **ulna**. The ulna is the lower arm bone that joins to the **humerus** (funny bone). The humerus is the upper arm bone. The joint between the two is a **hinge joint**. The wrist joint is a **slipping joint**, which has limited **rotating** movement.

13 What do you think the doctor told Shona when she saw this X-ray?
14 Copy the diagram below of an arm into your notebook and label the bones and joints.

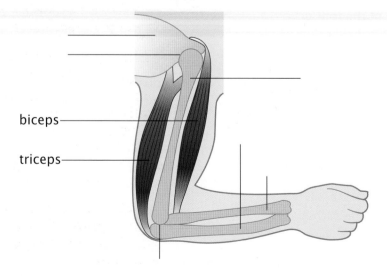

biceps

triceps

15 Describe the movement a hinge joint makes.
16 Why are joints needed in the arm?
17 Which muscle do you think contracts to move the lower arm up – the **biceps** or the **triceps**?
18 What connects muscles to bones – ligaments or tendons?
19 What connects the humerus to the ulna – ligaments or tendons?

The respiratory system

20 In teams do the quiz below. Check your answers and decide how to mark each correct answer. Compare your mark scheme with that of another team. Is it the same? If not, why not? Using your mark scheme work out what your team scored. What would you have scored using another team's mark scheme?

Quiz

Match definitions 1–3 to processes A–C:

A Gas exchange
B Respiration
C Breathing

1 The process of oxygen moving into the blood from the air in the alveoli at the same time as carbon dioxide leaves the blood and enters the alveoli.
2 The flow of air in and out of the lungs helped by the movements of the ribs and the diaphragm.
3 A chemical process inside cells that releases energy from glucose.

Aerobic respiration

Oxygen releases energy from glucose. 1 gram of glucose produces 15.6 kilojoules of energy. When we respire aerobically we have to breathe in oxygen and breathe out carbon dioxide. We also have to excrete (get rid of) the extra water created by adding it to our urine.

Anaerobic respiration

This happens when there is less oxygen available. 1 gram of glucose only produces 0.65 kilojoules of energy. When our cells respire anaerobically they also produce lactic acid. Too much lactic acid is thought to cause muscle cramps. Cells can only respire anaerobically for a very short time. Every cell in your body needs oxygen to live. Without it, a cell will die after just 4 minutes.

21 Which type of cell respiration gives the most energy from 1 gram of sugar – aerobic or anaerobic respiration?
22 Which type of respiration creates lactic acid, aerobic or anaerobic?

23 Why is the build-up of lactic acid painful?
24 When are you most likely to get cramp – sitting at your desk or running about? Why?
25 How long can a cell live without oxygen?
26 What are the waste products of respiration?
27 Which of these word equations is aerobic respiration, and which is anaerobic respiration?

glucose + oxygen → carbon dioxide + water + lots of energy

glucose → lactic acid + carbon dioxide + a little energy

Breathing

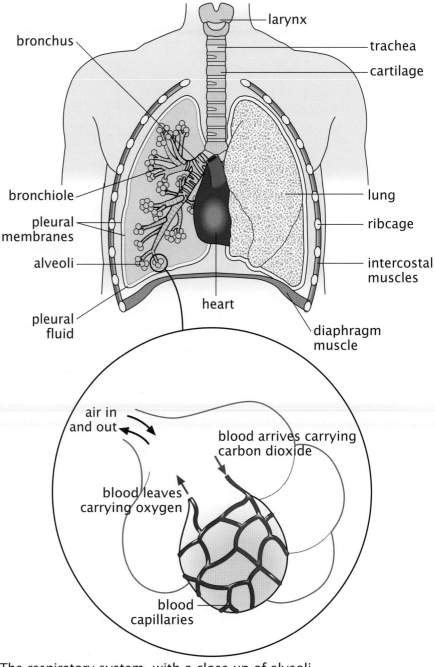

The respiratory system, with a close-up of alveoli.

Put your hands on your ribcage as shown in the diagram. Take a few deep breaths in and out.

28 Does the distance between your spine and ribs increase or decrease when you breathe in?
29 What happens when you breathe out?
30 Which did you feel took more effort – breathing in or breathing out?

Look at these drawings of how we breathe.

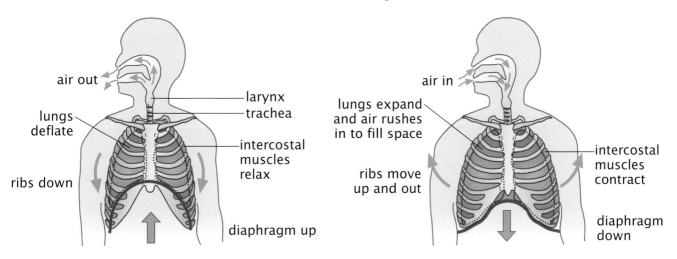

air out
larynx
trachea
lungs deflate
intercostal muscles relax
ribs down
diaphragm up

air in
lungs expand and air rushes in to fill space
intercostal muscles contract
ribs move up and out
diaphragm down

31 Copy and complete the following sentences by either filling in the missing words, or by crossing out the wrong words where there is a choice:

When you breathe in, your intercostal muscles contract and move the r…….. up and out. The d…………….. muscle c………… at the same time. It moves downwards. These two muscle actions increase/decrease the volume of the lungs. This raises/lowers the pressure inside the lungs compared with the air outside the lungs, so air rushes into the lungs through the t………….

To breathe out, the rib muscles contract/relax and the diaphragm also relaxes/contracts so the volume of the lungs d……………. Now the pressure is increased/decreased, so air is squeezed out of the lungs through the trachea and out of the n………. or mouth.

Time to think

Imagine that you are giving instructions to an oxygen molecule in the air on how to reach the blood system inside you. Use some or all of these labels to help you show the route:

- capillary
- trachea
- mouth
- bronchus
- alveoli
- bronchioles
- nose
- larynx
- lungs

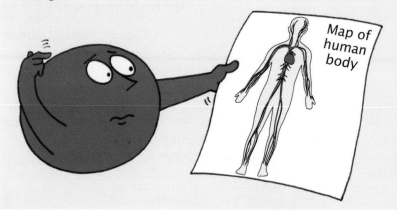

Breathing rate

This is the number of breaths you take in a measured amount of time. Look at the pictures below.

32 Which activities would increase your breathing rate?

33 Which activities might cause less oxygen to be available to cells?

→ *Keeping the respiratory system healthy*

Key words
* alveoli
* mucus
* secreted
* cilia
* phlegm

Lungs are like huge, delicate pink sponges. The air you breathe into your lungs contains all sorts of things, for example it always contains bacteria and viruses. It may also contain carbon particles if you live in an area where there is a lot of industry. The **alveoli** (air sacs) in your lungs are thin and can be easily damaged, so your body has several methods for protecting them from harmful things.

Special cells line the air tubes leading to your lungs. These cells make **mucus**. The mucus is **secreted** from the cells so that it forms a slimy layer over the inside walls of the air tubes. Dust and microbes get stuck in it. In between the mucus cells are other cells that are covered in tiny microscopic hairs called **cilia**. These cilia move backwards and forwards in waves, a bit like seaweed in water. They sweep the mucus up towards the mouth and nose, and away from the lungs. It reaches the back of the throat and you swallow it!

The digestive system destroys the dirt and microbes. If any dirt or microbes that have been trapped in the mucus do reach the alveoli they are quickly destroyed by white blood cells. When you get a cold or develop a cough, lots of thick yellow or greenish mucus is produced because of all the viruses being trapped. This is **phlegm** or snot.

The lining of the trachea.

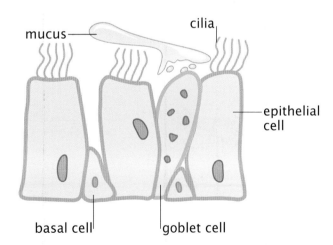

34 What chemical process produces carbon particles that might get breathed in? (HINT – Another word for carbon particles is soot.)
35 What makes the lungs look pink?
36 Why do you think they are described as 'like sponges'?
37 When you have a cold you produce lots of extra mucus. Why?
38 Why do you have to blow your nose when you have a cold?

Information processing   ## Healthy lungs

1 Check with a partner that you know what each of these words means. You can copy them into your notebook and mark them using the traffic light system – green for the ones you both know and understand, amber for the ones one of you knows about, and red for the ones you think both of you need to find out about.

- bacteria
- viruses
- alveoli

- mucus
- cilia
- phlegm

- microbes
- white blood cells

2 These words describe some environmental conditions:

- wet
- dry

- warm
- cold

Using a blue pen write down the conditions microbes like to live in. Using a red pen write down the conditions that are like the inside of your respiratory system. Is there a match? What can you deduce from this?

Time to think

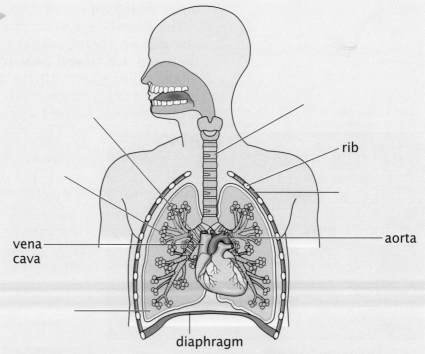

Copy this diagram and complete the missing labels.

Look at the checklist below of what you have studied so far in this chapter. Decide which of these you are confident about, and which you need more help to understand. Ask someone in your group to help you learn more about the things you are not sure about.

Checklist:

- the differences between fitness and healthiness
- how to increase health

- the organs of the respiratory system
- the differences between anaerobic and aerobic respiration
- how we breathe
- how the respiratory system protects itself
- the functions of the skeleton
- how to avoid sports injures
- how to plan an investigation to compare breathing rates or pulse rates
- how to carry out a survey
- the meaning of all the key words so far.

Smoking

Key words
* passive
* pneumonia
* bronchitis
* lung cancer
* nicotine
* addicted

Smoking causes 120 000 people to die in the UK every year. Hundreds more die from **passive** or 'second-hand' smoking. Passive smoking is breathing in air filled with smoke from other people smoking in the same environment. Treating smoking-related diseases costs the National Health Service £1.7 billion a year.

The diseases caused by smoking affect the breathing system, for example **pneumonia**, **bronchitis** and **lung cancer**. Smoking gives some people relief from stress because cigarettes contain a drug called **nicotine** which stimulates the brain and relaxes the muscles. Nicotine is a habit-forming drug, so people who smoke get **addicted** to it.

Inhaling cigarette smoke increases carbon monoxide levels in the blood stream. Carbon monoxide attaches itself to red blood cells in place of oxygen molecules, so the blood cells cannot pick up oxygen. People who smoke are often very 'short of breath'. This is because they cannot use the oxygen from each breath they take efficiently.

Smoke contains soot and tar particles. These stick to the lining of the respiratory system, building up mucus and leading to 'smoker's cough'. This damages the efficiency of gas exchange in the lungs. The heat from inhaled smoke burns the tiny hairs lining the nostrils. These hairs would normally help to trap dust and dirt and prevent them from getting into the respiratory system.

Smoking increases the heart rate and blood pressure. This causes stress that can damage the heart muscle over time. People who smoke double their risk of a heart attack compared with non-smokers. Cigarette smoking is the main cause of sudden death from heart disease.

Women who smoke when they are pregnant are more likely to have a spontaneous abortion (miscarriage) or stillbirth. Babies born to smokers are usually underweight and small in size, so they are not as strong as babies born to non-smokers. They may also be more likely to catch infections as their immune system may be damaged.

Information processing ## Diseases from smoking

1 Read the section on smoking again. Working in pairs, discuss which of these conditions you think smoking is likely to cause, and why.

- bronchitis
- pneumonia
- heart disease
- stress
- lung cancer
- stomach cancer

2 Make two lists with the headings 'Benefits of smoking' and 'Drawbacks of smoking'.
   a) Which is the longer list? Have other people put the same facts in each list as you?
   b) Use this information to make a 'No smoking' poster.

3 What different reasons might women have compared to men for giving up smoking?

Information processing ## Respiratory infections

Look at this table of data.

Groups of American soldiers undergoing physical training	Percentage of soldiers in each group who reported respiratory infections (for example colds and coughs)
Soldiers who smoked during their physical training course	25
Soldiers who began smoking during their training course	21
Soldiers who did not smoke at all	17

1 Which group of soldiers has the highest number of infections?

2 Which group of soldiers has the lowest number of infections?

3 What do you conclude from the table about the effects of smoking on health?

4 How do you think the data were collected?

Reasoning Correlations

In the 1960s cigarette manufacturers argued that statistics did not prove that smoking causes cancer. They are logically correct – just because there is a correlation between smoking and lung cancer it does not mean that one causes the other. It would be like saying that eating cereal for breakfast causes car accidents, because out of a sample of drivers who had car accidents, 78% had eaten cereal for breakfast. A correlation between two variables indicates that there is probably a link between them – they may be related. To see if they are, scientists look for other evidence to back up the correlation relationship.

1 Which of the graphs below indicate a strong correlation between the disease and smoking?

2 Which indicate some correlation, but it is not strong?

3 Which of the graphs indicate no correlation?

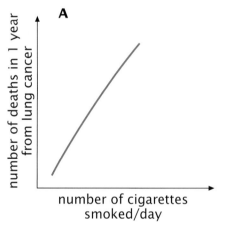

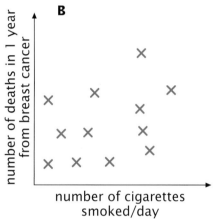

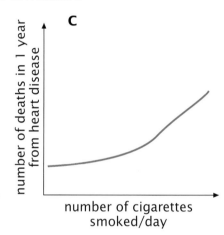

4 Here are two statements, both of which are true:

'In one year, more people are killed by diseases linked to smoking than die in all the road accidents in that year.'

'Every time you smoke a cigarette you shorten your life by an hour.'

a) Which is the best statement for putting people off smoking? Why?

b) Which statement would it be easier to provide scientific evidence for? Why?

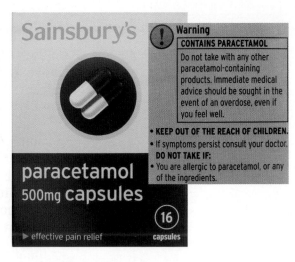

5 What other products carry health warnings?

Stopping smoking

Make a health campaign poster that includes a graph to show how much money people could save if they gave up smoking, and some of the things that they could buy with the money they saved. Add any other information that you think would help people to decide to give up smoking. Make sure the poster is both eye-catching and informative.

Smoking

1 Explain why each of these remarks is unscientific.

2 Discuss this question in your groups:

If smoking is so bad for you, why do people do it?

It's never too late to quit

Research shows that 2 years after giving up smoking, the risk of former smokers developing heart disease is reduced by 25%. After 10 years, the risk of developing heart disease is similar among former smokers and those who have never smoked. Quitting is difficult, but it is a positive step towards a healthier heart.

Drugs

The dictionary definition of a drug is:
'A medicinal substance, used alone or as an ingredient; narcotic, hallucinogen, or stimulant.'

(*The Concise Oxford Dictionary*)

Drugs are chemicals that change the way the body works. Medicines are drugs that help the body when you are sick, but like all drugs they are dangerous if misused. Examples of medicines are painkillers and **tranquillisers**. Cigarettes and alcohol are legal drugs for adults. They are known as **recreational** drugs. In the UK, you have to be 16 years old to smoke and 18 to drink alcohol legally. Caffeine is a drug you can have at any age. Other drugs, for example heroin and Ecstasy, are **illegal** for everyone in this country.

39 a) Decide which of these substances are drugs:

ginger	sage	nicotine
beer	Ecstasy	tar
aspirin	penicillin	ibuprofen
caffeine	alcopops	Vaseline
wine	banana	cannabis

b) Do the others in your group agree with you?

40 Which of the drugs in the list are legal and which are illegal to use?

Classifying drugs

Some **medicinal** drugs can be bought in supermarkets and pharmacies, whereas others can only be **prescribed** by a doctor.

All the products in the picture contain drugs. Annie has been asked to classify them each as recreational, medicinal, illegal or legal. Discuss which is which in your groups. Decide also which drugs can be bought 'over-the-counter' and which have to be prescribed by a doctor.

Evaluation   **School rules**

What are the rules about drug-taking in your school? What happens to pupils or staff who break the school rules about drugs? Do you think that these rules are fair or not? Why?

Damaging drugs

Key words
* addiction
* depressant
* hallucinations
* narcotics
* coma

Here is a table about some of the drugs that cause damage and are illegal. The amount of damage they cause in young bodies is much greater than in adults' because the tissues are still growing. Many of these drugs have very bad effects on brain development, and many lead to **addiction**. Some can cause death even when taken for the first time. The world of drug taking is a scary and dangerous place.

Official name	Other common names	Appearance	How it is ingested (taken into the body)	Effects
marijuana – the most widely used drug	cannabis, hashish, Mary Jane, herb, weed, grass, pot, chronic, joint, reefer, skunk	green, brown or grey dried crumbled leaves, like dried parsley	• smoked as hand-rolled cigarettes (a joint or nail) or in a pipe, or in a water pipe called a bong • can be mixed into foods, baked in cakes or brewed as a tea • sometimes mixed with crack cocaine, making it very dangerous	• a **depressant** – slows down the central nervous system • users lose concentration, find it difficult to learn, feel 'chilled out' • raises blood pressure • gives the user red eyes and a dry mouth • can make user sleepy or hungry • can cause paranoia and **hallucinations** • when smoked, it is as damaging to lungs as tobacco
heroin – grouped with the pain-relieving drugs known as **narcotics**, which include codeine and morphine, both legally prescribed by doctors	horse, smack, caballo (Spanish), big H, black tar, junk	• white or brown powder with a bad taste • black tar heroin looks sticky or like a hard lump	• can be mixed with crack cocaine – the mixture is called 8 ball • usually injected or smoked • if pure, it can be inhaled through the nose (snorted)	• burst of good feeling (rush) leading to a high level of relaxation, followed by drowsiness and sickness • users can stop breathing and die • repeated injecting leads to scarring called 'tracks' • addicts often share needles, increasing their risk of getting killer diseases such as hepatitis B and HIV/AIDS • can be addictive after only one or two doses • withdrawal symptoms include panic attacks, lack of sleep, chills and sweats, convulsions and seizures • it is easy to fall into a **coma** and possibly die with an overdose

Official name	Other common names	Appearance	How it is ingested (taken into the body)	Effects
Ecstasy – 3,4-methylenedi-oxy-*N*-methyl-amphetamine (MDMA)	XTC, X, Adam, E, roll	• made illegally as a 'designer' drug as tablets or powder • tablets may have a popular logo on them (such as a cartoon character) which makes them look like sweets	• can be swallowed as a pill or tablet, or snorted as a powder	• gives a 'high' by stimulating adrenaline production • can keep user active for days • can kill after one use • causes racing heart, dry mouth, stomach cramps, blurred vision, chills and sweats, sickness • the body can overheat during dancing leading to death • causes a decrease in the salts and minerals in the blood so the brain swells – this can cause permanent brain damage • destroys memory and thinking functions • literally 'mind-bending'
inhalants – for example glues, paint thinners, dry cleaning fluid, some felt tip marker pen inks, hairspray, deodorants, spray paint, whipped cream dispensers (whippets)	whippets, poppers, snappers, rush, bolt, bullet		• sniffed, snorted from containers or a plastic bag (bagging) or 'huffed' – holding an inhalant-soaked rag in the mouth	• give a 'rush' or 'high' • feelings of being drunk followed by sleepiness, staggering, dizziness and confusion • long-term use leads to headaches and nose bleeds, loss of sense of smell • oxygen to the brain is decreased, so brain function is damaged • can kill on first use

Time to think

1 Check that you know what the following words mean:

co-ordination
coma
tranquilliser
depressant

2 In your groups discuss these issues:
Which drugs do you think are the most dangerous for young people – cocaine, caffeine or cannabis? Why?

- What do you think 'addiction' is?
- Why do people get 'hooked' on drugs?
- Why do you think that drug addiction is increasing in people under 20?
- What do you think could be done by the government to help young people avoid being tempted by drugs?
- What do you think when you hear some people say that smoking marijuana is not as dangerous as smoking cigarettes?

→ *Addiction*

Drug abuse can lead to addiction. Addiction can be **physical**, **psychological** or both.

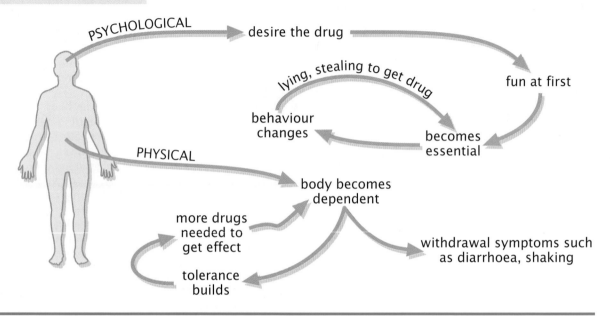

Reasoning Addiction

Read this information from a health clinic leaflet.

How to tell if a friend is addicted:

Have their sleeping habits changed?

They may sleep more or less than usual.

Have their eating habits changed?

Are they always hungry or have they lost their appetite?

Do they complain they are tired?

Do they feel sick?

Are they irritable and unpredictable?

Have they started arguing with their family all the time?

Have they lost interest in sports and hobbies they used to like?

If they are athletic, has their performance got poorer?

Have they become secretive?

Have they become depressed?

Have their school grades or marks got worse?

Are they taking less care with personal appearance?

Spots around the mouth/bad breath/red eyes?

Overall, are they becoming a stranger to you?

DID YOU KNOW?

Babies whose mothers are heroin addicts can become addicted to the drug before they are born. They have to undergo treatment to wean them off the heroin as soon as they are born. If they are not treated, this addiction can kill them soon after birth. However, nicotine is said to be even more addictive than heroin or crack cocaine.

1 Do you think this leaflet is helpful?

2 How could you improve it to make it more helpful to young people?

Alcohol

Key words
* alcohol
* hepatitis
* cirrhosis

Some of the effects of drinking too much **alcohol** include **hepatitis** and **cirrhosis**:

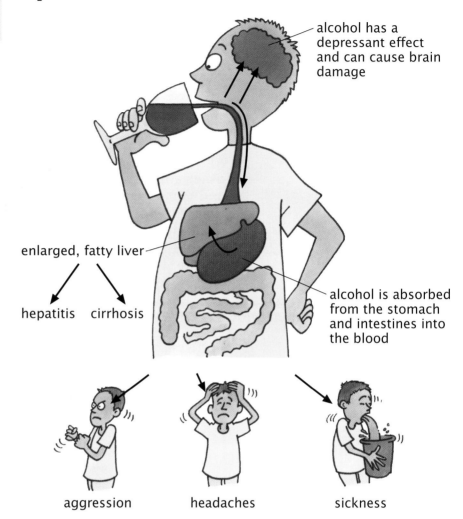

alcohol has a depressant effect and can cause brain damage

enlarged, fatty liver

hepatitis   cirrhosis

alcohol is absorbed from the stomach and intestines into the blood

aggression   headaches   sickness

Alcohol and the law

Age	What is legal	What is illegal
up to 16	no alcohol	it is illegal to buy alcohol anywhere, and it is illegal for other people to buy alcohol for you
16–17	you can buy or be bought beer and cider on licensed premises to drink with a meal in a restaurant area	you cannot drink beer or cider bought for you in the bar area or in public spaces
18 and over	you can buy alcohol and consume it in bars and restaurants; people selling you alcohol are entitled to ask for ID showing how old you are	you cannot buy alcohol for anyone under 18 or encourage anyone under 18 to buy alcohol

DID YOU KNOW?

Children who start drinking alcohol before they are 15 years old are four times more likely to become alcoholics than their non-drinking friends.

1 List all the effects of alcohol on the body.
2 How does the body get rid of the water and carbon dioxide made when alcohol is broken down?
3 Why does alcohol affect every organ in your body?
4 What does the word 'metabolism' mean?
5 Why is the liver the organ most likely to get damaged with excess alcohol consumption?
6 Why are alcoholics more likely to get injured than people who do not drink to excess?
7 How old do you have to be before you can drink alcohol in a pub?

Alcopops

Alcopops are made by mixing alcohol with fruit juices or other soft drinks like lemonade. They are brightly coloured and very sweet. There is concern in health organisations that these drinks are causing an increase in illegal teenage drinking of alcohol. The drinks are marketed by the alcohol manufacturers so that they appeal to young people. One in four deaths among 15 to 29-year-olds is caused by alcohol abuse.

Evaluation *What evidence?*

Alcopops rot teeth

The controversial fizzy alcopops drinks are so acidic that they can rot people's teeth. The danger came to light when John Brown, a 17-year-old from Huddersfield, went to the dentist complaining that his teeth hurt, particularly the morning after a night out with his friends.

He admitted that when he went out he and his friends drank beer and several bottles of alcopops, often vomiting because they got so drunk. His dentist capped his teeth and told him that the damage was caused by the acid in the alcohol mixing with the stomach acid in his vomit. John cut down on his drinking and his teeth have stopped rotting.

1 Why did the dentist think that the acid in alcopops might cause tooth rot?

2 What else could be the cause of tooth rot?

3 From this one example is it scientific to assume that alcopops cause tooth rot? How could more scientific evidence be collected?

4 How do alcohol manufacturers make alcopops appeal to young people?

Caffeine

Caffeine is a drug found in coffee, tea and chocolate, as well as some soft drinks, for example, cola. It comes from plants grown in the tropics – coffee comes from a plant called *Coffea arabica*, tea from *Camellia sinensis*, and cocoa from *Theobroma cacao*.

Coffee bar.

Picking coffee beans.

Tea plantation.

Cocoa pods.

The symptoms of caffeine poisoning

In very small doses, caffeine mildly stimulates the nervous system. Large quantities of caffeine can cause dizziness, stomach pain, nausea, diarrhoea, elevated pulse rate and low blood pressure, as well as drowsiness. Severe caffeine **poisoning** causes headaches, insomnia, tremors and constipation. Since caffeine **tolerance** varies from person to person, it is hard to predict just how much caffeine a person can drink before they develop any symptoms.

Luckily, caffeine poisoning is not fatal. Moderate consumption is, for many people, one of life's perks. However, some people are very sensitive to caffeine and need to avoid drinking it. It can be found in drinks other than tea and coffee, such as cola, so they need to read the ingredients labels very carefully.

Enquiry ## *Effect of coffee and tea*

1 Design and carry out an investigation to find out the effect of drinking one, two and three cups of coffee on a human pulse rate, compared with one cup of water.
How many people would you include in your investigation? What are the independent (input) variables? What is the dependent (outcome) variable?

2 Carry out a survey to find out how many cups of tea, coffee or cocoa people of different ages drink in a day.
How will you ensure that your data are **representative**?
(A representative sample of school children is one that is large enough to include all possible types of variation in the population, for example different ages, as well as both sexes.)
List the effects that large doses of caffeine can have on the body. Ask the people you interview if they are aware of the effects of caffeine. Show them your list. How do they respond?

3 Use the information you have obtained from these two investigations to design a poster about caffeine as a drug.

DID YOU KNOW?

Holly plants also contain caffeine. Their seeds, bark and leaves are all toxic, but the greatest concentration of caffeine is found in the berries. If you grow holly in your garden it is very important to keep children from eating the berries.

The digestive system

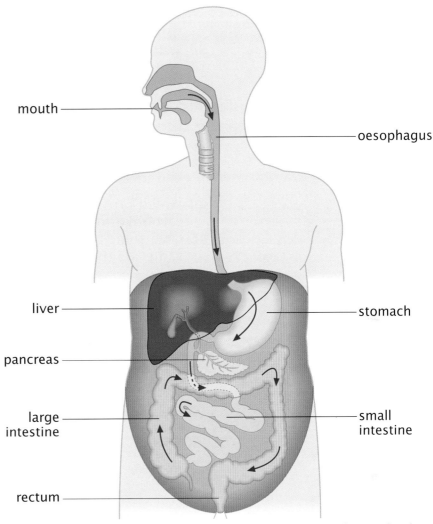

mouth

oesophagus

liver

stomach

pancreas

large intestine

small intestine

rectum

41 Copy out the parts of the digestive system from the list below and then write the correct function from the list by each part.

Parts of the digestive system
- Mouth
- Oesophagus
- Stomach
- Small intestine
- Rectum
- Large intestine

Functions
- Forms faeces for excretion.
- Makes enzymes that digest proteins, as well as enzymes that complete the breakdown of carbohydrates.
- Takes food into the digestive system and breaks it up with the teeth.
- Makes three types of enzymes (carbohydrase, lipase and trypsin) to break down carbohydrates, fats and proteins.
- Moves the food to the stomach.
- Stores faeces.

What do you know about diet?

42 List the different types of food that we need to have in our diet to keep us healthy (think back to your Year 7 work). What is each type for?

43 Copy and complete these sentences:

A good meal is one that contains a lot of .... but little ....

A bad meal is one that contains a lot of .... but little ....

Now compare your sentences with other people in your group. Do you all agree about what makes a good or bad meal?

44 Which provides the most energy in our diet – protein, carbohydrates or fat?

45 Give some reasons why two 16-year-old males of the same weight might need different amounts of energy.

Information processing — *Energetic activities*

The following table shows how much energy different activities use per day. Rank the activities from the most energetic to the least energetic, and make a graph to show this information in a visual way. Think about what type of graph you should draw – a pie graph, a bar chart or a line graph? Why?

Energy used for a variety of activities and ages

Activity	Gender	Age	Energy used in kJ
sleeping	man	40	7150
	woman	40	6400
office work	man	40	10 500
	woman	40	9500
car mechanic	man	30	13 000
	woman	30	12 800
builder	man	30	15 500
	woman	30	15 000
pregnancy	woman	25	10 000
breastfeeding	woman	25	12 600
playing	boy	8	6700
	girl	8	6050

Minerals and vitamins

As well as the major food types – carbohydrates, fats and proteins – the body also needs **minerals** and **vitamins** to keep healthy.

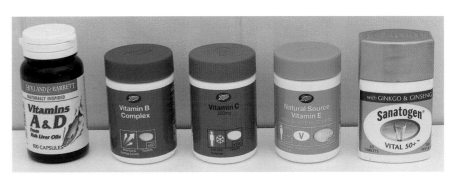

Vitamin or mineral	Source	Function	Deficiency disease
A	• vegetables, butter, egg yolk, liver	• healthy skin • helps vision in dim light	• lowered immunity • poor night vision
D	• butter, egg yolk • the skin synthesises it when exposed to sunlight	• regulates absorption of calcium and phosphate in food from the gut • helps deposit these minerals in the bones	• poor bone formation (rickets) • children have bowed legs and their bones break easily
E	• butter, wholemeal bread	• helps maintain healthy immune system	• nerve damage
K	• cabbage, spinach • made by bacteria in the gut	• aids blood clotting	• wounds bleed for a long time
B1, B2, B12	• wholemeal bread, yeast, liver	• general good health • formation of red blood cells	• lack of B1 leads to beri-beri, a disease that inflames the muscles • lack of B2 leads to pellagra, a skin disease • lack of B12 leads to anaemia
C	• citrus fruit, milk, fresh vegetables	• repairs damaged tissue • helps immunity	• scurvy – the skin flakes, gums bleed and wounds do not heal
Ca, Ph	• milk, cheese	• bones and teeth (see vitamin D)	• brittle bones and teeth
Fe	• liver, egg yolk	• healthy red blood cells	• anaemia
I, Na, K	• seafood, salt, leafy vegetables	• make the hormone thyroxine, which controls metabolism • help nerves and muscles function	• swollen thyroid glands (goitre) • muscle cramps

46 Check that you understand the information in the table by copying and completing this paragraph:

If you do not have enough iron in your diet your red blood cells will not pick up oxygen efficiently, and you may suffer from _____. Rickets is another disease caused by a lack of minerals. In this case they are _____. Your teeth will be weaker without these minerals. Phosphorus is necessary for the healthy growth of _____ and _____. Muscle cramps can be caused by a lack of _____ in your diet, but can also be caused by anaerobic respiration in your muscles, which creates _____ acid. Plenty of fruit in your diet prevents _____.

Evaluation   Diet

1 Review your diet this week. List all the minerals and vitamins that you think you have eaten. Note down the ones you may be short of. What will you try to eat for the rest of the week to make sure that you have enough of the necessary vitamins and minerals?

2 How does your analysis of your diet compare with a friend's? Do they eat a healthier diet than you?

3 Why does a 30-year-old female require less calcium in her recommended daily intake than a 15-year-old girl?

4 Why are water and roughage (fibre) also necessary to keep healthy?

Information processing   Vitamin C

Vitamin C is found in fresh fruit and vegetables.

1 Name three specific foods that you would eat to give yourself vitamin C.

2 Find out why vitamin C is a necessary part of a healthy diet.

3 What symptoms indicate that someone is not getting enough vitamin C in their diet?

DCPIP is a chemical indicator that is used to test for vitamin C.

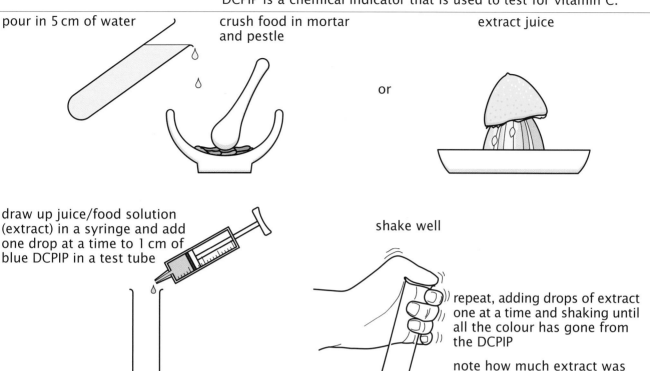

pour in 5 cm of water

crush food in mortar and pestle

extract juice

or

draw up juice/food solution (extract) in a syringe and add one drop at a time to 1 cm of blue DCPIP in a test tube

shake well

1 cm

repeat, adding drops of extract one at a time and shaking until all the colour has gone from the DCPIP

note how much extract was added from the syringe – if there is a high amount of vitamin C in the extract then less is needed

4 Make a list of the equipment that you would need to carry out a vitamin C test.

5 List the steps you would take.

Imagine you have compared some grapefruit juice with some apple juice to see how many drops of each turn DCPIP colourless. It takes five drops of grapefruit juice to turn 1 cm³ DCPIP colourless and ten drops of apple juice to turn 1 cm³ DCPIP colourless.

6 Which has the most vitamin C in it, the grapefruit juice or the apple juice?

Planning an investigation

7 Working in a group, plan an investigation to answer the following question:

Which contains the most vitamin C – freshly squeezed orange juice, concentrated orange squash or a carton of chilled orange juice?

8 Write down your proposed method. Be specific about how you will prepare all the juices, and the DCPIP quantities used. Explain how you would make this a 'fair' comparison between the juices.

Draw a table to organise the data you collect. You will be recording the type of juice tested and how many drops of juice make the DCPIP solution colourless.

Reasoning ## Diet and heart disease

A survey found the following data for the percentage of energy provided by fat in a typical diet in some countries, and the annual death rates in these countries for men.

	Deaths per 100 000 men	Percentage of total energy from fat
Finland	403	48
USA	346	51
Scotland	343	47
Australia	297	52
New Zealand	273	37
Canada	270	41
England and Wales	259	45
Norway	213	41
Czechoslovakia	201	36
Germany	194	30
Israel	148	31
Bulgaria	72	31
France	66	29
Romania	61	27
Spain	50	31
Hong Kong	34	26
Japan	34	28

The figures show that the more fat you eat, the more likely you are to die of heart disease.

Dr Smythe

The figures show no correlation between diet and heart disease.

Dr Jones

There is a correlation between percentage of fat eaten and death rate.

Dr Singh

Discuss with a partner which doctor you agree with.

What other information would you want before you could make a better, more informed conclusion about heart disease and fat?

Being 'out of balance'

To be healthy, all your body systems need to be in balance. **Anorexia**, **bulimia** and **obesity** are all disorders to do with overeating or undereating. They are caused by the digestive system being unbalanced. This in turn leads to an **imbalance** in what is absorbed into the blood system. Any imbalance in the blood affects all the other systems, particularly the heart.

47 Look at these drawings and make some notes that describe the symptoms of each eating disorder.

REDUCED LIFE SPAN

Obesity
- diabetes
- breast cancer in women
- shortness of breath
- high blood pressure
- polycystic ovaries
- gall bladder disease
- tiredness
- arthritis in back, hips, knees and ankles

LOW SELF-ESTEEM

Bulimia
- depression
- hormone imbalance
- dehydration
- loss of important minerals
- damage to oesophagus, kidneys and liver
- laxative use
- eating out of control (binges)
- vomiting

Anorexia
- perfectionist with low self-esteem
- periods stop
- may starve to death
- depression
- bones soften
- lowered immunity

Creative thinking   *Pregnancy advice*

In your groups, design a fact sheet for health visitors to give to couples intending to start a family. You will need to read back over this chapter to find all the information related to pregnancy. Explain the dangers of smoking, taking drugs (both illegal and legal), drinking too much alcohol or coffee, lack of exercise and poor diet.

How would you make sure that your leaflet was easy to understand, interesting and informative?

➡ *The body's defence against pathogens*

The diagram below should remind you of the many ways your body protects you from disease.

Key words
* antiseptic
* immune

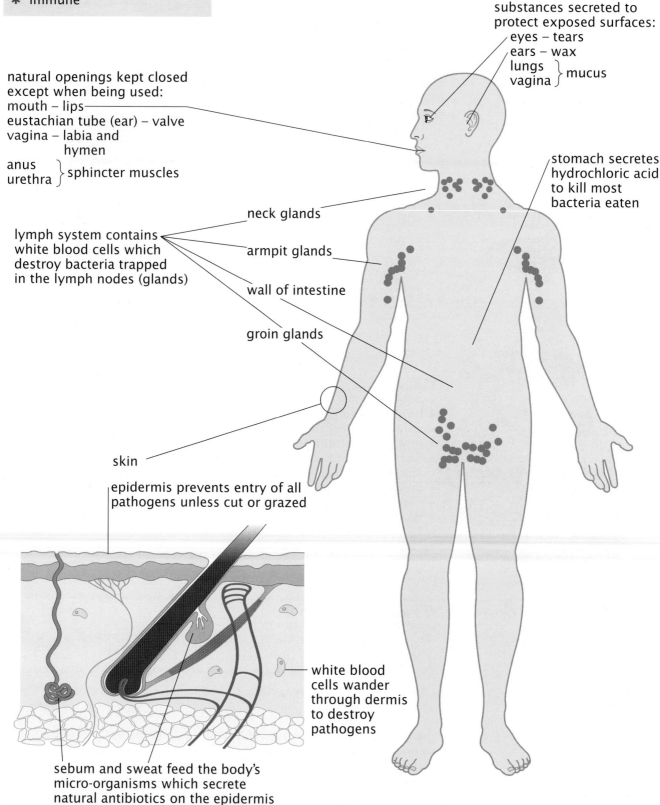

substances secreted to protect exposed surfaces:
eyes – tears
ears – wax
lungs
vagina } mucus

natural openings kept closed except when being used:
mouth – lips
eustachian tube (ear) – valve
vagina – labia and
          hymen
anus
urethra } sphincter muscles

stomach secretes hydrochloric acid to kill most bacteria eaten

neck glands

lymph system contains white blood cells which destroy bacteria trapped in the lymph nodes (glands)

armpit glands

wall of intestine

groin glands

skin

epidermis prevents entry of all pathogens unless cut or grazed

white blood cells wander through dermis to destroy pathogens

sebum and sweat feed the body's micro-organisms which secrete natural antibiotics on the epidermis

Think back to your previous work and see if you can answer these questions:

48 Name some useful drugs and the diseases or infections they treat.
49 What is an **antiseptic**?
50 How would you treat a grazed knee?
51 What is aspirin useful for?
52 What might cause food poisoning?

Creative thinking *Immune system*

Use these notes to make a leaflet for a local gym called 'Habits that weaken your **immune** system'. Use diagrams, tables or lists to summarise some of the information visually. Many people find visual presentations easier to remember.

Certain foods and environmental influences are damaging to the immune system, for example, too much sugary food, too much fat, excess alcohol, and smoking.

Overdosing on sugar
Eating or drinking 100 grams (8 tablespoons) of sugar, the equivalent of one 350 ml can of fizzy drink, reduces the ability of white blood cells to kill bacteria by 40%. The immune-suppressing effect of sugar starts less than 30 minutes after ingestion and may last for 5 hours. The ingestion of complex carbohydrates, or starches, has no effect on the immune system.

Excess alcohol
Harms the body's immune system in two ways:
1. It produces an overall nutritional deficiency, depriving the body of valuable immune-boosting nutrients.
2. Consumed in excess, alcohol, like sugar, can reduce the ability of white cells to kill bacteria. High doses of alcohol stop white blood cells multiplying. They inhibit the action of killer white cells on cancer cells.
One drink (the equivalent of 350 ml of beer, 150 ml of wine, or 30 ml of spirits) does not appear to affect the immune system, but three or more drinks do. Damage to the immune system increases in proportion to the quantity of alcohol consumed. Amounts of alcohol that are enough to cause intoxication are also enough to suppress immunity.

Food allergens
Some people have a genetic allergic response to otherwise harmless substances (such as milk or wheat). After eating lots of food allergens, the gut wall becomes damaged, enabling invaders and other potentially toxic substances in the food to get into the bloodstream and make the body feel generally unwell. This condition is known as 'the leaky gut syndrome'.

Too much fat
Obesity can lead to a depressed immune system. It can affect the ability of white blood cells to multiply, produce antibodies and move rapidly to the site of an infection.

Key words
* cancer
* tumours
* lymph system

→ *Cancer*

Cancer is the name given to a group of related diseases of cells. Cancer cells do not grow and multiply at a normal rate; they accelerate and grow out of control. All the extra cells can form into lumps called **tumours**. Tumours destroy normal cells around them. They can be broken up by drug and chemical treatments, or removed by surgery. Sometimes they may break up on their own without treatment. Cancer cells can travel around the body in the **lymph system**, causing tumours all over the body. Cancer in children is rare, but the risks of getting cancer increase with age. Imagine a football stadium full of children. The probability is that only one will develop cancer. These days, many cancers can be stopped and cured, and people who have had cancer can go on to lead normal, healthy lives.

We do not know why cells should 'go mad' and start multiplying into cancers, but we do know that smoking and alcohol increase the chances of getting cancer as you grow older.

→ *Stress*

Most people are exposed to much higher levels of stress than they realise.

53 Which of these situations cause stress?

You receive a prize at school.
Your bike has a flat tyre.
You go to a fun party that lasts until midnight but your parents do not know you will be out so late.
Your cat gets sick.
Your best friend comes to stay at your house for a week.
You get a bad cough.
You cannot do your science homework and it is too late to get help from a friend.
You know that your parents are planning a surprise birthday party for you.
Your parents are getting divorced.

All of the above can cause stress, as stress is caused by many different kinds of things: happy things, sad things, allergies and other physical things. Many people carry enormous stress loads and they do not even realise it. To most of us, stress is worry – worrying about being late for school, or about having enough pocket money to buy your friend a birthday present, or about your gran when the doctor says she may need an operation.

Your body has a much broader definition of stress than just worry. Your body thinks that stress is anything that means change in your life, or uncertainty. It doesn't matter if it is a 'good' change or a 'bad' change, both cause stress. Catching a cold, breaking an arm, a skin infection and a sore back are all changes to your body. Very hot or very cold climates can be stressful. Very high altitude may be a stress. Toxins or poisons, like alcohol or nicotine, are stresses. Each of these factors threatens to cause changes in your body's internal environment.

Hormonal changes also cause stress to your body. Puberty is a very stressful time. A person's body is changing shape, sexual organs begin to function and new hormones are released in large quantities.

Allergic reactions are a part of your body's natural defence mechanism. When confronted with a substance which your body considers toxic, your body will try to get rid of it by attacking or neutralising it. If it is something that you breathe in through your nose, you might get a runny nose and start sneezing. If it lands on your skin you might develop blisters. If you inhale it, you'll get wheezy lungs. If you eat it, you may break out in itchy red lumps in your mouth and all over your body. Allergic reactions are a stress, requiring large changes in energy expenditure on the part of your body's defence system to fight off what the body perceives as a dangerous attack.

Information processing   *Stress*

1 Read the section on stress again. Make a list of all the negative things that can cause stress, and all the positive things that can cause stress. Compare your list with a partner. Discuss any differences until you are sure you both know what might cause stress for some people.

2 What sort of physical problems are caused by stress?

3 Which organs of the body are affected by stress?

4 The number of people attending psychiatric clinics is much greater now than it was 50 years ago. Discuss what you think the reasons for this might be.

Adrenaline

The body prepares itself for important action or activity with the 'stress response'.

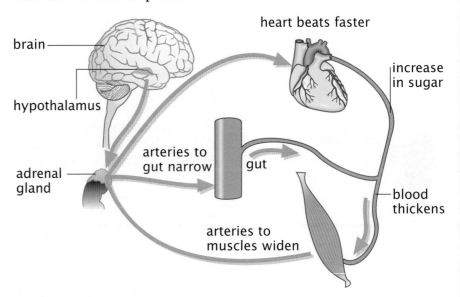

A chemical called **adrenaline** produces the stress response. Adrenaline is a **hormone**. A region in the brain called the **hypothalamus** controls its release by sending a message to the adrenal glands to release adrenaline into the bloodstream. The adrenal glands are on top of the kidneys.

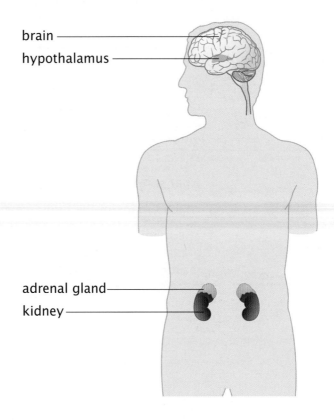

Location of the adrenal glands.

Adrenaline in the bloodstream very quickly causes the following short-lived changes in the body:

- the heart beats faster
- extra sugar is released into the blood
- the arteries to the muscles get wider
- blood thickens so that it will clot more easily.

54 In your group, discuss how you think each of these changes caused by adrenaline helps the body to prepare for action. Think about the last time you felt stressed. What caused the stress? How did you feel? List the ways in which your body responded to this stress.

55 Check that you know the answers to these questions:
Where is adrenaline made in the body?
Where is the hypothalamus?
What does it do?

Adrenaline is sometimes called the 'fight or flight' hormone.

Evaluation ## The effect of alcohol

One of the effects of stress is that the stomach can make too much hydrochloric acid. This can cause indigestion and heartburn. People suffering from stress sometimes claim that alcohol makes them feel happier or more relaxed. It can make them feel better, but it is likely to affect the stomach and the liver.

Nina, Su King and Karl did an experiment to investigate the effect that alcohol might have on the lining of the stomach. Here is part of their report:

We put six drops of dilute hydrochloric acid into five labelled test tubes. The hydrochloric acid had the same pH as stomach acid, pH 3.5. Here is a drawing of what we then did:

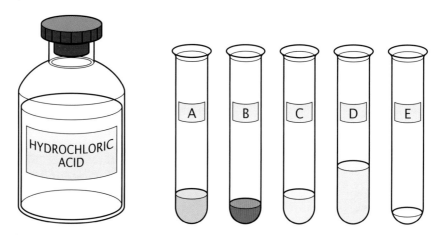

Test tube A contains 15 drops of lager, B 10 drops of whisky, C 15 drops of white wine, D 30 drops of water, and E contains only hydrochloric acid. This last tube is the control, so that this is a fair test. We then added 3 drops of Universal Indicator to each tube to find out the pH. We also found out the amount of alcohol in each alcoholic drink by looking at the labels on the cans or bottles, where it is given as a percentage.

Here are our results:

Type of drink	Lager	Whisky	White wine	Water	Hydrochloric acid
Percentage alcohol	5%	20%	12%	0%	0%
pH	3	2	2	3.5	3.5

1 Why did the pupils put hydrochloric acid into each tube?

2 Why did they use hydrochloric acid with a pH of 3.5?

3 Why did they say tube E was included?

4 What is the purpose of tube D?

5 Did they need both tubes D and E? Explain your answer.

6 What do you conclude from their experiment about the effect of alcohol on the stomach?

7 Some of these alcoholic drinks are likely to be more damaging than others; which ones are more damaging, and why? Use this drawing of the stomach to help explain your answer.

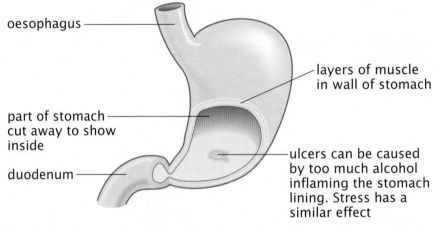

oesophagus

layers of muscle in wall of stomach

part of stomach cut away to show inside

duodenum

ulcers can be caused by too much alcohol inflaming the stomach lining. Stress has a similar effect

The stomach.

8 List at least three suggestions that the team could use to help them improve their investigation.

Research

Find out what activities, courses and services there are in your school and local community that aim to help people manage stress. You might find out about evening classes in activities such as tai chi or yoga, or find out where there are counsellors for marriage guidance or dealing with bullying.

Word play

Lots of magazine articles and television programmes refer to people's 'lifestyle'. In your group discuss what you think 'lifestyle' means. How would you describe your lifestyle? What similarities and what differences do you and your friends have between your lifestyles? How do you think you could improve your lifestyle?

Creative thinking Fit and healthy

9. What type of milk do you drink?

A full cream..............☐
B skimmed...............☐
C semi-skimmed.......☐
D none....................☐

Write down 20 questions for a 'fit and healthy' questionnaire that could be included in a health magazine. The questions should help readers see which category they are in – very fit, moderately fit or unfit.

Recommend some lifestyle-changing action for readers in each group.

Evaluation Fit and healthy

Steve Redgrave is an Olympic gold medal winner. He won his medals for rowing. He is also a diabetic. Would you say that he is fit and healthy?

- Are we healthier than our great-grandparents were?

What sort of information and evidence would you want to see to make your answer to this question 'objective', not just an uninformed opinion?

What do your parents think about this question?

Time to think

Think back over the work you have done in this chapter. What have you found out about health and fitness that you did not know before?

Form the same group that you did at the very start of the chapter, and repeat the activity that you did then:

- agree and write down the five most important things that you must do to stay healthy
- agree and write down the five things that you think are the biggest dangers to health.

Have these changed or are they the same as at the start of the chapter?

3 Energy and electricity

In this chapter you will learn:

➡ that energy conservation is a useful scientific accounting system when energy is transferred
➡ to describe some energy transfers
➡ about potential difference in electrical circuits
➡ about the hazards of high-voltage circuits
➡ how to compare the energy consumption of common electrical appliances
➡ how electricity is generated from fuels, including the energy transfers involved

You will also develop your skills in:

➡ identifying patterns and trends in measurement of voltage and using these to draw conclusions about the way voltage varies around a circuit
➡ relating energy transfer devices in the laboratory to everyday appliances
➡ extracting information from secondary sources and summarising and communicating it clearly

➡ ➡ ➡ WHAT DO YOU KNOW?

Key words
* fuels
* energy resources
* renewable
* non-renewable

You will have met the word energy many times already. Sometimes it will have been used scientifically and at other times it will have been used in everyday language.

1 Write a sentence where the word energy is used in everyday language and another where it is used scientifically. Compare your sentences with those of your neighbour.

2 Here is a list of **fuels**. Make a two-column table and give an example of where each fuel is used.

Fuel	Example of its use
gas	central heating in home
wood	
coal	
peat	
charcoal	
petrol	

3 **Energy resources** can be described as **renewable** or **non-renewable**. Copy and complete the table of energy resources below, showing whether they are renewable or non-renewable.

Energy resource	Renewable or non-renewable
coal	non-renewable
petrol	
geothermal	
hydroelectric	

4 Some people claim that wood is a renewable energy source, while others say it is non-renewable. What do you think? Explain your reasons.

5 On separate pieces of card, write down all the key words that you connect with energy. Here are some examples to start you off:

- fossil fuel
- solar
- joule
- coal
- food
- respiration

Now arrange the cards on a sheet of paper to produce a concept map. Remember to draw lines to link the words, and write a connecting sentence.

Wind farm – renewable energy.

Word play

Many scientific words are derived from Latin and Greek. Sometimes they start words (prefixes). Here are some prefixes that you will meet in this chapter. Write down any scientific words or phrases you know that start this way.

- therm-
- kin-
- trans-
- gen-
- hydro-
- electro-
- bio-

How is energy stored?

Key words
* chemical energy
* kinetic energy
* thermal energy
* potential energy
* elastic potential energy
* sound energy
* nuclear energy

Energy is an important concept because we need energy to live, to make things happen, and to do things. Because you cannot see energy, different people think of energy in very different ways. They make different thought models inside their heads.

Sometimes people find it useful to give special names for the different forms of energy. For example, you will find the following words used:

- **chemical energy**
- **kinetic energy**
- **thermal energy**
- **potential energy**
- **elastic potential** (spring) **energy**
- **sound energy**
- **nuclear energy**

1 Which of these words can you match to the thought bubble above?

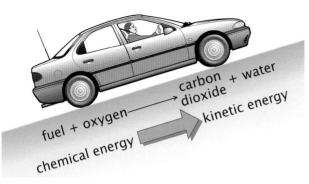

Chemical energy

This is the energy stored within the chemicals in a system. For example, when the fuel in a car combines with oxygen in the air it transfers energy to the car. The car can now do useful work such as go up a hill. Fuels are the main sources of chemical energy. When the car goes up the hill, chemical energy in the fuel is used to keep the car moving.

2 What is the source of our chemical energy?

Kinetic energy

This is the name we use to describe the energy something has when it is moving. As a skier travels down a slope, she gets faster and gains kinetic energy.

Thermal energy

When a solid is heated, the particles that make up the solid vibrate more. As they gain energy the temperature of the material increases. It has gained thermal energy.

Potential energy

Potential energy is the name given to the energy something has because of its position. Scientists use the term gravitational potential energy for this.

In the picture below the acrobat loses potential energy as he jumps down, and his partner then moves up, gaining potential energy.

Elastic potential energy (spring energy)

Here is another way in which energy may be stored. In the picture the elastic has to be stretched before the catapult can be used. The energy stored in the elastic is called elastic potential energy (spring energy). Can you think of other examples of devices that make use of elastic potential energy?

Sound energy

When being used, these loudspeakers are a source of sound energy.

Nuclear energy

This photograph shows a nuclear submarine. It uses nuclear energy which it gets from a nuclear reactor.

Wind energy

The photograph at the beginning of the chapter shows wind turbines in a wind farm. They use energy from the wind to generate electricity.

Clockwork radio

Trevor Baylis OBE was born in Kilburn, London, in 1937. In 1991 he saw a television programme about AIDS in Africa. An AIDS worker commented that one way to help prevent the disease from spreading any further would be to broadcast advice by radio, if only radios, and in particular batteries, were not so expensive. Baylis was inspired by what he saw and set about inventing a clockwork radio. In 1994 his first prototype was featured on BBC's *Tomorrow's World.* The radio worked for 14 minutes on just one wind-up. Finance expert Christopher Staines and South African entrepreneur Rory Stear acquired funding to make the radio, and the following year they set up BayGen Power Industries in Cape Town, South Africa, employing disabled workers to manufacture the Freeplay® wind-up radio. As well as the benefits of not having to rely on electricity, an environmental benefit of the clockwork radio is that there are no batteries to throw away, as these can lead to mercury poisoning.

Using springs to generate electricity was nothing new. What was so innovative was the fact that the electrical energy could be supplied over a long period of time rather than in a short burst. The production radio gives 40 minutes of play from a 20-second wind-up.

> Winding up the radio coils a spring

> The spring is attached to a gearbox connected to a dynamo

> When the spring is released, the gearbox allows the spring's energy to be slowly released to produce electricity

> The dynamo produces 3 volts at 55–60 milliwatts

Wind-up radios are very popular where access to electricity is restricted and batteries are expensive. They are especially popular in South Africa. Former President Nelson Mandela was so impressed with the radios that he has helped Trevor Baylis to publicise them.

1 Why is the wind-up radio environmentally friendly?
2 What other 'free' sources of energy could be utilised to run a radio?

Energy transfer

Look at the picture of the kettle:

energy from $\rightarrow$ energy in the hot water, the kettle
the electricity   and the surroundings

In this example energy is **transferred** by the electricity to the heating element and then to the water, the kettle and the surroundings.

Look at the picture on the right:

energy stored $\rightarrow$ energy in the movement of the person +
in our food   energy in lifting the person up the stairs

In this example energy is transferred from the food to the person.

Energy transfer diagrams

Energy transfer diagrams are a useful way of representing what happens in different situations. The diagram below represents the energy transfer in a kettle. In the diagram, the width of the arrow is **proportional** to the amount of energy – the wider the arrow, the larger the amount of energy. These branching diagrams are called **Sankey diagrams**, and they are named after the physicist who invented them.

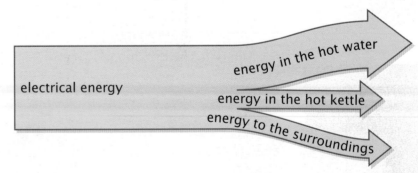

This diagram is for the person walking up the stairs:

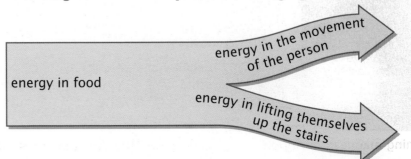

3 Describe the energy transfers in the two photographs below and draw an energy transfer diagram for one situation.

EXTENSION   **4** You will probably have already investigated the energy transfers shown in the diagrams below.

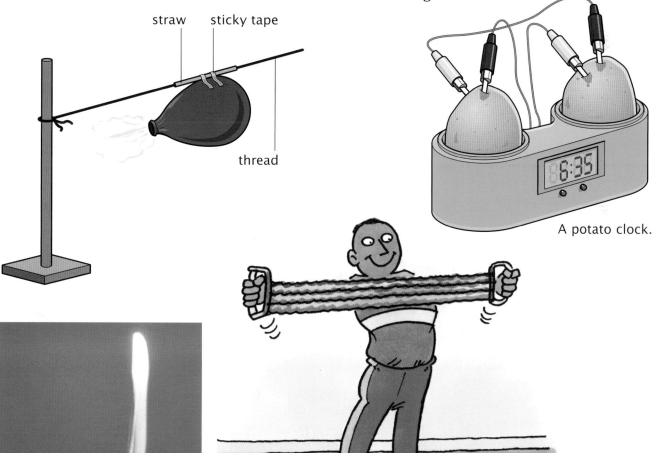

straw   sticky tape

thread

A potato clock.

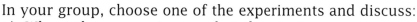

Burning magnesium ribbon.

In your group, choose one of the experiments and discuss:

a) Where the energy is stored at the start.
b) What happens to the energy?
c) Where does the energy end up?
d) Draw an energy transfer diagram (Sankey diagram) and annotate it.

5 Repeat this for a second experiment.

→ *Conservation of energy*

Key words
* conservation
* dissipated
* analogy

Energy can be transferred from one place to another and stored in different forms. The total amount of energy in a system remains constant. Each time it changes form some of it becomes heat. The heat spreads out in the system and it is difficult to reuse. Look back at the energy transfer diagram for the kettle on page 78. In this example, the amounts of energy at each transfer are shown.

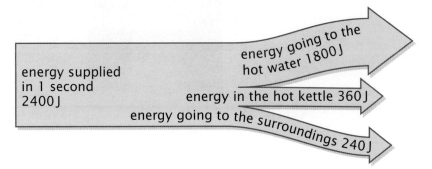

energy supplied in 1 second 2400J

energy going to the hot water 1800J

energy in the hot kettle 360J

energy going to the surroundings 240J

As you can see, the total energy going into the system is 2400 J and the total energy leaving is 1800 + 360 + 240 = 2400 J. The energy in the surroundings and the kettle is not useful – it is 'wasted' energy.

When energy is transferred, the total amount of energy before and after remains the same. No energy ever disappears. This is called the principle of **conservation** of energy. The energy that is spread out, usually as thermal energy, is wasted energy. It is not useful. When the energy is spread out in this way it is said to have been **dissipated**.

One way to explain energy is to use an **analogy** (a comparison). Think about a birthday cake shared out amongst six people. When a seventh person arrives, each of the six pieces has a small piece cut out of it to make a seventh piece. The total amount of cake provided remains the same. In this example the cake is analogous to the energy. It is shared out into smaller amounts but the total amount remains the same.

Here is another example. Suppose a rich aunt gives one of her young relatives a £50 note. This could be used to buy a CD player. However, if the money were shared out amongst eight relatives, each would receive only £6.25 each. The total amount of money being shared has not changed, but it has been spread out from just one person to many people. They in turn may share their portion out to yet more people. There would now be an even less useful amount for each person. Similarly, when energy is transferred, it finally ends up in a less useful form. In the case of energy, it usually ends up heating our surroundings.

→ *Energy and power*

It is useful to know not just how much energy is transferred, but how quickly this is done. The energy transferred in every second is called **power**.

$$\text{power} = \frac{\text{energy transferred}}{\text{time taken}}$$

The unit of power is the **watt**. A more powerful device can do a job more quickly than a less powerful one.

The unit of power is named after James Watt (1736–1819).

→ *Electricity*

There are many situations where energy is transferred via electricity from one place to another. In a torch, the battery transfers energy to the **electrons** in a circuit, which carry it to the lamp where the energy is transferred from the electrons to light and heat in the lamp. The lamp gives out light and gets hot.

6 Think of a device where the electricity transfers energy to:

a) produce sound
b) produce movement of air
c) melt butter.

Reasoning *Power*

Imagine that energy is like a can of fizzy drink. On a hot summer's day a shop might sell 200 cans of drink, while on a cold day it might only sell 100.

The rate of sales varies on different days. The rate per day will also vary between big shops, like supermarkets, and small shops, like newsagents.

Power is the *rate* at which devices transfer energy from electricity. Cookers, heaters, irons and kettles have high power ratings. Radios, lamps and telephones have low power ratings.

Explain to your partner how the fizzy drink model explains power. Decide whether this is a good way of thinking about power or not.

1 Look at the details in the table from the consumer magazine *Which?* showing a range of hairdryers.
   a) Which is the most powerful?
   b) Is the most powerful necessarily the best hairdryer?
   c) Is it the most expensive?

Hairdryers						
	Babyliss Salon Professional 1013	**Boots** 1600 Coolshot	**Braun** Silencio PX 1600	**Remington** Compact Turbo D2200	**Revlon** Professional 1800 9003	**Vidal Sassoon** Salon Professional VS-481
Price (£)	30	20	12	9	24	30
Country of origin	China	China	Ireland	China	China	China
Weight (g)	710	620	390	360	680	810
Wattage (kW)	1.2	1.6	1.6	1.4	1.8	1.3
Drying time	◖	◖	◖	◖	○	◖
Quiet operation	○	○	◖	○	○	◖
Ease of use switches/controls	○	◖	●	●	○	○

key
best ←——→ worst
● ◖ ○ ◖ ○

Information processing

Power rating

Here is a list of some different power rated devices found in the home:

torch bulb	2 W
electric fan heater	1000 W
Morphy Richards kettle	2025 W
light bulb	100 W
Indesit W84 washing machine	1850 W
Bosch SPS 20 dishwasher	3200 W
Hinari CW102 toaster	800 W
Krups coffee maker	2165 W
Belling microwave oven	1200 W
Bosch PSB electric drill	600 W
Thomson TV	115 W
Panasonic DVD player	15 W

Look at the information shown above. Think of a suitable way of representing this information in a chart. You may wish to use a spreadsheet.

Key word
* joulemeters

Working out electricity bills

Different devices transfer different amounts of energy in a given time (power). For example, a light bulb may be rated 60 W. This means that it transfers energy at the rate of 60 joules each second (J/s). Meters that measure energy transferred are called **joulemeters**.

A joulemeter measures how much energy is transferred.

The power rating plate on a stereo.

If you look at different household electrical appliances you will find that they have a plate showing their power rating. Other useful sources are adverts or *Which?*-type reviews.

Think about an electric fan heater. The power rating is 1 kW (1000 W). This means that:

in one second, 1000 J are transferred,
in one minute, 1000×60 J $= 60000$ J are transferred,
in one hour, $1000 \times 60 \times 60$ J $= 3\,600\,000$ J are transferred,
in 5 hours, the number of joules transferred is
$\quad 5 \times 1000 \times 60 \times 60 = 18\,000\,000$ J.

Instead of joules, electricity companies use another unit for calculating energy. They call it the kilowatt-hour (kWh) or sometimes simply 'a unit'. So if a 1 kW electric fire is used for 5 hours the number of units of electricity used is $1 \times 5 = 5$ kWh.

7 If a 7 kW electric shower is used for 30 minutes a day, how many units would it use in a week?

To find the cost of the units of electricity, you use the following formula:

total cost (in pence) = power (in kW) $\times$ time (in hours)
$\qquad \times$ cost of a unit (in pence)

Household electricity meters measure in kWh.

Information processing *Energy transfer*

The table below shows the power rating of a kettle. To find out how much energy it transfers we also need to know how often (the frequency) and the length of time for which it is used. Copy out the table. Add further devices, putting the most powerful at the top and the least powerful at the bottom. You may wish to enter the results into a spreadsheet.

Device	Power rating (kW)	Times used per day	Estimated time switched on	Total energy used
kettle	2	10	6 minutes	2 kWh

1 Work out how much energy each device uses in
  a) a week
  b) a month
  c) 6 months.

2 If a kWh (unit) of electricity costs 10p, how much would the bill be for:
  a) a week
  b) a month
  c) 6 months?

→ *Power and efficiency*

Key word
* efficiency

When energy is supplied to a kettle of water only some of the energy heats up the water.

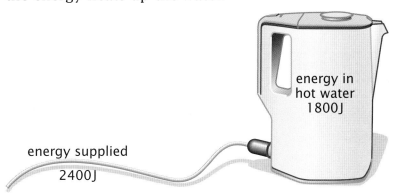

energy in
hot water
1800J

energy supplied
2400J

8 a) How much of the energy supplied is not used to heat the water in the kettle?

b) What fraction of the energy supplied is transferred to the water?

This is called the useful energy.

Scientists define **efficiency** as:

$$\frac{\text{useful energy}}{\text{total energy}} \times 100\%$$

In this example, the efficiency is:

$$\frac{1800}{2400} \times 100\% = 75\%$$

Different styles of kettle.

100% efficiency is impossible as heat energy always gets lost to the kettle and the surroundings. The more efficient things are the less energy is wasted. Designers work to improve both the efficiency and style of kettles (some examples are pictured on page 85), and other household devices.

Time to think

Copy and complete each statement using the following key words:

> **power, million, efficiency, kinetic energy, joule, non-renewable, renewable, watt, 1000.**

Definition

The scientific unit of energy is the _____.

The scientific unit of power is the _____.

When something is moving we say that it has _____.

The formula: $\dfrac{\text{energy transferred}}{\text{time taken}}$ calculates _____.

In SI units, kilo means multiply the basic unit by _____.

The formula: $\dfrac{\text{useful energy}}{\text{total energy}} \times 100\%$ calculates _____.

In SI units, mega means multiply the basic unit by _____.

Energy resources that will not run out are known as _____.

Gas is an example of an energy source that is _____.

DID YOU KNOW?

The work done by the beat of a fly's wing is one-millionth of a joule.
The work done by the single beat of a human heart is 0.5 J.
The energy content of the nuclear bomb dropped on Hiroshima was 80 million megajoules (MJ).
The energy output of a power station in a year is about 10 000 million megajoules (MJ).

→ *Current and voltage*

How many of these questions can you answer without help? Compare your answers with others and make a note of any points that you need to learn.

9 Which is the **series** circuit and which is the **parallel** circuit?

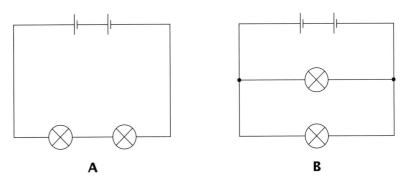

10 What does an **ammeter** measure? What does a **voltmeter** measure?

11 In the circuit below, are the ammeters connected in series or parallel? Is the voltmeter in series or parallel?

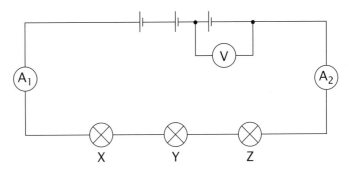

12 The ammeter A_1 reads 0.2 A. What does ammeter A_2 read?

13 A voltmeter is connected across the first cell as shown. It reads 1.5 V.

a) The voltmeter is then disconnected and reconnected across two cells as shown. What will it read now?

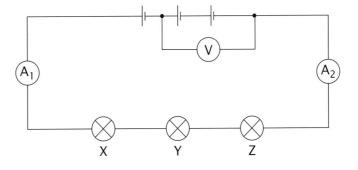

b) The voltmeter is then disconnected and reconnected across the three cells as shown. What will it read now?

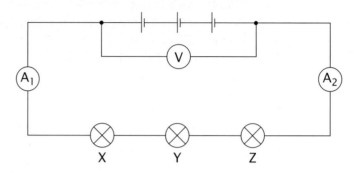

c) The voltmeter is now disconnected and reconnected across lamp X. What will it read now?

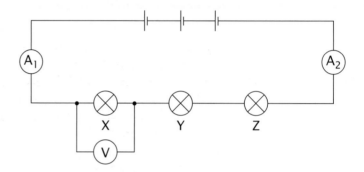

d) The voltmeter is now disconnected and reconnected across lamp Y. What will it read now?

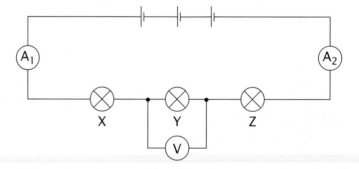

Remember to connect the ammeter in series with the lamps and to connect the voltmeter in parallel with the lamps. You do not need to break into the circuit to connect the voltmeter.

➡ *Voltage and energy*

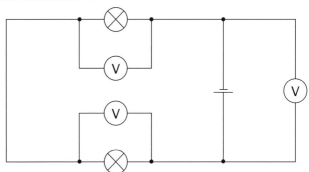

Key words
✷ model
✷ resistor
✷ resistance

In Book 1 we used a simple concrete and lorries analogy to help us to think about electricity. To understand what voltage is about let us look again at our model. Look at the electric circuit below.

Charged particles move round the circuit. These charged particles are called electrons. Electrons are given energy by the cell, and they transfer this energy to the lamp. If there were two identical lamps, the charged particles would transfer half of their energy as they passed through the first lamp, and the other half as they passed through the second lamp. (This energy is radiated by the lamps.) More particles passing through the lamp means that more energy is transferred.

In our concrete and lorries analogy, we will suppose that the firm has to maintain a continuous supply of concrete to two building sites at a steady rate. To do this, the lorries visit each site in turn and deposit half of their load of concrete at each site.

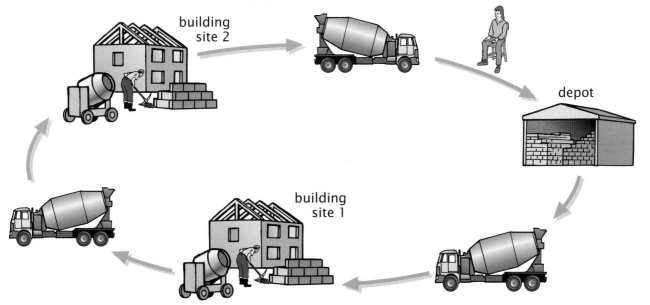

In the electric circuit, the voltage of the cell is a measure of the amount of energy that the cell can transfer to the particles. The voltmeter reading across the lamps is a measure of the amount of energy that is transferred to that lamp by the particles passing through it.

Reasoning

Models

Copy and complete the table below.

Electric circuit	Building circuit
battery	depot
lamps	
	lorries
wire	
ammeters measuring current flowing	person by side of road counting rate at which lorries pass
voltmeter measuring energy transferred by charged particles	site manager checking the amount of concrete left by the lorry

The example of lorries and concrete is just a **model** to help explain what happens in the electric circuit. A model will have its limitations, and while it will help us to explain simple situations it is less useful for more complex ones. We can use lots of different models to help explain the same concept. Can you remember or invent other models to explain your ideas about electricity?

A **resistor** is an electrical component. It opposes the flow of electricity. The bigger the **resistance** of the resistor, the smaller the electric current that can flow. Resistance is measured in ohms. The abbreviation for ohm is the Greek letter Ω. Adding a resistor to a circuit reduces the electric current.

Evaluation

Using a voltmeter

A group of students performed an experiment using resistors and a voltmeter. They were investigating the relationship between resistance and voltage in a circuit. They were provided with a selection of resistors with resistances of 100 ohm, 220 ohm and 330 ohm, a 3 V battery, connecting wires, and a digital voltmeter.

They were also provided with a resistor whose value was not known. The resistors they were given were labelled as follows:

A = 100 ohm
B = 100 ohm
C = 100 ohm
D = 220 ohm
E = 220 ohm
F = 330 ohm

X is unknown.

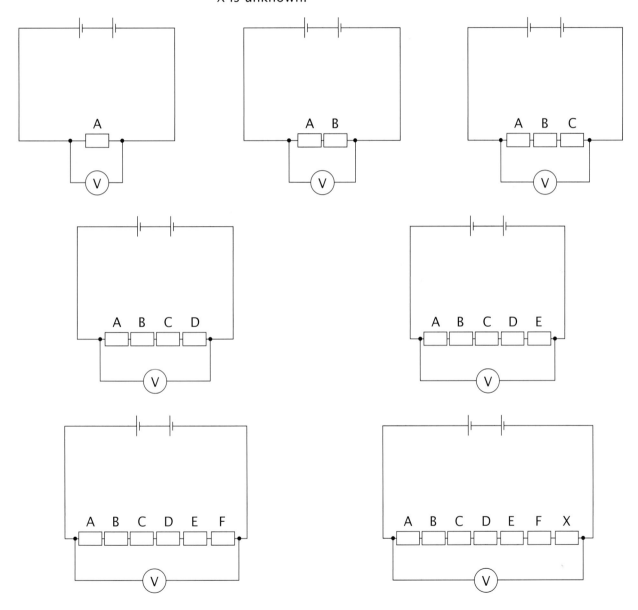

This is the report of one group of pupils:

We connected all the resistors in series as in the diagram. We measured the voltage across resistor A first, then resistor A and B and then resistors A, B and C and so on. We put the results in the table. This is shown below.

Resistors	Value of resistor (ohm)	Voltage (V)
A	100	0.25
A and B	200	0.49
A, B and C	300	0.74
A,B,C and D	520	1.28
A,B,C,D and E	740	1.82
A,B,C,D,E and F	1070	2.47
A, B, C, D, E, F and X	1070 + X	3.00

We then plotted a graph of resistance against voltage.

1 What do you think the pupils were trying to find out?

2 Can you suggest a title for their experiment?

3 In each experiment what was the input (independent) variable?

4 What was the outcome (dependent) variable?

5 Which variable goes on the horizontal axis?

6 On graph paper plot the graph using the results they obtained. Describe the shape of the graph.

7 What sort of relationship do these results suggest?

8 Use the graph you have drawn to estimate the resistance for a voltmeter reading of 3.0 V.

9 What is the value of the unknown resistor X? Explain how you obtained this answer.

Transferring energy at high voltage

High voltages allow more energy to be transferred by the electric current as it flows around the circuit. This is why high voltage devices and cable can be dangerous to humans. Even mains electricity at 230 V can be lethal and should be carefully handled. Small voltages are not harmful. If you touch both ends of a 1.5 V dry cell it will not harm you. The resistance of your skin is high enough to ensure that even with a 12 V car battery only a small current will flow through should you touch its terminals.

You may have seen equipment similar to this:

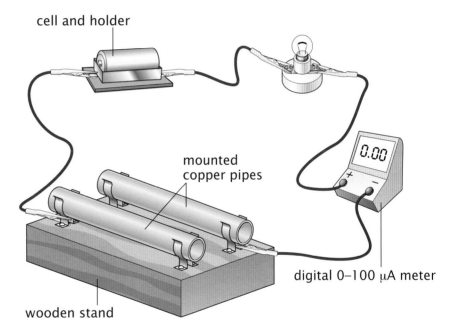

cell and holder

mounted copper pipes

digital 0–100 µA meter

wooden stand

This demonstration circuit shows the conditions needed for the human body to be a conductor: a volunteer gripping the two copper pipes will complete the circuit.

SAFETY!

You should NEVER touch the mains as this could be lethal!

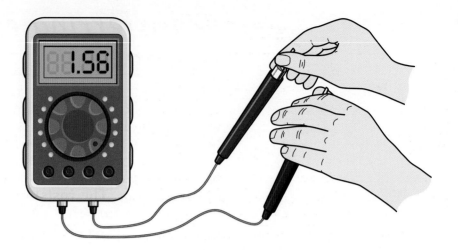

This alternative demonstration uses a digital multimeter to measure the resistance between your hands.

The size of a current depends on the resistance in the circuit, and the battery voltage.

The resistance that your body has depends on a number of factors. The resistance between your little finger and thumb is slightly different from that between your hand and foot. The main thing that affects your resistance is the amount of hard dry skin on the surface, and whether or not your skin is wet. Dry skin has a resistance many times greater than wet skin. Dry, hard skin may have a resistance of 10 kilohms whereas wet skin could easily be as low as a few hundred ohms. This is why you should NEVER use electrical equipment, for example a hairdryer, in a bathroom. If your skin is wet, resistance is lowered, and handling a hairdryer could be fatal.

SAFETY!

You should NEVER use electrical equipment in a bathroom.

Every year in the UK about a hundred people are killed by electric shocks. These are often received from household appliances such as electric lawn mowers, hedge trimmers, and hairdryers being used in the bathroom.

DID YOU KNOW?

A shock current greater than about 50 thousandths of an amp (50 mA or 0.05 A) will probably start the heart beating in an irregular fashion. This is fatal if it is not corrected very quickly. The nervous impulses from the brain to the muscles instructing the body to move are electrical. If a large electric current flows through the body it interferes with this nervous stimulation, and a person holding a live conductor cannot let go. This is called the 'no let go' current.

Creative thinking *Shocking electricity*

Current (mA)	Effect
1	threshold of feeling, current just detectable
1.2–2	tingling sensation in the hands
1.2–2.8	sensation that the hands have gone to sleep
2.8–3.5	slight stiffening of the hand
3.5–4.5	considerable stiffening of lower arm muscles
4.5–5.0	feeling of cramp in the lower arm and slight trembling of the hands – this is accepted as the maximum harmless current
5.0–15.0	unpleasant cramping of the lower arm – limits of ability to 'let go' are reached
15–20	release is impossible, this cannot be tolerated for more than 15 minutes
20–40	serious and very painful contraction of the muscles, breathing stops but will normally resume if current is interrupted
50–200	ventricular fibrillation (a state of the heart which leads directly to death)
over 200	tissues and organs burn

In groups, design a series of hazard warning signs using some kind of scale to represent the different current effects.

Whilst it is the current in your body that causes the electric shock, a greater voltage provides a bigger push. Higher voltages are potentially more dangerous. The voltage of the electric mains is 240 V, which is potentially lethal.

→ *Transmitting electricity*

Mains electricity is usually produced at 25 000 V. It is then transformed (changed) to 275 000 V (or even higher) to travel through the National Grid system. Overhead cables carry the high voltage electricity to all towns and cities. However, to use the electricity in our homes the current is transformed back down to 230 V. This happens at substations, and it is sent to homes and businesses through underground cables.

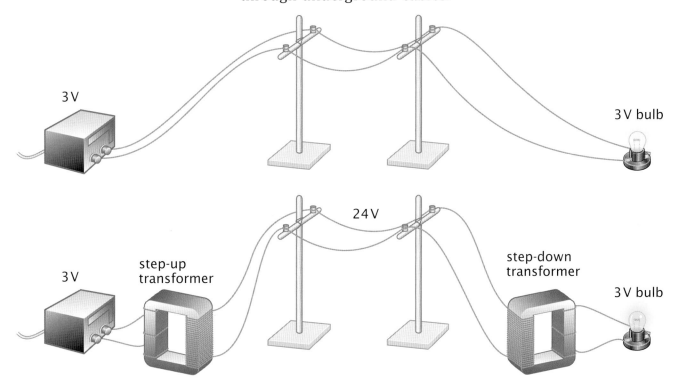

Energy is wasted in the long wires carrying the energy to a distant village and so less energy is available to light the lamp in the village. With higher voltages, a given electric current can transfer more energy.

Information processing | *Power station*

The diagram opposite shows the main features of a coal-fired power station. The coal is delivered by rail and stored until it is needed. It is then taken to the pulverising mills where it is ground into a fine powder. This powdered coal is mixed with warm air and burnt. The furnace heats the boilers and the water inside them is turned into steam. This high-pressure, high-temperature steam passes into the turbine where it strikes the blades, making them rotate at 3000 revolutions per minute. This turbine turns the generator to produce electricity. The transformer steps the voltage up from 25 000 V to 275 000 V and feeds the electricity into the National Grid. In the power station the steam is turned back into water in the

condensers, where it is passed over a series of cold pipes. From here the water is returned to the boiler. The warm water from the condenser passes through the cooling towers where it is cooled.

1 On a sheet of paper draw the main parts of the power station. Label each feature and use the information above to explain its function.

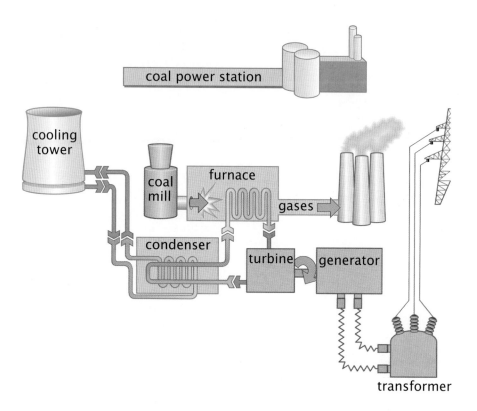

The diagram above shows coal being burnt to heat the water to turn it into steam which makes the turbines rotate. Other power stations burn gas or oil to create the heat while nuclear power stations use the heat created when atoms of uranium split up. In hydroelectric power stations there is no heat produced. The turbines rotate because of the force of the water passing over them.

2 Which power stations are using fossil fuels?

3 Divide the sources of energy into renewable and non-renewable.

4 Draw a block diagram to show how you think electricity is generated by wind farms.

Creative thinking ## No electricity

Imagine you lived in a world in which there was no electricity. List in order the things you would miss the most. Compare your list with others in your group. Would you expect adults to have a similar or different list from yours? How might your list be different if you lived near the North Pole?

Research

Internationally, not all countries think the same way about energy policy. Find out about the Kyoto protocol, and what the attitude of the US government is.

There is much information now available about alternative ways of generating electricity. Various leaflets exist about these alternative methods, and there is plenty of information on the internet. Some alternative methods of generating electricity are from:

solar power
wind farms
biogas
waves
geothermal energy
nuclear energy
combined heat and power (CHP)

Choose one of the types mentioned above and produce your own leaflet about it.

Enquiry ## Solar energy

The pictures below show two different devices which transfer energy from the Sun.

Solar panels use radiation from the Sun to provide hot water.

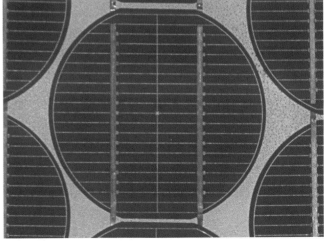

A solar cell uses energy from the Sun to provide electricity.

Choose one of the devices to plan an investigation. The questions to be investigated are:

What affects the temperature of the water?

What affects the output from a solar cell?

1 There are a number of variables that you could change. Make a list of them.

2 Plan which question you will investigate. Decide which variable you will change (the independent variable), and which variable you will observe (the dependent variable).

3 What equipment will you need?

4 How will you collect and record the data?

5 How will you present the data?

Time to think

Think back over the work you have done in this chapter. What have you found out about energy and electricity that you didn't know before? Which parts did you find interesting?

Repeat the activity you did at the start of the chapter where you were asked to write down on a piece of card a list of all the key words that you connect with energy. Cut out the key words and arrange them on a sheet of paper to produce a concept map. Remember to draw lines to link the words and write a connecting sentence.

Compare your concept map with the one that you produced at the beginning of the chapter. Has it changed or is it the same as the one you originally made?

4 Forces and space

In this chapter you will learn:

➡ **that gravity is a force of attraction between objects and that this force depends on their masses and how far apart they are**

➡ **that larger objects like the Earth have greater gravitational pull than smaller objects**

➡ **that gravity gets less the further an object moves away from the Earth's surface and this influences space travel**

➡ **how weight is different on different planets**

➡ **what satellites are and how they are used**

➡ **how forces affect the movement of objects as they fall**

➡ **how streamlining reduces resistance to air and water and how this resistance increases with the speed of the object**

You will also develop your skills in:

➡ **using a model of gravitational attraction to describe how stars, planets and satellites are kept in their orbits in relation to one another**

➡ **describing how ideas and evidence about the nature of the Solar System have changed over time**

➡ **researching secondary sources to find out about recent space exploration and how the Universe might have begun**

➡ **using data to compare gravitational forces and weight differences on different planets**

➡ **plotting and interpreting graphs about the movement of objects**

➡ ➡ ➡ WHAT DO YOU KNOW?

1 On your own decide which pupils shown on page 101 are stating the truth, as we know it, and which pupils have 'misconceptions' – wrong scientific ideas.

2 Now compare your answers with someone else in your group. If the two of you disagree about any statement being true or false, find out which one of you is right.

A The Moon has no gravity because it has no air.

B Gravity acts down.

C Rockets are propelled through space by their exhaust gases pushing out behind them.

D It takes the Earth twenty-four hours to spin around once.

E Tides in oceans are caused by the pull of the Moon's gravity.

F The Sun is the centre of the Solar System.

G When an object is not moving, no forces are acting on it.

H Heavy objects fall faster than light objects.

I The Sun is the largest object in the Solar System.

J All stars are the same distance from the Sun.

K A football will fall faster than a tennis ball because it is larger.

Measuring

3 Which of these instruments measures mass, and which measure force?

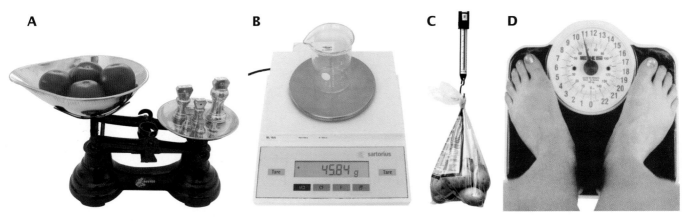

A   **B**   **C**   **D**

4 Here are drawings by Shona and Sohail to show their ideas about the pull of gravity.

Shona's drawing:

Sohail's drawing:

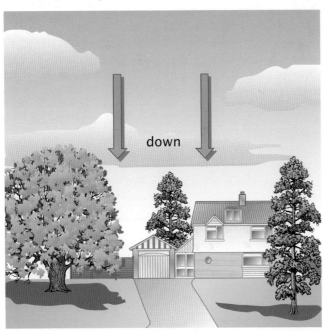

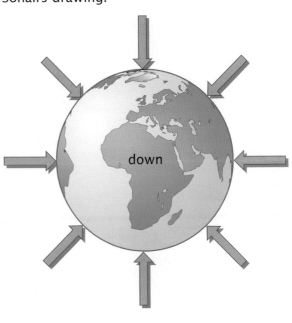

a) Why do you think Year 1 pupils would choose Shona's drawing to show the meaning of 'down'?

b) Which drawing best represents the way a scientist might think about gravity? Talk about your answers and explain why you think that.

5 Copy each of the drawings below and add arrows indicating the forces that you think are acting on the objects.

A

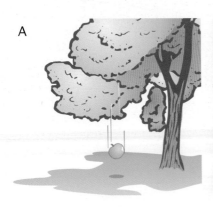

B

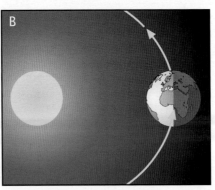

C

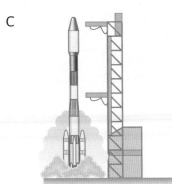

D

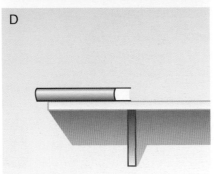

E

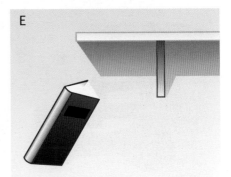

→ *Astronomy*

Key words
* astronomy
* astrology

Newton, Galileo, the Egyptian scholar, Ptolemy, and the Mayan civilisation in Central America were all interested in **astronomy** – the scientific study of stars, planets and the Universe.

1 In your groups, discuss what you know about any of these people.
   Astrology is the use of the zodiac – the arrangement of stars and planets to foretell the future. It is not thought of as a science.

2 Do you know your astrological sign?
3 Lots of magazines and newspapers have weekly or daily horoscopes. Think of some ways you could test if these predictions are accurate and scientific.

Word play   Sort the list of key words below into alphabetical order. Put a tick by any you think you already know the meaning of. Look up dictionary definitions of the others.

Key words
* rotated
* heliocentric
* geocentric
* celestial
* Solar System
* orbits
* axes
* astronomical
* ellipse

How our ideas about astronomy changed with time

In pairs, read this brief history of astronomy to each other. Decide between you who reads which parts out loud.

The earliest written records about astronomy were probably written three hundred years before Christ was born. They were found in Mesopotamia. This is the present-day Middle Eastern country of Iraq. Early records show that people thought the Earth was the centre of the Universe and that the stars and planets, including the Sun, **rotated** around us. In the third century BC, Aristarchus of Samos studied the Earth, Sun and Moon and put forward the idea that the Sun, and not the Earth, was at the centre of the Universe. This **heliocentric** (helios is Greek for Sun) view was rejected by the people of his day.

Stonehenge in Wiltshire, England, was built between 3000 and 1500BC. Some of the larger stones weigh over 45 tonnes. There are lots of theories that it was built for astronomical calculations of the Sun and Moon.

Aristotle, one of the most famous Greek philosophers was born in 384BC, and he started his own academy in Athens. He developed a theory of gravity but it is his model of the Universe, with the Earth at the centre that is best known. This is the **geocentric** (or Earth-centred) theory. Another famous astronomer was Ptolemy, who was born at Pelusium in Egypt in about 100AD. He collected together the historical works and ideas of Aristotle and Hipparchus, another Greek astronomer. Aristotle and Ptolemy's geocentric theories were respected so much that they were unchallenged up until the sixteenth century.

It was Nicolaus Copernicus who finally challenged their theories. He was born in the Polish town of Thorn in 1473, and became a professor at the University in Rome, Italy. He returned to Poland, and it was here that he developed his heliocentric model based on Aristarchus's ideas. He could not prove that his theory was correct, and he was also concerned that his ideas contradicted the views of the powerful authority of the Church. The Church said it was a matter of faith that the Earth was in the centre of the Universe, because humans were the most important of all God's creations and He had made the Earth for them. Copernicus' work was published in 1543, just before he died. It was called 'On the revolutions of the **Celestial** Bodies'. In it he described the Sun as the centre of the **Solar System**. The planets revolved around it in circular **orbits** at varying distances, and also rotated about their **axes**.

The next major contributions to the study of astronomy were by Tycho Brahe, Johannes Kepler and Galileo Galilei. They were all born within a period of 30 years.

Brahe (1546–1601) was a Danish nobleman and the pioneer of accurate **astronomical** observation. His work was all done without the aid of a telescope, because it had not yet been invented.

Kepler (1571–1630) was born at Weil in Germany. In 1600 he accepted an invitation to work with Brahe, succeeding him as 'Imperial Mathematician' of Denmark when Brahe died. One of the important laws he stated, based on his observations of the movement of planets, was that the path of a planet around the Sun was an **ellipse**.

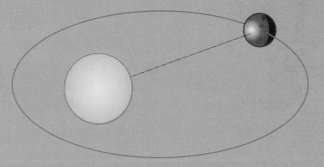

Galileo was born in Pisa on 18th February 1564. When he heard of the invention of the telescope he designed and built one for himself. He was the first person to use a telescope systematically for astronomical observations and records. He observed the moons of Jupiter, and saw that their movement around Jupiter was a miniature model of the Solar System. He saw that Venus had phases similar to those of the Moon, as Copernicus might have predicted. The Church said that this was heresy, because it contradicted the teaching of Aristotle, and in 1616 Galileo was warned to stop teaching that Copernicus's theory about the heliocentric system was correct. The Inquisition tried Galileo when he was 68. His book was placed on the 'Index' of forbidden books, where it remained until 1824. He was also sentenced to house arrest for the remainder of his life. It was not until 1990 that Pope John Paul II officially accepted that the Church had been wrong to oppose his scientific method and his findings.

Galileo compared the motion of heavy objects and light ones. He described mathematically how far an object fell in a given time, and was then able to verify experimentally that this description was correct. He was able to show that a heavy object and a light object both fall at the same rate. The story of the experiment at the leaning tower of Pisa is well known. Galileo released a large and a small mass from the top of the tower and they reached the bottom at the same time. Galileo is considered by many scientists and philosophers to be the founder of experimental science.

The leaning tower of Pisa.

DISCORSI
E
DIMOSTRAZIONI
MATEMATICHE,
intorno à due nuoue scienze
Attenenti alla
MECANICA & I MOVIMENTI LOCALI,
del Signor
GALILEO GALILEI LINCEO,
Filofofo e Matematico primario del Sereniffimo
Grand Duca di Tofcana.

Con vna Appendice del centro di grauità d'alcuni Solidi.

IN LEIDA,
Appreffo gli Elfevirii. M. D. C. XXXVIII.

Sir Isaac Newton (1642–1727), was born the year Galileo died. His thinking was very important for the development of today's ideas about mechanics and planetary motion. Newton showed that the entire Universe obeyed the same laws of nature, as published in his *Mathematical Principles of Natural Philosophy* (or *The Principia* as it became more commonly known) in 1687. He proved that the mechanics that determined how bodies fall on Earth also explained the regular motions of the planets. According to folklore it was an apple falling from a tree that suggested to Newton his ideas about the force of gravity. He guessed that the Earth's gravity extended out into space, gradually getting weaker, and it was this force that kept the Moon in orbit around the Earth.

Word play

Look at your alphabetical list of key words again. Tick the ones you are now sure you know the meaning of with a green pen. Compare your list with other people's and see if they can help you learn the meaning of any un-ticked words. Circle the words that describe movement.

Information processing *Astronomers*

Draw a table with three columns. In the first column write a list of the names of people that have influenced the study of astronomy with their ideas. In the second column write down the dates when they lived and died. In the third column make a note of their important ideas.

Time to think

Here is a self-test to check how well you understand the ideas in this chapter so far.

1 Who believed in the heliocentric theory?
2 Who believed in the geocentric theory?
3 What is the main difference between these two theories?
4 Which do you believe, and why?
5 What forces keep the Moon orbiting the Earth?
6 Is it true to say that the Moon rotates around the Earth because of gravity?
7 What is the shape of the orbit our Earth makes around the Sun? Draw it.
8 What instrument did Galileo construct?
9 How did he use it in a way that had never been done before?
10 Why do many people who study physics think that the leaning tower of Pisa is a famous landmark?
11 Why was Tycho Brahe an important person in the history of astronomy?
12 Why were Galileo and Copernicus afraid to talk or write about their theories publicly?

Work with a partner to check your answers and agree on a mark scheme for this test. Give each other a mark and a suggestion for improving performance.

Gravity

Key words
* mass
* weight
* gravity
* matter

Make sure that you know these important definitions:

The unit of **mass** is the kilogram.

The unit of force is the newton.

There is a difference between mass and **weight**.

Mass is a measure of the amount of 'stuff' present in an object. It tells us about the number of particles that are in the object.

Weight is a force. It tells us about the pull of **gravity** on the object.

DID YOU KNOW?

We call the metric system of units the SI system (French for Systeme Internationale) because it was devised in France during the time of Napoleon. The standard unit of mass is 1 kg, the mass of a lump of metal (a platinum-iridium alloy) kept at Sèvres near Paris, France.

4 In pairs make a revision list of the important facts about gravity in the following two paragraphs.

Any two objects that have mass have an attractive force between them. This attractive force is what we call gravity.

If one object is big, like the Earth, the attractive force is also big. If you drop an apple it is attracted towards the Earth by the force of gravity. The Earth is also attracted towards the apple by the same force at the same time, but because the Earth is so massive its movement towards the apple is too tiny to be detected. The force of gravity on a mass of 1 kg on the surface of the Earth is about 9.8 N. To make calculations easier we can round this up to 10 N. As you travel away from the Earth the pull of gravity gets less.

Gravitational force pulls us towards the Earth, and without it we would float about. It was Sir Isaac Newton who came to the conclusion that gravitational force exists between all objects, or **matter**. Matter can be defined as anything that is affected by gravity, i.e., that has weight or would have weight if it were near the Earth or another star or planet. Gravity is responsible for holding the Moon in its orbit about the Earth and planets in orbit around the Sun.

Word play

Newton said this:
'If I have seen further than other men it is because I have stood on the shoulders of giants'.
What do you think he meant by this?

Information processing ## Gravity

1 Look at the graph below which shows how the gravitational force changes with distance from the Earth. What happens to the size of the force as the distance from the Earth gets greater?

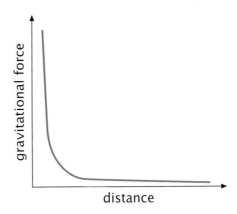

2 Imagine a 6 kg bag of potatoes. The force of gravity on the Earth is about 10 N per kg, so the force of gravity on one 1 kg of potatoes is 10 N. What is the force of gravity, in newtons, on the 6 kg bag of potatoes?

3 On the Moon the force of gravity is only one-sixth that of the Earth. If you took the potatoes to the Moon (highly unlikely!) what would be their mass? What would be the gravitational force on the potatoes on the Moon? What would be the weight of the potatoes on the Moon in newtons?

Enquiry *Mars experiment*

Key word
* newton meter

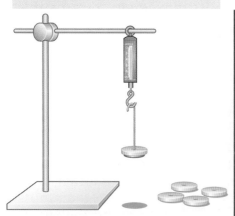

Measuring the gravitational pull.

Mass (kg)	Weight (N)
0.2	0.75
0.4	1.49
0.6	2.24
0.8	2.98
1.0	3.73

If we took a **newton meter** to Mars we could measure the gravitational pull of Mars. Future visitors to Mars could perform this experiment.

Instructions:

1 » Suspend the mass hanger from the newton meter as shown in the diagram.

2 » Add a mass of 0.2 kg and note the reading on the newton meter.

3 » Record the results in a table.

4 » Continue the experiment by adding extra masses of 0.2 kg up to 1 kg in total and recording the readings from the newton meter.

Results for this experiment might look like those in the table on the left.

1 Use the results to plot a graph of the mass against the gravitational pull of Mars. (The independent variable (input) variable goes on the horizontal axis.)

2 What is the shape of the graph?

3 What is the pull of Mars on a mass of 1 kg?

4 Predict what the reading would be for a mass of 0.5 kg.

5 If the gravitational pull were 6 N, what would be the size of the mass?

6 Is the gravitational pull of Mars greater or smaller than the gravitational pull of Earth? Can you think why this may be so?

Reasoning *Jupiter*

On Jupiter, gravity is about 2.5 times that of the Earth. Which top-pan balance is showing the Jupiter mass of a 5 kg bag of potatoes? How did you work this out?

The centre of gravity of an object is the point inside an object where there is as much mass on one side as the other. In a balance beam this would be called the pivot or fulcrum. Men and women have a different centre of gravity, because of their different body build.

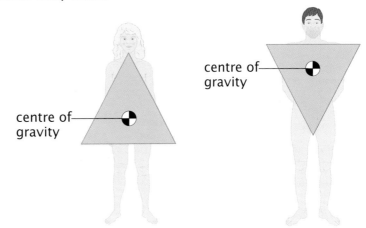

centre of gravity

centre of gravity

Centre of gravity

Test this out at home. Stand with your toes touching a wall. Put one foot behind the other and walk three paces away from the wall. Ask someone to put a stool between you and the wall. Lean over and put the top of your head against the wall so your legs are at about a 45° angle.

Grip each edge of the stool and pick it up and hold it against your chest. Now try to stand up. Get some adults to try it too.

What do you expect the difference between men and women to be?

→ *Planet facts*

Planet	Relative mass of planet if Earth equals 100* units	Average distance from the Sun (million km)	Pull of gravity on 1 kg mass on the planet's surface
Mercury	6	60	4
Mars	10	230	4
Venus	80	105	9
Earth	100*	150	10
Saturn	9 500	1 400	11
Moon	1	150	1.7
Jupiter	31 700	770	26

*In fact the Earth's mass is 6000 million million million tonnes.

5 Why do you think the table gives Earth as having a mass of 100 units?
6 Which planet has the biggest mass?
7 Which planet is closest to the Sun?
8 What is the pull of gravity on 1 kg of flour on Earth?
9 What would it be on Mars?
10 Rachel weighs 42 kg. What would be the pull of gravity on her if she were on Mars?
11 On which of these planets could you jump the highest? Why?
12 The first man on the Moon was the astronaut Neil Armstrong. His body pushed down on the Earth with a force of 750 N. What force made his footprints in the Moon's surface dust?
13 Is this statement true or false? 'The further a planet is from the Sun, the bigger the pull of gravity on it.' Explain your answer.

→ *A brief history of space exploration*

Date	Spacecraft	Achievement
October 1957	Sputnik 1	• launched by Russia • orbited Earth every 96 minutes
November 1960	Sputnik 2	Russia launched the first living organism into space – the dog Laika
April 1961	Vostok 1	Major Yuri Gagarin, a Russian, is the first man in space
February 1962	Friendship 7	John Glenn is the first American to orbit Earth
June 1963	Vostock 6	Valentina Tereshkova, a Russian, is the first woman in space
March 1965	Voskhod	Russian astronaut Alexei Leonov takes the first walk in space
December 1968	Apollo 8	James Lovell, William Anders, Frank Borman, from the USA, are the first people to fly around the Moon

Date	Spacecraft	Achievement
July 1969	Apollo 11	Neil Armstrong takes the first human steps on the Moon, followed by Buzz Aldrin
April 1971	Salyut 1	▪ Russia launches the first space station ▪ it orbits for 23 days but all three of the crew are killed when the return flight burns up on re-entry into the Earth's atmosphere
July 1971	Apollo 15	lands on the Moon and the first moon buggy, an electric car, travels 17 miles on the Moon
May 1973	Skylab	first American space station launched
July 1975	Apollo 18 and Soyuz 19	first joint American and Russian space mission as the two spacecraft link up
April 1981	Columbia Space Shuttle	first flight of a new programme for transporting astronauts to space stations
January 1986	Challenger space shuttle	the American spacecraft exploded just over a minute after its launch, killing all seven crew
May 1973	Skylab 1 and 2	▪ unmanned space lab was launched, followed by launch of first manned space lab ▪ a crew met up with Skylab 2, where they made some repairs and carried out experiments ▪ Skylab was abandoned in 1975 ▪ in 1979 Skylab fell to Earth, scattering wreckage from the Indian Ocean to western Australia
February 1986	Mir space station	Russia launches the space station Mir
May 1991	Mir programme	Helen Sharman visits Mir as a prize in a contest to become Britain's first astronaut
1998	International Space station	the first two models of this international space station are launched and joined together in space
April 1990	Hubble project	a space telescope first designed in the 1970s is launched and continues still to provide high-quality information about outer space
August 1999	Mir programme	▪ the 27th crew to Mir lands back on Earth ▪ no replacement crew is sent up
February 2001	Mir programme	Mir space lab completes 15 years in orbit, surpassing its planned life of less than 5 years
November 2000	International Space Station programme	the first crew (of two Russians and one American) go to the station
March 2001	Mir programme	▪ Mir burns up as it is made to descend to a lower orbit ▪ most of the lab burns up over the South Pacific between Australia and Chile, although 30 tons may have survived re-entry through Earth's atmosphere to fall into the Pacific Ocean
February 2003	Columbia programme	after many successful routine space flights, a Columbia spacecraft explodes on re-entry to Earth's atmosphere, killing all seven crew
August 2003	International Space Station programme	▪ Russian cosmonaut Yuri Malenchenko is the first person to marry while in space ▪ he exchanged vows 240 miles above New Zealand aboard the International Space Station with Ekaterina Dmitriev who was on Earth, at the Johnson Space Centre at Houston
late 2004	Atlantis space shuttle	this is the planned next manned flight to take crew to the International Space Station

14 Which of the following events were carried out by Russians and which by Americans?

First man on the Moon
First woman in space
First animal in space
First Earth orbit
First space vehicle on the Moon
First space walk
First space lab launched
First wedding in space

Research

Find out why the Americans called all their Moon mission spacecraft 'Apollo'.
Find out what the 'Atlantis' spacecraft is named after.
Find out what NASA stands for.
Find Helen Sharman's home page and use it to write a short biography of her life that could go in a reference book about space travellers. The editor says it cannot be longer than 150 words.

I believe this nation should commit itself to achieving the goal, before this decade is out, of landing a man on the Moon and returning him safely to Earth. No single space project in this period will be more impressive to mankind, or more important in the long-range exploration of space; and none will be so difficult or expensive to accomplish.
        John F. Kennedy, Special Joint Session of Congress, 25th May 1961

Who was John F. Kennedy, and which spacecraft achieved Kennedy's aim?

Space disaster

In February 2003, the spacecraft Columbia was destroyed. NASA scientists think that a piece of fuel-tank insulation that fell off at launch may have damaged one or more ceramic tiles. Temperatures on the left side of the shuttle rose significantly before it burst into flames, and this could have caused more tiles to fall off.

Falling foam "caused shuttle disaster"

A DRAMATIC experiment appears to have confirmed the leading theory for the Columbia space shuttle disaster: that it was fatally damaged by a falling piece of foam insulation during its launch on January 16.

NASA investigators say that the debris from the orbiter's fuel tank could have punched a hole in a critical heat shield. ... The results appear to remove any doubt that the foam, which struck the leading edge of Columbia's wing in the first seconds of launch, was ultimately responsible for its disintegration over Texas ...

From *The Times* 9th July 2003

The space shuttle Columbia.

15 When the space shuttle is travelling through space it does not heat up in the same way as it does when it returns to Earth. What causes the space shuttle to get hot on re-entry?

16 What type of energy does the shuttle have as it re-enters the Earth's atmosphere?

Because astronomical distances are so enormous, special units are used to measure them. The Astronomical Unit (AU) is the average distance of the Earth from the Sun. It is about 150 million km.

The parsec is another unit of distance. It is even bigger than the AU and 1 parsec is about 200 000 AU or 30 000 000 000 000 km. The third unit used is the light year. This is how far a ray of light will travel in a year. As light travels at about 300 000 km/s, it would travel about 9 461 000 000 000 km in a year.

150 000 000 km

1 AU

Earth orbiting the Sun.

The Hubble project

The launch of the Hubble Space Telescope is probably the most important event for deepening our understanding of the Universe since Galileo made his observations. The project is named after Edwin Hubble, who in the 1920s discovered that the galaxies were moving away from each other. The further away they are, the faster they are going. He concluded that the whole Universe was expanding and that at one stage everything started from one point. The Hubble telescope orbits 600 kilometres (375 miles) above Earth, working around the clock to unlock the secrets of the Universe. It uses state-of-the-art instruments to provide stunning views of the Universe that cannot be made using ground-based telescopes or other satellites. Astronauts can take it apart, replace worn out equipment and upgrade its instruments in space.

Edwin Hubble.

Before Hubble, distances to far-off galaxies were not well known. Questions such as how rapidly the Universe is expanding, and for how long, created great controversy. Now we are beginning to answer these questions. Every day, Hubble archives 3 to 5 gigabytes of data and delivers between 10 and 15 gigabytes of information to astronomers all over the world. It has now travelled about 1.489 billion miles – nearly the distance from Earth to Uranus. It circles the Earth about once every 97 minutes.

Photo taken using the Hubble telescope.

The Big Bang theory

Key words
* Big Bang
* Big Crunch
* stead state theory

The **Big Bang** model is a modern theory to explain the origin and evolution of our Universe. It is based on a large amount of evidence, including Hubble's original observations, so most people believe that this theory is correct. It says that 12 to 14 billion years ago the Universe came into existence at a specific moment in time. It started with an enormous explosion. Both time and space were created in this huge blast.

Just after the Big Bang, all the material in the Universe was packed into a tiny volume. The Universe has since expanded from this hot, extremely dense state into the vast and much cooler Universe of today. We can detect and measure remnants of this hot dense matter, which some scientists call 'cosmic background radiation'.

One question that many scientists ask is 'Will the Universe continue to expand?'. There seem to be two possibilities: either it will continue to expand forever, or it will stop expanding and the Universe's own gravity will begin to pull it all back together. This has been called the **Big Crunch**. This is something that we needn't worry about, as this will be a long time in the future!

There are some scientists who do not believe in the Big Bang theory at all. They prefer the idea that the Universe always has been and always will be. This is known as the **steady state theory**.

Modelling the Big Bang

An analogy based on baking a fruitcake may help to explain the Big Bang theory. Think of the Universe as a fruitcake mix of raisins, currants and cherries in a cake mixture. The mixture is poured into a cake tin, which it does not fill. The cake is put into the oven to bake. Imagine that you are a raisin inside the cake. As it bakes, the cake rises and all the other bits of fruit move further and further away from you. No matter where in the cake you are, everything around is moving away at the same rate.

17 In this analogy what could the cake mix be compared to?
18 What is the fruit supposed to represent?
19 Think about the cake baking. What will happen to it eventually? Does this suggest what might happen to our Universe in millions of years to come?

Creative thinking **End of the Universe**

Write a short drama called 'The end of the Universe'. You might like to find out what author Douglas Adams imagined in his book *The Hitchhiker's Guide to the Galaxy*.

Every day 1000 tonnes of meteor dust fall on the Earth. Meteorites are very important for scientists to study. They, along with Moon rock brought back by the Apollo and Lunar missions, are evidence of a Universe beyond Earth.

→ *Satellites*

Key word
∗ satellite

Sputnik 1.

We call an object orbiting a planet a **satellite**. Some are natural, like our Moon. Others are manufactured, and these are artificial satellites that have been put there by us.

Today we have many different uses for satellites. There are communications satellites, spy or military satellites, navigation satellites, weather satellites, science research satellites and many others. A space station is a satellite like any other, except that it can house people for long periods of time.

The world's first manufactured satellite was Sputnik 1, launched by Russia in October 1957.

In 1965 the world's first commercial communication satellite was launched. This was Early Bird. It didn't have a battery, so it only worked when its solar panels received light from the Sun.

Polar satellites are satellites that travel over both of the poles. As the Earth turns on its axis, the satellite passes over a different area of the planet with each orbit.

Some satellites have equatorial orbits. These satellites are placed a lot further out than polar satellites. If they are placed at 36 000 km, the satellite will take 24 hours to make one orbit. This is useful for communications satellites.

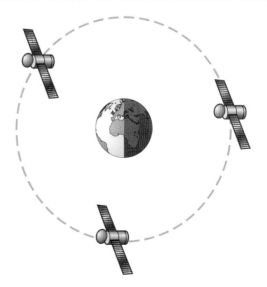

Spy satellites are widely used today to collect information about battlefields and possible military targets. They can take very detailed pictures on which it is possible to pick out individual people on the ground. Other military satellites monitor the Earth for signs of hostile activity, such as the launch of a missile or a nuclear explosion. These defence satellites are able to monitor large sections of the Earth's surface, and usually have a polar orbit.

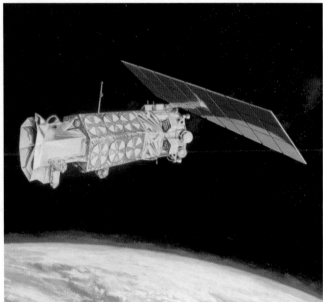

A defence satellite.

Satellite image showing light pollution.

Weather satellite image.

Weather satellites help us to forecast the weather. Weather satellites look at air movements and cloud cover. They monitor storms and hurricanes. Weather satellite information contributes to the improved accuracy of our weather forecasts, and we now know what weather to expect not only tomorrow but also in two days' time or even a week. Weather satellites also act as remote dataloggers. They can take readings of temperature, pressure and humidity.

Satellites also help scientists to study the Earth's surface. They can monitor the growth of crops, and the size of the polar ice caps. They are also useful in identifying the location of resources such as ore and coal.

Satellites detect these things by analysing light and other radiation which is reflected and emitted from surface features. Each feature, for example a building, an ocean or a forest, has a different signature of reflected and emitted radiation.

Other satellites are used to look away from the Earth to study space. Such an example is the Hubble Space Telescope. It is able to observe distant galaxies without any interference from the Earth's atmosphere.

20 Read the information above about artificial satellites. Draw a two-column table as shown below and complete the columns using the information from the passage.

Type of satellite	Key features

Evaluation *Space research*

America and Russia have spent billions of pounds on space research. Do you think this is a worthwhile use of money?
To help you decide:

1 Find out about discoveries that have been made through space research that have improved daily life. Teflon is one example.

2 List what we would not have if there were no artificial satellites.

3 What else could the money be used for, if not invested in space research? In your opinion, would it be better spent in these other ways?

Why satellites stay in orbit

Key words
* circular motion
* tension

To understand the motion of satellites, we need to think about **circular motion**. This is an experiment that can be tried outdoors.

21 Look at the diagram on the right. Imagine that a rubber bung on a string is released at point A. Where does the bung go after its release? Why? Discuss this with your neighbour and make a sketch to explain your reasoning.

In the same way that the **tension** in the string is providing the force for the bung to move along a circular path, so the Earth provides the gravitational force to keep the Moon orbiting the Earth.

Newton described a 'thought' experiment to explain the motion of satellites. Imagine firing a cannon ball from a cannon. The bigger the charge firing the cannon the faster the cannon ball would go, so the further it would travel before it fell to the Earth. If it were travelling fast enough it would fall to the Earth at the same rate as the Earth curved away, so the cannon ball would keep going round the Earth, eventually returning back to where it started.

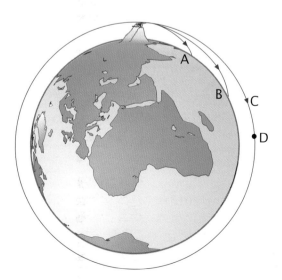

22 In real life there are other factors that would need to be taken into account. Can you think of any?

→ # *Rockets*

Key word
* thrust force

The picture below shows a water rocket. You may have seen one. It consists of a plastic 1.5-litre drinks bottle, about a quarter filled with water and connected to a foot pump. As air is pumped in the pressure builds up and the tube connecting the pump to the bottle comes off. Water is ejected from the bottle. There is a reaction force on the bottle. As well as this **thrust force** acting on the bottle, there is another force acting on the bottle. This is its weight. To get off the ground the force acting upwards must be greater than the weight of the water rocket.

Another simple rocket is the balloon rocket, also shown in the picture below.

water rocket

balloon rocket

23 Explain how the balloon rocket works.

To lift a rocket into space, a lot of energy needs to be supplied. As the rocket travels further away from the pull of the Earth's gravity, the force on the rocket from the Earth becomes less. It will now become more affected by other objects in the Solar System.

24 A rocket needs to carry all its fuel. The rocket that carried the British astronaut Helen Sharman into space burnt kerosene and oxygen. It cannot, for example, use ordinary air to 'burn' its fuel. Why not?

In recent years rockets have been launched into space to enable us to gather information about our neighbouring planets. For example, the photo here shows a picture taken of the far side of the Moon, which we cannot see from Earth. It is thought to show the presence of water.

The far side of the Moon.

Information processing

Using a Rokit

Write some short instructions on how to use the Rokit that can be put inside a box to make it into a gift for someone.

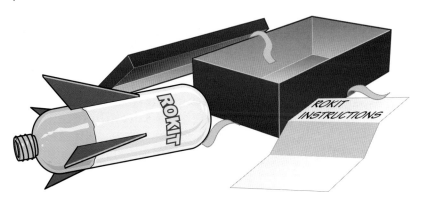

→ # Moon facts

The Moon is 400 000 km from the Earth and it has a diameter of 3500 km. It takes the Moon 27.25 days to orbit the Earth once.

Moonlight is not light from the Moon, it is light from the Sun that is reflected off the Moon. The gravitational pull from the Moon as it orbits the Earth causes large masses of water to move, making tides. Unlike the Earth, the Moon has no atmosphere and there appears to be no water. The surface temperature varies between 100 °C and −155 °C.

Reasoning ## Phases of the Moon

Here is a diagram showing the phases of the Moon, and a drawing modelling the movement of the Moon around the Earth. Redraw the Moon orbit model with the correct phase of the Moon at each of the points labelled 1 to 8.

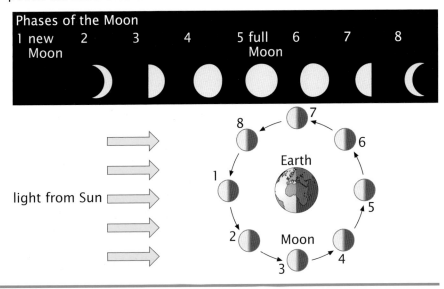

Stars

DID YOU KNOW? Our Sun is a star and it has been burning for about 5000 million years. It is about half-way through its life.

A **star** is made of a mass of gas and particles that collapse together under their own gravity and pull towards each other into a giant ball. As the matter falls inwards, it speeds up. The ball shrinks and heats up so that eventually the star glows red. As it goes on collapsing inwards it gets smaller and hotter. Nuclear fusion begins as hydrogen is burnt up, and it glows yellow. Big stars suddenly explode at the end of their life to form supernovae, which can be as bright as 100 million times our Sun.

A **galaxy** is a collection of about 100 000 million stars. There are probably about 10 000 galaxies in our Universe. Galaxies are usually spiral or elliptical.

Spiral galaxy.

Ellipitical galaxy.

Time to think

1 We have looked at the gravitational forces acting between two objects (such as Mars and a satellite, or an apple and the Earth). There are two main factors that affect the size of the gravitational attraction; one is how far apart the two objects are, and the other is the mass of the objects.
Copy and complete these sentences.
The further apart two objects are placed, the .... (greater/smaller) the size of the gravitational force.
The greater the mass of an object, the .... (greater/smaller) the gravitational attraction on another object.
2 Write an explanation of the differences between a star, a planet, the Moon and an artificial satellite.

Creative thinking **Postage stamps**

Select any space event or fact that you find particularly interesting, and design two or three postage stamps to commemorate the event. Make a class display of all the designs.

→ *Measuring speed*

In Book 1 we covered some work on **speed**. To measure the speed of something we need to take two measurements: the distance travelled and the time taken. Speed is measured in metres per second, m/s, in science but a car speedometer will usually show miles/hour, mph. Other units for speed are km/hour. The speed shown on a car speedometer gives us the instantaneous speed – this is the speed that we are travelling at the instant we look at the speedometer. This is *not* the same as the average speed, which is found by using the following equation:

$$\text{average speed} = \frac{\text{total distance travelled}}{\text{total time taken}}$$

25 Different sites on the internet suggest different routes for a car travelling from Birmingham to Southampton. One route, via the M40 and A34 has a total distance of 216 km. The time taken is 3 hours. What is the average speed in km/hr? Show your working. The second route is by taking the A46, M5 and M4. The total distance is 237 km and the time taken is 2.5 hours. What is the average speed using this route? Which is the fastest route? Which is the furthest route? What advantages are there in taking the first route? What advantages are there in taking the second route?

26 A car takes the first route. It takes the driver 40 minutes to cover the first 20 km, then a further hour to cover the next 80 km on the motorway. The final 16 km takes the driver 20 minutes. Using the graph as a guide, plot a distance–time graph of the journey.

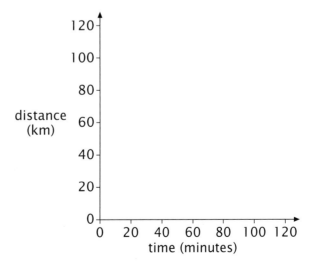

27 Calculate the average speed for each section of the journey. Over which part of the journey was the car going fastest? Over which part of the journey was it going more slowly?

Information processing *Looking for patterns*

Look at the information provided in the table. The data show information on a number of races at a recent International Athletics meeting.

Men (M)/ Women (W)	Race distance (m)	Race time (min:s)	Race time (s)	Last lap distance (m)	Last lap time (s)	Race speed (m/s)	Last lap speed (m/s)	Type of race
W	3000	8:26.53	506.53	400	59.95	5.92	6.67	flat final
M	800	1:44.55	104.55	400	52.83	7.65	7.57	flat heat
M	110	12.99	12.99			8.47		hurdles
W	400	48.65	48.65			8.22		flat final
M	800	1:43.45	103.45	400	53.91	7.73	7.42	flat final
W	800	1:56.10	116.10	400	59.67	6.89	6.70	flat final
M	10 000	27:21.30	1641.30	400	65.02	6.09	6.15	flat final
M	200	19.76	19.76			10.12		flat final
W	200	21.33	21.33			9.38		flat final
M	1500	3:40.89	220.89	400	52.62	6.79	7.60	flat heat
M	3000	8:05.51	485.51	400	57.63	6.18	6.94	steeple final
W	10 000	31:05.21	1865.21	400	66.38	5.36	6.03	flat final
W	100	12.38	12.38			8.08		hurdles final
M	1500	3:38.09	218.09	400	53.64	6.88	7.46	flat semi-final
M	1500	3:35.96	215.96			6.95		flat final

1 Do runners run faster or slower at the end of the race? Is there a pattern in the results?

2 What types of races are run at a faster speed?

3 Do men always run faster than women?

This table gives information on the fastest production cars and their **acceleration** (acceleration is the change in speed over time).

Car	Acceleration (0–100km/h) (seconds)	Top speed (km/h)	Mass (kg)
Callaway Sledgehammer Corvette	3.9	408	1665
2001 Lotec Sirius	3.7	400	1280
1998 Ferrari F50 GT	3.3	380	909
2003 Lamborghini Gallardo	4.0	308	1614
2003 Alfa Romeo 147 GTA	6.3	246	1355

4 Use a spreadsheet to produce a suitable chart of the information.

5 Is the fastest car the one with the greatest acceleration?

6 Is there any relationship between the mass of the car and its acceleration?

Enquiry *Measuring the speed of a trolley down a slope*

Key word
* terminal velocity

This experiment uses light gates to measure the speed of a trolley running down a runway. You may have seen a similar experiment yourself.

When the card attached to the trolley breaks the infrared beam of the timing gate the timer starts recording. As the card leaves the gate the timer stops. The software records and displays the time and can show the speed of the object if the length of the card is known. In an experiment using this equipment, the trolley was released from different distances above the light gate to see how this affected the speed recorded at the light gate.

1 What would you expect to happen to the speed of the trolley as it runs down the slope?

The results obtained by investigating this are shown below:

Distance from light gate (cm)	Speed (cm/s)
10	5
20	10
30	
40	20
50	25
60	29
70	31

2 What were the key variables in this experiment? What was the input (independent) variable and what was the outcome (dependent) variable? Which variables were kept constant?

3 Use the results above to plot a graph. Plot the independent variable along the horizontal (*x*) axis.

4 As you can see the pupils forgot to write down one of the readings. How could you make a good estimate of what it was? What do you think it might have been?

5 Describe the shape of the graph you have plotted.

6 Can you explain why it changes shape the way it does?

7 What estimate would you make for the **terminal velocity** of the trolley?

Enquiry *Planning an experiment*

In the experiment described on the previous page the pupils kept the slope constant and altered the position of launch of the trolley. Another group of pupils used the same equipment but performed different experiments. They kept the point of release unchanged, but they increased the angle of slope.

1 Write down a series of instructions for someone to perform this experiment. List the equipment that they would need.

2 What do you predict would happen to the speed of the trolley in such an experiment? Can you give a reason for this?

3 What readings would you take?

4 Show how you would record the results.

Interpreting graphs

Key words
* velocity
* direction

The graph shows the actual distance–time graph for a car making a journey. Discuss the shape of the graph with a partner and write a paragraph about the motion of the car using words such as: speeding up, stops, slows down, goes at a steady speed.

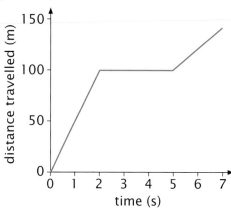

Lots of people use the words speed and **velocity** without realising that they have two different meanings. Speed and acceleration are two other scientific concepts that people wrongly assume mean the same thing. Scientists must define them clearly to use them as part of their models about the Universe. The following thought exercise will help you to understand the difference between them.

Think about a model train going at a steady speed around a track. It is travelling at a constant speed of 15cm/s. Imagine a second train on a parallel track travelling in the opposite direction, also at a constant speed of 15cm/s.

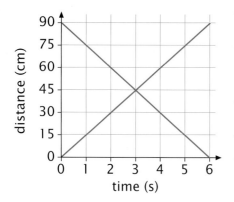

When they pass one another in front of you, one train is moving from your right to your left and the other is going from left to right. The trains have the same speeds but different velocities. If the one going to the left has a velocity of +15cm/s (towards you), the one going to the right has a velocity of −15cm/s (away from you). So whilst speed gives us information about how fast something is travelling, velocity also gives us some information about the **direction**, as well as speed. If one of the trains was getting faster and faster as it went past you, it would be accelerating.

You may have used a motion sensor to plot a graph on a computer screen as you move towards or away from the sensor. As well as plotting a distance–time graph, the equipment can be set up to plot a velocity–time graph. The first graph below shows the motion of a person walking at a slow steady speed towards the sensor. The second graph shows the equivalent velocity–time graph for the motion.

28 How far away is the pupil at the start?
29 How far does he travel in 5 s?
30 What was his average velocity?

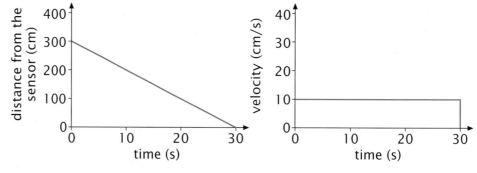

Air cushioned vehicles – hovercraft

Hovercraft are vehicles that depend on the low resistance of air compared to water. The vehicles 'float' on a cushion of air. You may have made a model hovercraft or seen a linear air track or magnetic pucks floating on a cushion of carbon dioxide from 'dry ice'. Examples of these are shown in the photographs.

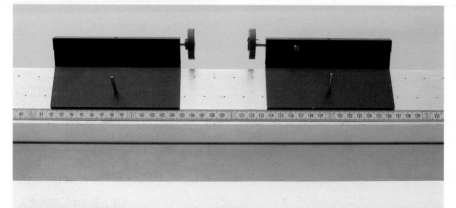

A linear air track.

You may have played air hockey with similar disks.

In diagrams of objects moving you are often asked to show the direction of the forces acting on the object. It is important that you do not confuse the direction of motion of the object with the force.

31 Copy the drawing of the sky diver as he has just left the plane. Draw an arrow to show direction of motion. In a different colour draw arrows to show the direction and relative size of the forces acting on the sky diver.

32 When the parachute opens, draw the direction of motion of the sky diver. How is the speed different?

33 Draw arrows to show the direction and relative size of the forces acting on the sky diver now.

34 The picture below shows a tennis ball just after it has left a person's racket, at the top of its trajectory, and just before it hits the floor. For each position, copy the diagram and mark in the direction of motion of the ball. In a different colour mark the direction and relative size of the forces acting on the ball in each position.

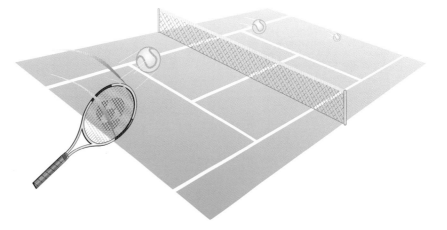

When Concorde was cruising at supersonic speeds, the tip of its nose could reach a temperature of 127 °C. The characteristic 'droop nose' was designed to streamline the aircraft and keep air resistance to a minimum as it flew through the air at twice the speed of sound (1350 mph). At these speeds, the entire aircraft heated up so much that its length expanded by about 15 centimetres. To help reflect and radiate this heat, Concorde was painted with 'high-reflectivity' white paint.

Enquiry ## Investigations

Plan one of the following investigations.

Terminal velocity investigation

Imagine you are investigating the factors that affect the terminal velocity of a falling object. To do this you could drop a sphere through a long tube containing a liquid.

Think about the things you could change, what you could measure and what you could keep the same.

How would you present your results?

How would you know if the object has reached its terminal velocity?

How could you use a datalogger as an alternative approach?

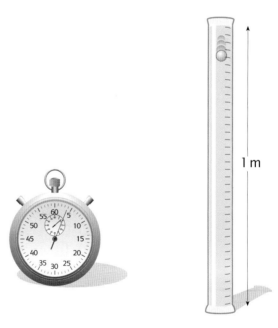

1 m

Investigating friction

Imagine you are investigating the force of friction between a block of wood and a surface. Write down a list of the things you could change. Decide on the things you will change, what you will keep the same and what you will measure.

Decide how you will present your results.

Time to think

1 Working on your own, think back over all the work you have done in this chapter. What topics have you found most interesting. Why?

Which topics do you think will be hard to revise? How can you make your revision of these topics more effective?

2 Look at the four graphs that some Year 9 pupils drew to represent this statement:

'A lift travels up a building with five floor levels. It stops at each floor for three minutes.'

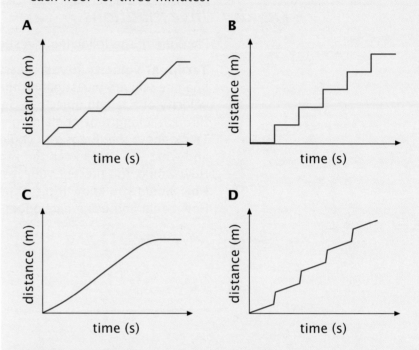

Which of the four graphs is correct? Why?

Write three comments, one for each of the other three pupils to tell them where their thinking has gone wrong.

Do this exercise in a pair:

Draw a speed-time graph and make up five questions to check someone else's ability to read and understand the graph. Try answering another pair's questions.

3 Discuss these statements in your pair and decide which of these statements are 'true', 'false' or 'it depends'. Note that they are not all factual statements; some are about your opinions:

a) The Moon radiates moonlight.

b) Galileo was the most important astronomer who ever lived.

c) Velocity only describes how fast something is travelling.

d) Tides are caused by the pull of the Earth's gravity as it rotates about the Moon.

e) Space programmes are a waste of money.

f) Gravity is a force so it is measured in newtons.

g) All objects always fall to Earth at the same speed.

h) Laika was the first animal in space.

5 Patterns of reactivity

In this chapter you will learn:

➡ to establish and use a reactivity series for metals
➡ to represent chemical reactions by word and symbol equations
➡ that although metals react in a similar way with oxygen, water and acids, some react more readily than others

You will also develop your skills in:

➡ making predictions using the reactivity series
➡ presenting data in a way that enables patterns to be described
➡ identifying and controlling variables in an investigation of the reactivity of different metals

➡➡➡ WHAT DO YOU KNOW?

1 Look at the photos and explain what has happened to each object.

Before	After	Time lapse	Conditions
iron		1 week	left outdoors
gold		over 2000 years	buried underground
lead		6 months	left outdoors

Before	After	Time lapse	Conditions
silver		2 years	left indoors, uncleaned
copper		1 year	left outdoors
potassium		2 seconds	left indoors
sodium		4 seconds	left indoors

2 Look at the photographs of potassium and sodium.

   a) Describe one piece of evidence that shows that these two elements could be metals.

   b) Describe one piece of evidence that shows that these two elements could be non-metals.

   c) i) Which group of the periodic table are these two elements in?

     ii) From their position in the periodic table, are the two elements metals or non-metals?

3 Freshly cut sodium reacts with oxygen in the air. Write a word equation for this reaction.

4 What makes copper go green?

In your group, look at the above cartoon and discuss the three explanations.

a) Decide if each answer is either:

- definitely correct
- could be correct
- definitely wrong.

Give a reason for each decision.

b) If you have decided that an answer 'could be correct', you will need some more evidence to make a definite decision. Discuss what sort of evidence you might need.

5 Try to list the seven metals in order of their increasing reactivity. Use the evidence in the table.

6 Freshly cut calcium also reacts with oxygen in the air. Give a word equation for this reaction.

→ *Reacting metals with water*

Key word
* tarnish

Some metals react with water. Other metals **tarnish** in damp air. When metals tarnish in air they are reacting with the oxygen <u>and</u> the water.

Some metals such as potassium react vigorously with water.

Some metals such as copper do not seem to react at all with water.

This is how potassium is stored.

1 Which metals, apart from potassium, would you expect to react vigorously with water? Give a reason for your answer.

2 List all of the possible pieces of evidence that you might see if a chemical reaction occurs between a reactive metal and water. Share your ideas with others in your group.

3 Why are metals such as potassium and sodium stored under oil?

Lithium in a beaker of water containing Universal Indicator solution.

4 This is part of a pupil's results table for the reaction of some metals with water:

Metal	Observations	Test on the gas	Test on the remaining solution
Lithium	The metal floated, giving off bubbles of gas. It eventually disappeared.	The gas popped when ignited	Turned Universal Indicator dark blue (pH 14)
Sodium	Metal whizzed across the surface	Gas ignited from heat of reaction	Turned Universal Indicator dark blue (pH 14)

a) Which piece of evidence under 'Observations' might be unexpected for a metal?

b) Which gas is formed in the reaction?

c) Where has the lithium gone? Has it really disappeared?

d) i) What type of substance has a pH of 14 in solution?
   ii) Can you give the chemical name of one example of this type of substance?

e) Write a word equation for the reaction of lithium with water.

Uses of the periodic table

Key words
* compounds
* combining power
* bond

One feature of the periodic table is the arrangement of the elements into vertical groups. This feature means that it is very useful for predicting how the elements will behave.

Group 1
lithium
sodium
potassium
rubidium
caesium

5 What is the link between the order of the group 1 metals in the periodic table and their reactivity with water?

Group 2
beryllium
magnesium
calcium
strontium
barium

6 Predict which group 2 metal is the most reactive with water.

Another important use of the periodic table is to help with the writing of formulae. All elements in the same vertical group form **compounds** with other elements that have the same simple ratios of atoms. This is because they have the same **combining power**. The table below shows some of the metals in group 1 and the formulae of some of their compounds.

Metal	Metal chloride	Metal oxide	Metal sulphate
lithium (Li)	LiCl 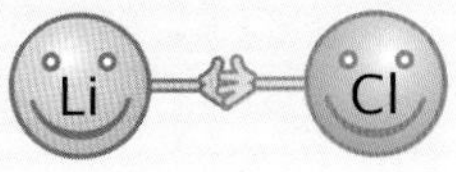	Li_2O 	Li_2SO_4 
potassium (K)	KCl 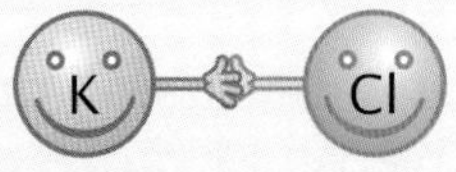	K_2O 	K_2SO_4 
caesium (Cs)	CsCl 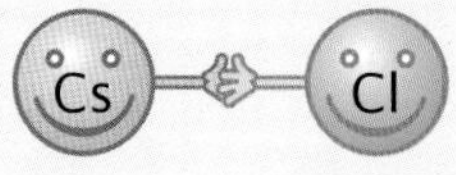	Cs_2O 	Cs_2SO_4 

Note that the three group 1 metals all have one 'hand' to form a **bond**.

7 For the three group 1 metals shown in the table, what is the ratio of:
  a) metal to chlorine in the metal chlorides
  b) metal to oxygen in the oxides
  c) metal to sulphate (SO_4) in the sulphates?

8 Sodium (Na) and rubidium (Rb) are also in group 1. Write down what you think is the formula of:
  a) sodium chloride
  b) rubidium oxide
  c) sodium sulphate.

Check your ideas with others in the group.

Another important use of the periodic table is to help with the writing of word equations. Generally, all elements in the same vertical group have very similar equations for their reactions with a given substance. For example, the word equations for the reaction of two group 1 metals with water are shown below:

sodium + water → sodium hydroxide + hydrogen

rubidium + water → rubidium hydroxide + hydrogen

9 Write a word equation for the reaction of:
  a) potassium with water
  b) caesium with water.

Summary

Using the evidence looked at so far, the metals can be placed in a 'league table' with the most reactive at the top:

Metal	Reaction with water	Time to tarnish
potassium	explosive	2 seconds
sodium	vigorous	4 seconds
lithium	quite fast	8 seconds
magnesium	slow	some hours
iron, zinc, copper	very slow	days or months
silver	does not react	months
gold	does not react	does not tarnish

The evidence we have does not enable us to put the metals copper, iron and zinc in order. We need more evidence to be able to compare them. This can be obtained from observing the reactions of metals with acids.

Reacting metals with acids

10 In Chapter 1 you saw that most metals react with acids.
  a) What is the gas formed?
  b) What happens to the magnesium?
  c) Write a word equation for the reaction of magnesium with hydrochloric acid.
  d) Write a general word equation for the reaction of metals with acids.

Magnesium reacting with hydrochloric acid.

Enquiry *Planning*

Plan an investigation to find out the correct order of reactivity of the metals copper, iron, magnesium and zinc with sulphuric acid. Key parts of your plan are:

- to decide what you are going to measure to determine the order of reactivity
- to decide which **variables** must be kept the same to make it a fair test.

Summary

Using evidence from the reactions of metals with acids, the league table now looks like this:

Metal	Reaction with water	Time to tarnish	Reaction with dilute acid
potassium	explosive	2 seconds	react explosively
sodium	vigorous	4 seconds	
lithium	quite fast	8 seconds	
magnesium	slow	some hours	dissolve, giving off hydrogen gas
zinc	very slow	days or months	
iron			
copper			
silver	does not react	months	no reaction
gold	does not react	does not tarnish	

more slowly ↓

This is called the **activity series** for metals.

Time to think

In your own words, explain what is meant by the activity series for metals. Compare your explanation with two or three other people. Pool your ideas to write a group explanation for the activity series for metals.

Enquiry ## Quality of evidence

Key words
* quantitative
* qualitative
* valid
* accurate
* reliable

Evidence that involves measurement is called **quantitative**. Evidence that does not involve measurement is described as **qualitative** – it just has descriptions such as 'quite fast' or 'fairly fast'.

1 a) Which of the evidence in the table on page 135 is quantitative?
  b) Which of the evidence is qualitative?

Key words used in describing the quality of evidence are **valid**, **accurate** and **reliable**. Their scientific meanings are similar to their meanings in everyday use, as shown below.

2 James, Kath and Susan spent a rainy afternoon at Susan's house playing darts. James suggested that they should decide who was the best player by throwing six darts at the 'bull's eye'. The results are shown below:

James

Kath

Susan

a) Describe the dart throws for each player.
b) Who had the most accurate set of throws?
c) Who had the most reliable set of throws?
d) Who had the least reliable set of throws?
e) Who was reliable but not very accurate?
f) Do you think that the sample size was large enough to make a decision about the best darts player? Discuss your ideas with others in your group.

Evaluation ## Order of reactivity

In an investigation into the question 'What is the order of reactivity of the metals copper, iron, magnesium and zinc?', groups of pupils followed these instructions:

- Take some sieved metal grains of copper metal.
- Add some dilute hydrochloric acid.

- Measure the volume of hydrogen gas produced after a time.
- Repeat the experiment for the other metals.

Clara and John planned and carried out their investigation as shown below:

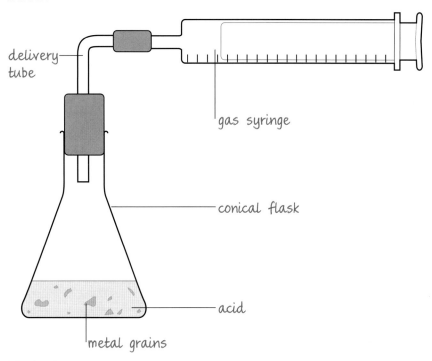

delivery
tube

gas syringe

conical flask

acid

metal grains

Method

- We weighed out 1.00 g of metal grains each time, using an electronic balance.

- 20 cm³ of dilute acid were measured each time, using a conical flask.

- The metal was added to the acid, a rubber bung with a gas syringe was fitted as shown in the diagram, and the stopwatch was started.

- After 1 minute the volume of hydrogen gas was measured.

- This was repeated two more times for each metal.

Results

Metal	Volume of gas (cm³) produced in 1 min			
	Exp 1	Exp 2	Exp 3	Mean
copper	0	0	0	0
iron	7	17	6	10
magnesium	42	47	37	42
zinc	9	10	8	9

Conclusion

We think that the order of reactivity of the four metals starting with the most reactive is: magnesium, iron, zinc, copper.

1 What did Clara and John use to measure the volume of gas? Is the volume of gas an input (independent) or outcome (dependent) variable?

2 Clara and John thought carefully about their plan.
  a) What did they do to make the final result for each metal more reliable?
  b) What did they do to make it a fair test?

3 The results of Clara and John's experiment were not as accurate as those of other groups.
  a) Which part of their method might have had the worst effect on accuracy?
  b) What would you do to improve this part of the method? Discuss your ideas with others.

4 Which metal has the most reliable set of results? How did you decide this?

5 a) Which single result from the table would you say was definitely odd (anomalous)?
  b) How has this result affected the conclusion?

6 Is the conclusion:
  a) accurate from the viewpoint of the 'correct' answer?
  b) valid from the viewpoint of the evidence used? Explain your answers.

→ *Reacting metals with oxygen*

Pure oxygen is a very dangerous substance because almost any material will readily burn in it.

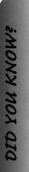

The first fatal accident in the NASA space programme happened in 1967, when three astronauts were testing an Apollo command module on the ground. The sealed spacecraft contained an atmosphere of pure oxygen, and a short circuit in some electrical wiring started a fierce fire, killing all three men. Following an inquiry, the cabin atmosphere was changed to a mixture of nitrogen and oxygen.

Enquiry *Predicting*

You have seen that the periodic table is very useful for predicting reactions and equations. The activity series can also be used to make predictions.

1 Predict two metals which will burn fiercely in oxygen.

2 Predict two metals which might not burn in oxygen. Compare your answers with others in your group.

The word equations for the burning of some metals in oxygen were looked at in Book 1. The word equation for magnesium burning in oxygen is:

magnesium + oxygen → magnesium oxide

3 Predict the word equation for the burning of the following metals in oxygen:
a) barium
b) calcium.

4 Scientists are always looking for patterns in evidence and links between ideas. Both metals in Question 3 burn strongly in oxygen. Can you see a link between this pattern and the periodic table?

Summary

In groups, look back at your explanation about the activity series and check that it still fits with the latest patterns that you have looked at.

→ *Displacement reactions of metals*

Tug of war – guess who wins!

Key word
∗ displacement reaction

So far we have seen that some metals are more reactive than others in their reactions with water, dilute acids and oxygen. In this section we will find out if one metal can win a tug-of-war against another metal compound. For example, can magnesium take away the sulphate from copper sulphate to form magnesium sulphate and copper? This is called a **displacement reaction** – the copper has been displaced from the copper sulphate.

11 Explain what has happened in this reaction. Write a word equation.

magnesium ribbon

Enquiry *Planning*

Can the activity series predict which displacement reactions will occur?

In order to test this question, you need to plan a series of reactions. You might be given the following materials:

solids: copper, iron, magnesium and zinc

solutions: copper sulphate, iron sulphate, magnesium sulphate and zinc sulphate

1 **Prediction:** From the list above, predict which metal will displace all of the other metals from solutions of their compounds, and give a reason why.

2 **Choosing equipment:** How many test tubes would you need to carry out *all* of the different combinations of possible reactions? Write out the possible combinations. Compare your ideas with others in your group.

3 **Presenting evidence:** Design a simple results table to show which combinations produced a displacement reaction.

Enquiry *Considering evidence*

The table below shows the observations made by a pupil for some displacement reactions.

Test	Metal	Metal compound	Observations
1	zinc	copper sulphate	blue solution went colourless; brown coating formed on the silver-coloured zinc
2	iron	zinc sulphate	iron stayed shiny and silvery
3	magnesium	iron sulphate	grey coating on the silver-coloured magnesium

1 In which of the tests did displacement occur?

2 What is the pattern shown by the above results?

3 Is there enough evidence to be confident about your answer to Question 2?

4 Write word equations for the combinations that did react.

5 Name a metal that is *not* in the above table that you think will:
   a) be displaced from its compounds by copper
   b) displace copper from copper sulphate.
   Explain why you think this. Compare your ideas with others in your group.

Key word
* Thermit reaction

Activity series

Look at the activity series on the right. Note that it has more metals than we have looked at so far.

potassium
sodium
lithium
calcium
magnesium
aluminium
zinc
iron
lead
copper
silver
gold

12 Copy out the activity series and highlight the metals that we have not looked at so far.
13 For one of these metals explain how you think it is going to react compared to the metals above and below it.
14 For the following pairs of substances, decide if a reaction will occur between them:
   a) lead and silver nitrate solution
   b) zinc and iron oxide
   c) magnesium and sodium sulphate solution.

EXTENSION 15 Write word equations for the identified displacement reactions in Question 14.
16 Tin is a metal which reacts only slowly with warm, dilute acid. It displaces lead from lead nitrate solution.
   a) What is the likely position of tin in the activity series?
   b) Give an example of a reaction that would be needed to confirm your answer. Explain your choice.

Displacement reactions are useful to separate some metals from their compounds. These reactions can also be useful in other ways.

The photograph shows a displacement reaction where so much heat energy is released that the displaced iron is molten. It runs out of the container and into the gap between the two parts of the rail, welding them together. This is called the **Thermit reaction** and the mixture contains powdered iron oxide and aluminium.

17 a) Write a word equation for the above Thermit reaction.
   b) Suggest an alternative metal to aluminium that would still displace iron from its oxide and be reactive enough to release enough heat energy to melt the iron. Explain your choice.

Welding railway lines with a displacement reaction.

18 An AA cell (battery) has a voltage of 1.5 V. The electrical energy is obtained from a chemical reaction inside the cell. Different chemical reactions produce different voltages. The following table gives values for some different cells made by dipping two different metals into a dilute acid. For any pair of metals, one is the positive and the other the negative terminal.

Metal 1 (+)	Metal 2 (−)	Voltage (V)
silver	copper	0.46
copper	iron	0.78
copper	zinc	1.10
silver	zinc	1.56
zinc	magnesium	1.60

a) Which pair of metals produced the highest voltage?
b) Try to identify a pattern for the combinations of metals that give a high voltage.
c) Predict a pair of metals that will give a higher voltage than any in the above table.

Time to think

Divide a sheet of paper into quarters. In each part write one of the following headings:

- Reaction with oxygen
- Reaction with acid
- Displacement reactions
- Activity series

Check back through the work that you have done so far and make notes under each of the four headings. Compare your notes with others in your group. Add or improve your notes to provide you with a good summary.

Key words
* antiquity
* ore
* native state
* anneal
* smelting

The history of metals

The first metal that humans used was gold, in about 6000 BC. Over the next 7000 years only six more metals were discovered: copper, silver, lead, tin, iron and mercury. These metals were used by the ancient Egyptians, Greeks and Romans, and are known as the seven metals of **antiquity**.

Most metals can only be obtained by extracting them from rocks containing a compound of the metal (a metal **ore**). However, five of the above metals can be found in their **native state** as the pure metal. These are gold, copper, silver, iron (in meteorites) and mercury.

6000 BC	gold
4000 BC	copper, silver
3500 BC	lead
1800 BC	tin
1500 BC	iron
750 BC	mercury
1400 AD	zinc
1500	platinum
1735	cobalt
1751	nickel
1783	tungsten
1791	titanium
1807	potassium, sodium
1808	barium, calcium, magnesium
1827	aluminium
1898	radium
1940	plutonium

discovery dates of some metals

Gold nuggets are easily panned from the gravel beds of streams. Stone Age people discovered that these nuggets could be hammered into shape to make jewellery and ornaments, but not tools. This is because gold is too soft.

Panning for gold.

Silver was discovered later than gold. It tarnishes slowly, forming a black coating. Silver is slightly harder than gold but it is still too soft to make tools.

Copper is harder than silver but it can still be hammered into shape. It was the first metal used to make tools such as knives and arrow heads. However, there were two problems:

1 When copper is hammered, it becomes brittle and it breaks easily. The answer was to **anneal** the copper – heat it and let it slowly cool down.
2 There was not enough native copper around. However, copper is found in many ores. The answer was to make more copper by **smelting** – extracting the metal from its ores by heating it with charcoal. This was first done in Asia in about 4000 BC. A high temperature of approximately 800 °C is needed, such as that found in a pottery kiln.

Lead is not found in its native state, but its main ore, galena (lead sulphide), is common. The ancient Egyptians used this black material as eye make-up.

The smelting process for lead is relatively easy because the temperature needed is reached in a simple wood fire (600 °C). Since lead melts at 327 °C it is easily separated from any solid impurities. It can be filtered and poured off. Lead is too soft to use for tools. Its main uses were for containers and lead piping for water.

Tin is not found in its native state. It is extracted from its ores by smelting. Tin was used to make bronze, by melting it with copper.

The ancient Egyptians used galena, the main ore of lead, as eye make-up.

Iron is only found in very small amounts in its native state in meteorites. The ancient Egyptians called it 'black copper from heaven'. Meteoric iron was five times more expensive than gold and it was used to make jewellery. It is difficult to extract it from its ores by smelting because a high temperature is needed (at least 1200 °C). Also, the iron formed has impurities from the rocks ('slag') and it is difficult to separate them.

Mercury is found in its native state in volcanic areas. It is also easily extracted from its ores by smelting at relatively low temperatures and is easily separated from the impurities. Mercury had limited uses but people were fascinated by its appearance. The chemical symbol for mercury is Hg, which comes from the Greek word *hydrargyros*, which means liquid silver.

1 What happens to silver when it tarnishes?
2 Why are nuggets of gold easily identified in the gravel beds of streams but nuggets of silver are not?
3 What is smelting?
4 Why is lead easily separated from any solid impurities after smelting?
5 For the seven metals of antiquity there are large differences in the amount of energy needed to extract them from their ores. Some are even found in their native state.
  a) Name a metal found in the native state.
  b) Name a metal that needs little energy to extract it from its ores.
  c) Name a metal that needs a lot of energy to extract it from its ores.
  d) What is the relationship between the energy needed to extract a metal from its ores and the position of the metal in the activity series?
  e) From the information about mercury, where would you place it in the activity series (page 141)?
  f) Why is gold found only in its native state?
  g) Bronze is an alloy of copper. Why did the Bronze Age come before the Iron Age in history?
6 In a group, make a game, PowerPoint presentation or poster that would help other people learn more about these metals.

In 1855 the prize exhibit in the Paris Exhibition was a small bar of the newly discovered metal, aluminium, displayed in a glass case. It was so precious that the emperor of France had a set of knives and forks made from it.

In 1999, the worldwide production of aluminium was 24 million tonnes. Its uses include cooking foil, milk bottle tops and window frames.

Mercury and its compounds are very toxic. It not only causes kidney damage and loosening of the teeth it also damages the brain. Many years ago mercury salts were used to make the felt material used for hats. Many of the workers making the hats started to behave strangely, hence the phrase 'mad as a hatter', and the Mad Hatter character in Lewis Carroll's *Alice in Wonderland*.

Alloys

Key words
* alloy
* steel
* bronze
* casting

An **alloy** is a metallic material made from a mixture of two or more elements. The elements are usually metals, but the non-metal carbon is an essential part of the alloy **steel**.

Bronze is an alloy of copper and tin. The earliest samples of bronze were found in an area which is now Iraq, and date from 3000 BC. Bronze was made by mixing copper and tin ores together before smelting. Bronze is much harder than copper, and bronze objects are made by **casting**. This involves pouring the molten mixture of copper and tin into a mould (cast).

Steel is an alloy of iron and carbon. Modern steels contain other elements such as nickel and tungsten. Iron smelting started around 1500 BC in Turkey, where it was made in furnaces. Depending on the

The bronze spear head and axehead pictured here date back to the Bronze Age, 5000 years ago.

The Delhi iron pillar.

conditions, the product was pure iron or steel. Steel is harder than iron and it can be made even harder by quenching – plunging the hot steel into water.

The new technology of steel-making slowly spread from Turkey. It had reached China by 600 BC and Britain by 100 BC. The ancient metal workers developed extraordinary skills. In Roman times, the best steel was imported from India and there is an iron pillar dating from 400 AD that still stands in Delhi, India. It shows very little sign of corrosion.

Arab metal-workers produced the famous Damascus swords that were renowned for their hardness, strength and sharpness.

A Damascus sword.

Research

Use the internet, CD-ROMs and reference books to find out about some modern alloys.

- What are they made out of?
- What are their properties?
- What are they used for?
- What have they replaced?

Use your information to produce a poster on 'Modern alloys'.

Word play

Copy and fill in the word puzzle below.

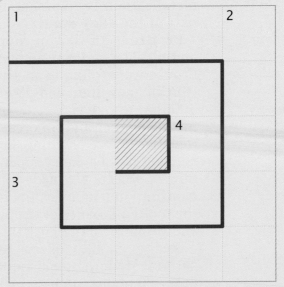

Clues:

1 Found as nuggets in streams.

2 First discovered in 1827 AD.

3 A treatment to make a metal less brittle.

4 To heat an ore with charcoal.

Now make up your own word puzzle about metals using the words alloy, native, ore, mercury and tin. Swap your puzzle with a partner and see if they can do it.

Time to think

In the *Thinking Through Science* books you have seen that scientists try to make sense of the world around them in various ways, for example:

- sorting – arranging observations, ideas or things into groups with different characteristics. For example different types of chemical reactions and different types of forces.
- listing – arranging things in order according to a chosen characteristic. For example, the reactivity of metals and the surface temperature of the planets of the Solar System.

Working in groups:

1 think of one other example of sorting, and note down the characteristics that identify each group
2 think of one other example of listing, and note down the characteristics that determine the arrangement.

Share your ideas with others in your group. Test another group by giving them your list or group and ask them what they think the characteristic is that formed the list or group. Can they add another example to your list or group?

3 'The periodic table could be described as a combination of sorting and listing.' Discuss this statement and see if you can explain what it means, giving some examples.

6 Environment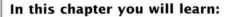

In this chapter you will learn:

→ to identify the causes and effects of acid rain and how they can be reduced
→ to describe how the appearance of landforms and or buildings may change over time, and to review the factors that cause chemical weathering
→ the importance of photosynthesis to humans and other animals
→ about the role of chlorophyll, chloroplasts and leaves
→ that carbon dioxide enters the leaves and water enters the roots of plants to make glucose in the process of photosynthesis
→ how photosynthesis produces plant biomass

You will also develop your skills in:

→ using secondary sources to investigate the factors that affect the pH of rainwater
→ evaluating strengths and weaknesses in the evidence obtained
→ representing the sequence of reactions for acid rain formation using flow diagrams, equations and concept maps
→ linking the theories of earlier scientists with our understanding (Priestley and van Helmont)

→ → → WHAT DO YOU KNOW?

1 This table contains data on different soil types: clay, sandy, chalk, peat and loam.

Soil type	Advantages	Disadvantages	How to improve
clay	▪ usually very fertile, with lots of nutrients	▪ poor drainage, heavy to work ▪ rock hard when dry, horribly sticky when wet	▪ add organic matter and maybe gravel to improve the drainage
sandy	▪ easy to work and easily improved	▪ free draining so it dries out quickly ▪ relatively infertile	▪ add organic matter and use fertilisers
chalk	▪ good drainage (usually), while being moisture-retentive ▪ moderate fertility	▪ shallow and stony ▪ not suitable for azaleas and other lime-haters	▪ add organic matter
Peat	▪ lots of organic matter	▪ wet and acidic	▪ may need drainage ▪ add concentrated fertiliser and possibly lime
Loam	▪ easy to work ▪ good drainage ▪ good fertility ▪ plants love it		▪ further enrich by recycling garden plants as compost ▪ use fertilisers

a) Why would adding gravel improve the drainage of clay soil?

b) Why do clay and organic soils hold nutrients better than sandy soils?

c) Which plants would grow well in chalky soil?

d) Which type of soil would you mix with a sandy soil to reduce the drainage?

e) Why would the free draining of sandy soils be a disadvantage to farmers or gardeners trying to grow crops and plants?

f) Suggest a disadvantage of loamy soils.

2 One of the easiest ways to identify a soil is to take some soil in your hand, wet it thoroughly and rub it between your fingers. Try and match up the descriptions with the soil types below.

Description	Type
it makes a shiny smooth coating on your fingers and is greyish-brown in colour	loamy
very gritty and a pale brownish colour	clay
crumbly and dark, but not especially gritty, smooth or shiny	sand

3 A pupil suggests that the use of acid would help to show the presence of chalk or limestone in a soil.

a) What gas is produced when an acid is added to chalk?

b) What reaction is taking place?

c) What is the chemical name for chalk? Write a word equation for the reaction between hydrochloric acid and chalk.

d) Which other rock types would react with acid in a similar way to chalk?

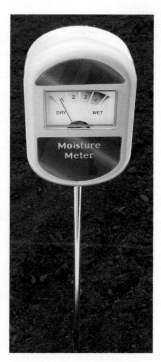

Testing soil for acidity and moisture.

Different plants grow best under different conditions. One factor that must be considered when choosing plants or crops for the garden is the level of acidity in the soil. Soil testing kits are often used by gardeners to measure soil pH.

This table gives the ideal soil pH for a range of plants.

Plant Type	Optimum soil pH
azalea, rhododendron, camellia, mountain laurel	5.0–5.5
most shrubs and shade trees	6.0
fescue, Bermuda grass, Saint Augustine grass	6.0–6.5
centipede grass	5.5
rose	6.5
berries and most fruit trees, except blueberries	6.0–6.5
most vegetable and field crops	6.0–6.5

4 What does the pH measure? Suggest the name of the indicator used in the soil testing kit.

5 Which plant prefers the most acid soil?

6 Which plants would not grow well in a pH 6.0 soil?

7 A farmer noticed that after a soil test the pH was 3.5. He added gardener's lime to increase the soil pH. What type of chemical is lime? What type of reaction is taking place?

8 Sodium hydroxide has a pH of 14. What does this tell you about this reagent? How would you convince the farmer that it would not be sensible to add this to the soil to alter its pH?

9 Look carefully at the components of the soil testing kit. Describe how you would carry out a soil test. What extra equipment would you need?

10 The soil in which a houseplant was growing was tested and found to have a pH of 8.5. The *Gardeners' World* magazine recommends a slightly acidic soil for this plant species. Which of these household reagents would you suggest to remedy the problem? Explain your reasons.

Household reagent	pH
fruit juice	4
ammonia cleaning fluid	11
toothpaste	8
lemonade	5
milk of magnesia	9

➡ *What happens to building materials over time?*

Key words
* ✴ physical weathering
* ✴ chemical weathering
* ✴ minerals
* ✴ biological
* ✴ acid rain
* ✴ igneous
* ✴ sedimentary
* ✴ metamorphic

Soil contains rock fragments that have been broken down very slowly over many many years. Rocks may seem very hard but they are softened and broken down as they are attacked by frost and rain. This is called weathering.

Physical weathering breaks down the rock into smaller pieces of the same type of rock. In **chemical weathering** the chemical composition of the rock is changed to produce new **minerals**. **Biological** action causes both physical and chemical weathering. Roots growing through cracks in rocks widen the cracks as the roots extend deeper into the rocks. Acids from plants such as lichens help to dissolve rocks and break them down into fragments. The actions of humans have also contributed to weathering in particular through the effects of **acid rain**.

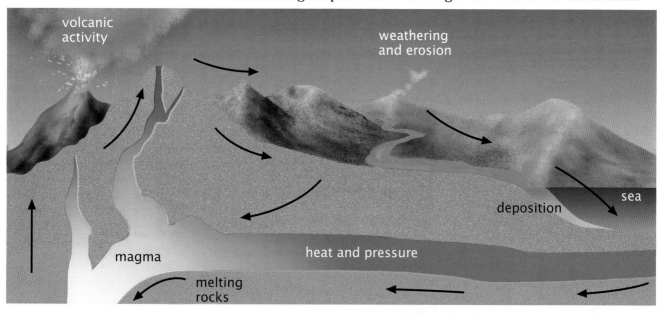

1 a) Classify the rocks in the diagram on the previous page as **igneous**, **sedimentary** or **metamorphic**.
  b) Copy out and complete these sentences using the words below to help you.

Igneous rocks change over time into _____ rocks by the following sequence:

1 _____ 2 _____ 3 _____
4_____ and 5_____.

Sedimentary rocks can change into _____ by the effect of _____ and/or _____.

weathering, heat, deposition, erosion, burial, transport, pressure, metamorphic, sedimentary

2 Study these photographs of a Cornish cottage built from granite, and a house in the Cotswolds built from limestone.

  a) Which of these buildings is more at risk from chemical weathering? Agree two or three points in your group and compare them with other groups.
  b) Decide which type of weathering has affected the Cornish building. Give reasons for your choice.
  c) What evidence is there from the photographs that biological weathering has occurred?

3 This photograph shows a family home in southern Spain.

Average monthly temperature (°C)												
	Jan	**Feb**	**Mar**	**Apr**	**May**	**Jun**	**Jul**	**Aug**	**Sept**	**Oct**	**Nov**	**Dec**
Madrid	9	11	15	19	22	27	31	32	25	18	13	9
London	3.9	4.2	5.7	8.5	11.9	15.2	17.0	16.6	14.2	10.3	6.6	4.8

Average monthly rainfall (mm)												
	Jan	**Feb**	**Mar**	**Apr**	**May**	**Jun**	**Jul**	**Aug**	**Sept**	**Oct**	**Nov**	**Dec**
Madrid	45.1	43.2	36.8	45.4	39.7	25.2	9.4	10.0	29.3	46.4	63.9	47.0
London	48.9	38.8	39.3	41.4	47.0	48.3	59.0	59.6	52.4	65.2	59.3	51.2

a) What difference is there between the average rainfall in Spain and in the UK?
b) How much hotter is the average temperature in southern Spain compared to the UK?
c) Where would you most likely expect to see:
   i) freeze-thaw weathering
   ii) weathering due to expansion and contraction of rocks
   iii) chemical weathering due to acid rain?

Creative thinking   *School survey*

Take some photographs or make drawings of local buildings, showing examples of weathering. Build up a class record and use this to make a display or PowerPoint presentation to inform others about weathering.

➡ *How pure is rainwater?*

Key words
* solvent
* respiration
* photosynthesis
* chlorophyll
* fossil fuels
* carbon cycle

Remember how scientists use the word pure? Pure water is made up of water molecules only. Water is an excellent **solvent**. It will dissolve many chemicals, including many of the gases which are found in the air. These gases may occur naturally in the atmosphere but are also produced by human activity. Increases in carbon dioxide levels can be harmful to living and non-living things.

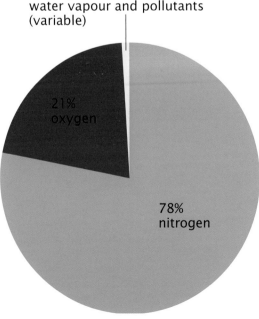

noble gases, carbon dioxide, water vapour and pollutants (variable)

21% oxygen

78% nitrogen

The percentage of gases found in air.

During **respiration** in both plants and animals, carbon dioxide and water are released into the atmosphere.

4 Write the word equation for the process of respiration.

Carbon dioxide is released into the atmosphere by a combination of natural and manufacturing processes. If the carbon dioxide builds up it can result in acid rain. A chemical reaction takes place between water molecules and carbon dioxide to produce a weak acid called carbonic acid (H_2CO_3). This makes rainwater slightly acidic.

5 Write the word equation for this reaction.
6 Suggest a value for the pH of acid rain. What colour would Universal Indicator turn in
  a) pure water
  b) acid rain?

Plants play an important role in maintaining the balance of carbon dixoide and oxygen in the atmosphere. **Photosynthesis** is the process that results in the removal of carbon dioxide from the atmosphere.

7 Here is the word equation for photosynthesis:

  carbon dioxide + water → sugar (glucose) + oxygen

  a) How does the chemical **chlorophyll** help this process?
  b) Which gas is released into the atmosphere by photosynthesis?

A group of students are surprised at the low level of carbon dioxide in the atmosphere.
  Sophie comments, 'What about the burning of **fossil fuels**? All fossil fuels and many other fuels contain carbon. As these fuels are used they are releasing more and more carbon dioxide into the atmosphere.'

The diagram opposite shows how carbon dioxide is recycled in nature. It is called the **carbon cycle**.

8 Use the diagram to explain how the balance of carbon dioxide and oxygen is maintained in the atmosphere.
9 Suggest how this diagram could be altered to show how the burning of fossil fuels affects the level of carbon dioxide in the atmosphere.

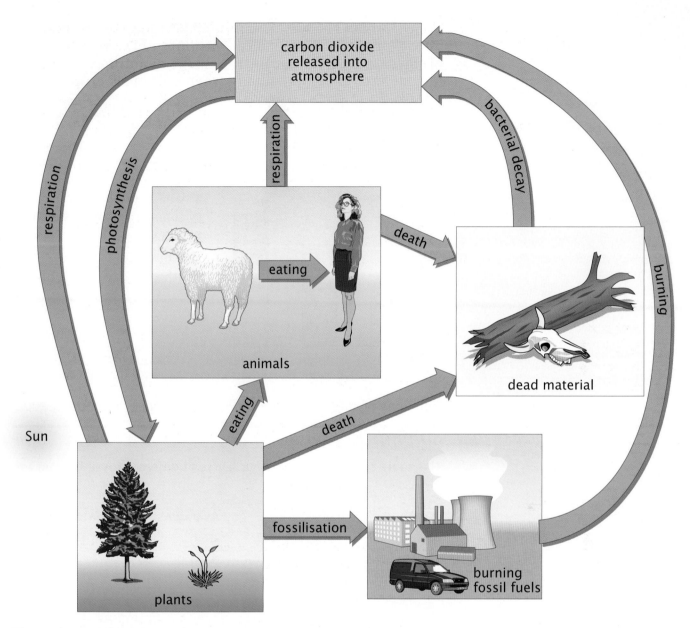

The carbon cycle.

→ *What causes acid rain?*

Key words
* oxidation
* oxidised
* pollution

Analysis of acid levels in the atmosphere shows that the pH level can be as low as 4. This low pH is due to both natural and manufacturing processes. Fossil fuels, including coal, oil and to a lesser extent gas, contain sulphur in different forms. The sulphur in fuel becomes sulphur dioxide on burning by combining with oxygen. This is an example of an **oxidation** reaction.

Sulphur dioxide (SO_2) is a colourless gas. It is soluble in water and can be **oxidised** inside water droplets in the atmosphere to form sulphuric acid (H_2SO_4), which falls as acid rain.

Throughout the world, emissions of the gases sulphur dioxide and nitrogen oxides contribute to the international problem of acid rain **pollution**. Large quantities of sulphur dioxide are released naturally when volcanoes erupt.

10 Look at the bar chart below. What is the main difference between the emissions of sulphur dioxide and nitrogen oxides?

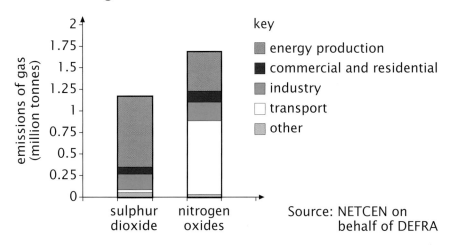

Source: NETCEN on behalf of DEFRA

Emissions of sulphur dioxide and nitrogen oxides in the UK in 2002.

Information processing ## Sulphur in fuels

This table compares the sulphur levels of different fossil fuels in the UK.

Fuel	Average sulphur content (%)
UK coal	1.6
imported coal	0.8–1.0
oil	2.9
gas	trace

1 Which gas is involved when sulphur is oxidised?

2 Write a word equation for the combustion of sulphur to produce sulphur dioxide

3 Which of the fossil fuels listed would you recommend as the most environmentally friendly? Give reasons for your choice.

4 Copy and complete this flow chart showing how the sulphur contained naturally in fossil fuels is converted into sulphuric acid which falls as acid rain. Add as much detail as you can on the arrows.

sulphur + ? → sulphur dioxide + ? + ? → sulphuric acid

Key word
* catalytic converters

Acid rain damage

The problem of acid rain is not a recent development, but our awareness of the damage caused by acid rain is much greater nowadays.

This famous temple was built over 2000 years ago. The damage that is clearly visible is largely due to the pollution caused by cars and other vehicles in Athens – the most polluted city in Europe.

The Parthenon of Athens.

Many other countries have also noticed an acceleration of damage to their cultural heritage. The Taj Mahal in India and monuments in Krakow, Poland and Italy are continuing to deteriorate. In Sweden, medieval stained glass windows are thought to have been affected by acid rain.

The Taj Mahal, India.   The Colosseum, Rome.

Buildings have always been at risk to attack by weathering – the effects of rain, wind, sun, and frost. Acid rain can speed up the rate of this damage.

In 1970, the release of nitrogen oxides from road transport in the UK was 0.8 million tonnes, and by 1990 emissions had risen to over 1.30 million tonnes. In 1999 they were 0.7 million tonnes lower than in 1970. This was mainly because of improvements in motor vehicle technology, such as the use of **catalytic converters**, and the use of cleaner fuels.

11 Present this data on nitrogen dioxide levels as a bar chart.
12 What do you understand by the term 'cleaner fuels'?

13 This question is about the sources of nitrogen oxides.

- Nitrogen from the air burns when temperatures are high enough.
- Nitrogen oxide is produced in motor vehicle engines and power station furnaces.
- Burning nitrogen in air forms various nitrogen oxides.
- These oxides react with water and oxygen in the atmosphere to produce nitric acid.

a) Present the data as a flow chart.

b) Copy and complete these word equations:

nitrogen + _____ → nitrogen oxide
nitrogen oxide + _____ + _____ → nitric acid

c) Copy and complete this paragraph:

Nitrogen and sulphur and _____ are all non-metal elements. When they burn in air (oxygen) they are _____ to produce a compound called an _____. These oxides are usually _____.

Use these words: oxidised, acidic, oxide, carbon.

Information Processing Evaluation

Pupils were investigating the question 'Which building materials are most affected by acid rain?'.
Ronnie's work is shown below.

Method

Place pieces of different building materials in $1\,cm^3$ of $1\,M$ sulphuric acid. Leave them in a warm room until the next lesson.

Results

Material	Observations	
	Before treatment	After 7 days
iron	shiny dark grey solid	iron broken up, some rusting
aluminium	light grey solid	little change, some bubbles
wood	light brown solid	material darkened, some flaking
zinc flashing	shiny grey solid	very little solid left
glass	transparent, clear solid	no effect
rubber seals	flexible brown solid	slight darkening
stainless steel	shiny silver solid	no effect
copper pipe	shiny brown solid	no effect
plastic guttering	flexible, white solid	no effect

Conclusions

My results show that some materials are more likely to be attacked by acid rain than others. Overall, metals are more likely to be attacked by acid than non-metals.

1 Copy out and complete the following table:

Building material	Metal/ Non-metal	Use in buildings	Useful properties

2 Summarise the useful properties of metals. Are there any other useful properties that you could add to your list?

3 Place the metals in order starting with the metal *most* affected by acid.

4 Compare your order with the activity series on page 141. How do they compare?

5 Explain why the acid has no effect on stainless steel but badly affects iron.

6 In the conclusion Ronnie states that 'Overall, metals are more likely to be attacked by acid than non-metals'.

Do you think the results give enough evidence to prove this?

7 In order to make the investigation more convincing, which other building materials would you include in the investigation? Work in groups to create your list.

8 How useful is Ronnie's data for answering the question set? Decide between very useful, of limited use or not useful. Give reasons for your choice.

9 A 5-year research programme in the UK has suggested that if sulphur dioxide emissions were reduced by 30%, savings over 30 years could be as high as £9.5 billion. Suggest how these savings could be made. Think about which materials are most at risk.

DID YOU KNOW?

In 1856, Robert Angus Smith – the scientist who first used the term acid rain – wrote:

'It has often been observed that the stones and bricks of buildings crumble more readily in large towns where much coal is burnt. ... I was led to attribute this effect to the slow but constant action of acid rain.'

Acid rain

During the winter of 1952 an area of high pressure settled over London. The wind dropped and the air grew damp; a thick fog began to form. The Great London Smog lasted for five days and led to around 4000 more deaths than usual. The cold weather meant that many coal fires were burnt which produced sulphur dioxide, smoke and dust. As a result of the thousands of deaths, the Clean Air Acts of 1956 and 1968 were passed. This prevented the burning of smoky fuels in certain areas.

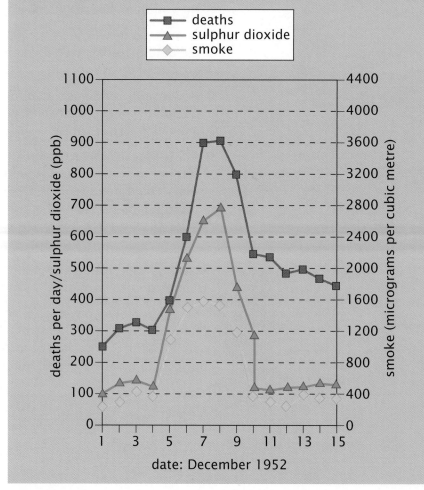

1 On which date did the effect of the pollution begin to show an impact on the number of deaths?

2 Estimate the number of people who died in London between the 4th and 11th of December.

3 What was the highest number of deaths in any one day?

4 What is the relationship between the levels of sulphur dioxide and smoke and the number of deaths during this period? Compare your answer with others. Whose summary of this is best?

5 After which date did the weather conditions begin to improve? Suggest a reason for your answer.

In 1990 changes to the Clean Air Act set rules to cut the release of sulphur dioxide from power plants down to 10 million tonnes by 1st January 2000. However, from the 12th to the 15th of December 1991 similar weather conditions to those of December 1952 prevailed in London, trapping a harmful mixture of fumes and particles. It was estimated that this smog caused around 160 more deaths than normal for the time of year.

Since 1952 industry has moved out of central London and the burning of coal has decreased. However, the use of motor vehicles has increased and has become one of the main sources of air pollution.

Exhaust fume emissions (per vehicle kilometre)

Vehicle	Carbon monoxide	Hydrocarbons	Nitrogen oxides	Smoke particles (carbon)	Carbon dioxide
petrol car with a catalyst	42	19	23	–	100
diesel car without a catalyst	2	3	31	100	85

6 The release of exhaust fumes has been measured per vehicle kilometre. Explain what this means.

7 Which pollutant increased in London between 1952 and 1991?

8 Look carefully at the figures for the exhaust fumes emissions. Despite much debate over which car is cleaner, petrol or diesel, weighing up the advantages and disadvantages is not always clear cut. Draw up a table comparing the advantages and disadvantages of each type of fuel.

9 The formation of carbon monoxide and smoke particles is due to the incomplete combustion of the fuel. Which gas is necessary for combustion? Explain how incomplete combustion occurs.

10 Write a word equation for the formation of carbon dioxide. What type of combustion is this? Explain your answer.

Word play How would you explain the use of the term 'smog'? From which two words has it been made?

How can the pollution problems caused by acid rain be solved?

Key words
* catalyst
* leached
* downwind

Reduce levels of nitrogen oxides

These gases are produced during combustion. Nitrogen is not present in fuels (it comes from the air), so cleaning fuels does not help. These are some of the ways levels of nitrogen oxides can be reduced:

In power stations
- get rid of excess air by using the least amount of air needed for combustion
- lower the combustion temperature.

In cars
- recycle exhaust fumes, which lowers oxygen content and lowers burning temperature, so producing less nitrogen oxides
- catalytic converters in exhaust systems in cars change carbon monoxide (CO) to carbon dioxide (CO_2), nitrogen oxides to nitrogen, and hydrocarbons to water and carbon dioxide. The **catalyst** used is a precious metal such as platinum.

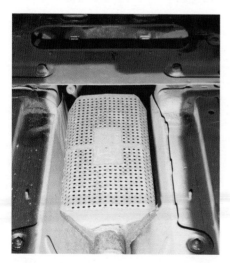

Catalytic converter in a car.

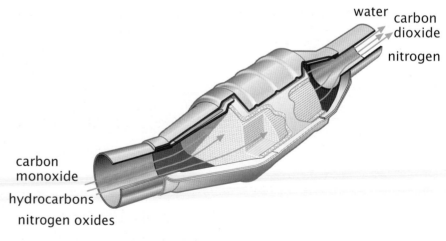

water
carbon dioxide
nitrogen

carbon monoxide
hydrocarbons
nitrogen oxides

Section through a catalytic converter.

14 What effect will reducing the amount of reactant (oxygen) available have on the amount of products (nitrogen oxides)?

15 How will lowering the temperature affect:
   a) the speed of the reaction
   b) the amount of nitrogen oxides produced?
16 Suggest one reason why catalytic converters may be expensive.
17 A gas produced by the catalytic converter is also a greenhouse gas.
   a) Name the gas.
   b) Write the word equation for the production of this gas.
   c) Why is this reaction called an oxidation reaction?

Reduce levels of sulphur dioxide

These are some ways we can reduce levels of sulphur dioxide in the air:

- burn less fossil fuel (this is conservation, and substitute fuel sources need to be found)
- switch to low sulphur fuels, such as petrol labelled ULS, which stands for ultra low sulphur fuel. Coal with less than 1% sulphur is not as readily available and is much more expensive
- fuel desulphurisation – this takes place before combustion, but it is expensive and is still being developed
- sulphur reduction during combustion by adding lime to coal during combustion
- flue gas removal – as gases are released from the chimney, a mixture of finely-ground limestone and water is sprayed onto the gases.

18 Two of the methods listed above use lime (CaO) and limestone (calcium carbonate, $CaCO_3$) for the removal of sulphur dioxide. Sulphur dioxide is an acid gas whereas lime and calcium carbonate are antacids.
   a) What type of chemical is an antacid?
   b) Name the type of reaction that is taking place.
   c) Can you name the salt produced in each reaction?

Treat damaged areas

In many cases, the damage already caused has to be treated. Here are two of the most commonly used methods:

- fertilise damaged conifers with calcium, magnesium, potassium, zinc and manganese since these elements are **leached** out of soil by the action of acid rain
- spread lime (CaO) on affected lakes and forests (this is a method that is already used and is working, but is very expensive).

19 Suggest why spreading lime onto polluted lakes is so expensive.
20 Under what conditions would leaching be most likely?

This map shows the areas that are currently affected by acid rain (heavily or moderately), and could be affected by acid rain in the future. Most damage is **downwind** of the sources of heavy sulphur dioxide and nitrogen oxides emission.

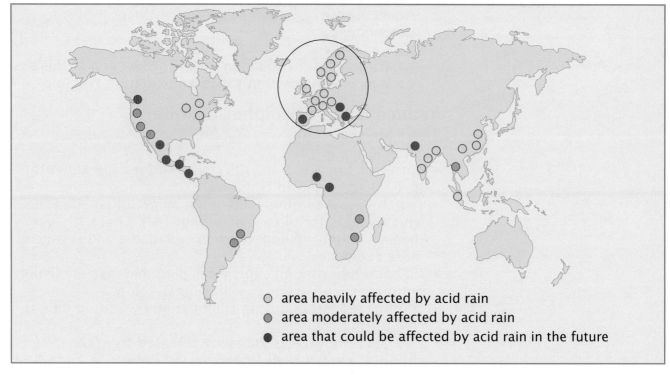

○ area heavily affected by acid rain

◉ area moderately affected by acid rain

● area that could be affected by acid rain in the future

21 Use an atlas to identify which parts of the world are heavily affected by acid rain.

22 Decide whether these areas are urban areas (towns and cities) or rural areas (countryside) and forest.

23 What are the likely sources of pollution in large towns and cities?

24 Look carefully at any rural areas which have been heavily or moderately affected by acid rain. Suggest a likely source of this pollution.

25 Decide which methods of prevention are most likely to be successful in:
   a) urban towns and cities
   b) countryside areas.

26 One of the countries marked in light green on the map opposite is Spain. Suggest how Spain could be affected by acid rain in the future. Where is the most likely source of the acid rain?

Since the 1960s, the problem has become worse in rural areas because the tall factory chimneys allow the wind to transport pollutants far away from their sources. In 1984 it was reported that almost half of the trees in the famous

Black Forest in Germany had been damaged by acid rain. This is one of the most dramatic examples of acid rain damage to trees. This is how the problem has developed:

- damaged fir trees were identified in the early 1960s
- during the 1970s, 30% of the fir trees had died
- by the mid-1980s more than 50% of spruce, pine, beech, and oak trees were damaged or dead
- currently more than 90% of the fir trees are damaged or dead.

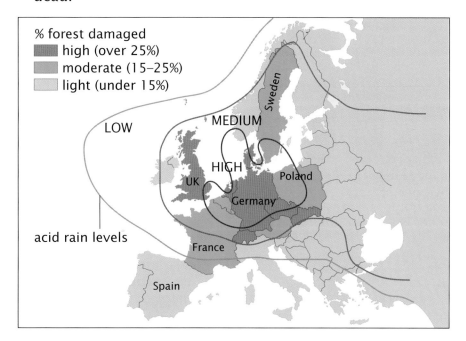

27 Look again at the map of Europe above. Which countries are heavily affected by acid rain?
28 what sort of damage do you think is being done to:
   a) buildings
   b) peoples' health
   c) crops
   d) lakes and rivers?
29 Two of the most seriously affected areas receive large amounts of acid rain which is transported from other parts of Europe:
   a) southern Scandinavia (downwind of Britain and West Europe)
   b) industrial parts of central and western Europe (also downwind of east Europe).
   Suggest the most likely source of this acid rain and how it is transported such long distances.

Enquiry Effect of acid rain

Key word
* secondary sources

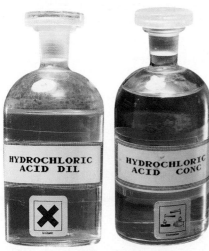

Both of these bottles contain hydrochloric acid. Suggest why one bottle is corrosive but the other is labelled irritant.

A group of students had been studying the cause and effects of acid rain, and were trying to decide on a title for their enquiry. Jonathan wanted to use the title: 'Is acid rain dangerous?'.

1 Jonathan has used the word 'dangerous'. What other words could be used to describe the hazards which are linked with acids?

2 Can you suggest an improvement to this question? Rewrite his title as a question that can be investigated scientifically.

Some teams were interested in finding out why the pH of rainwater might vary.

3 What factors affect the pH of rainwater? They might include:

- location
- wind direction.

In your group discuss what other factors need to be considered.

4 Daisy suggested that the method of data collection (collecting evidence) would limit how much data was made available for their analysis (considering evidence). This would influence the size of their sample. Suzy suggested that in order to find an answer to their question they could:

- collect results by testing rainwater samples in the laboratory
- use **secondary sources** such as databases, CD-ROMs or the internet.

   a) Which method would allow repeat measurements to be carried out?
   b) Which method would allow the pupils to collect data from different parts of the UK, Europe or even worldwide?
   c) Which method would allow pupils to collect a wider selection of data?
   d) What is the disadvantage of using data from secondary sources?

5 By using the sources of data available you could investigate the following questions:
   a) Is there a link between the acidity of the rainwater and the volume of the rainwater?
   b) Is the rainwater more acidic when the wind blows from the east?
   c) Is there a link between the acidity of the rainwater and the season?

Think up some more questions which you could investigate.

Enquiry *Analysing data*

Here are research data from three different groups.

Group 1
The data show the rainfall collected in one particular day at 42 different locations across Great Britain and Ireland.

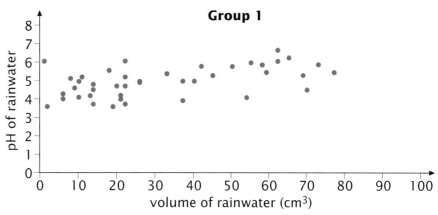

1 The pupils have presented their data as a scatter graph.
   a) What question do you think this group was investigating?
   b) Is there a link between the volume of rainwater and the pH?
   c) What additional information do you need in order to interpret these results?
   d) How else could this data be presented?

Group 2 and Group 3
Two groups collected data on rainfall and pH levels in their local area. They carried out their study during April.

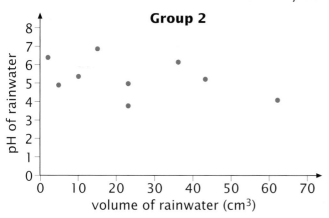

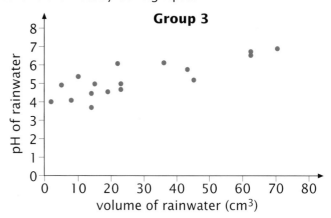

2 How much bigger is the group 3 sample compared to group 2?

3 Both sets of pupils stated: 'When there was less rainfall, the pH is higher. It is less acidic.' Look carefully at each set of results. Do you agree with this statement? Explain your decision.

4 Group 3 were concerned that a small sample might provide misleading results. Which group has the more reliable evidence?

5 Look at the *y* axis. What advice would you give to both groups about the presentation of their scatter graph?

How does acid rain affect aquatic organisms?

Key words
* biodiversity
* toxic
* tolerate

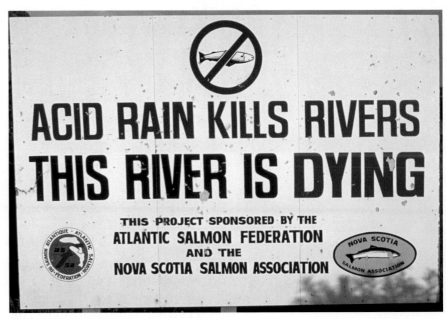

30 What does this sign mean? Is the river water dying?

In Norway, scientists started seeing an increase in the number of dead fish in lakes and rivers at the beginning of the twentieth century. Currently at least 20% of their lakes have no fish, and most of the lakes in Norway are damaged.

Acid rain causes a variety of effects that harm or kill individual fish, reduce fish population numbers or completely remove fish species from a body of water. This decreases **biodiversity**.

Word play

Bio means life.
Diversity means variety.
Explain what is meant by the phrase 'decrease biodiversity'.

As acid rain flows through soils, aluminium is released from the soil into the lakes and streams, resulting in a lower pH and a higher aluminium level in the water. Both low pH and increased aluminium levels are directly **toxic** to fish. This may not kill individual fish, but it leads to lower body weight and smaller size, and makes the fish less able to compete for food and habitat.

31 What is meant when we describe a substance as toxic?

Some types of plants and animals are able to **tolerate** acidic waters. Others, however, are acid-sensitive and will die as the pH falls. Generally, the young of most species are more sensitive to environmental conditions than adults. At a pH of 5, most fish eggs cannot hatch.
At lower pH levels, some adult fish die. Some acid lakes have no fish living in them at all. The chart below shows that not all organisms can tolerate the same amount of acid; for example, frogs can put up with water that is more acidic (has lower pH) than can trout.

Organism	pH tolerance
trout	5.0
bass	5.5
perch	4.5
frog	4.0
mayfly	5.5
snail	6.0
tadpole	5.5

32 Explain why smaller, lighter organisms might be less competitive.

33 Choose a word or phrase in the text above that means the same as tolerate.

34 'Being smaller and lighter could be an advantage', suggested Fran. Do you agree? Explain why.

35 What will happen to the fish population if the acidity of the water gets as low as pH 5?

36 Suggest why the frog population may decrease before the pH level drops below 5.

37 Snails will not tolerate pH levels lower than 6. What will happen to any organisms that prey on snails once the pH has dropped below this level?

38 Scientists often use sampling techniques to estimate the numbers in a population. How would environmental scientists use the data in the table to judge the water quality of a freshwater lake?

What is happening to the environment?

It is vital that we learn lessons from the past and protect both ourselves and our environment from further harm. There are national air quality and water quality monitoring systems in place to inform us of levels of air and water pollution. Information on each of the five main pollutants is gathered every hour from over 110 automatic monitoring sites.

The five main pollutants are:

- sulphur dioxide
- nitrogen dioxide
- ozone
- carbon monoxide
- smoke particles.

Levels of the five main air pollutants that can cause immediate health effects are given a numerical index. The index is used during weather reports to give a warning to people who are more likely to be at risk from pollution. Such sensitive individuals are people who suffer from heart and lung diseases, including asthma, particularly if they are elderly. The pollution index has a scale from 1–10.

Pollution band and numerical index	Health effect
1–3 (low)	effects are unlikely to be noticed, even by people who know they are sensitive to air pollutants
4–6 (moderate)	mild effects are unlikely to require action, but sensitive people may notice them
7–9 (high)	- sensitive people may notice significant effects, and may have to act to reduce or avoid them (for example, by reducing time spent outdoors) - asthmatics should find that their inhaler reverses the effects of pollution on their lungs
10 (very high)	the effects of high levels of pollution on sensitive people may worsen when pollution becomes very high

Air pollution levels vary from area to area and from day to day. Levels of pollution can be influenced by a number of things, such as:

- local landscape features and surroundings
- local and regional sources of pollution
- seasonal variations and main weather conditions.

1 Classify the locations and weather conditions in the table below as either higher pollution or lower pollution.
   a) Grade them as high pollution level or low pollution level.
   b) Reclassify each location/weather condition more specifically as:

   A – low
   B – moderate
   C – high
   D – very high.

Location/weather condition
Cities and towns in deep valleys
In winter, in cold, still, foggy weather, particularly vehicle pollutants in large cities
Smoke control area or areas with high levels of gas or electricity used for heating
Busy roads with heavy traffic next to high buildings and busy road junctions
Residential roads with light traffic
Windy or wet weather at any time of year
In summer, during sunny, still weather, particularly with respect to ozone levels in suburban and rural areas
Rural areas away from major roads and factories (for most pollutants except ozone)
Cities/towns on hills
High levels of solid fuel, for example coal and wood, used for heating in the local area

2 Pupils have mixed up the health effects of these three groups of pollutants. In groups, decide how the pollutant and the health effects should be matched up.

Pollutant	Health effects at very high levels
nitrogen dioxide sulphur dioxide ozone	fine particles can be carried deep into the lungs where they can cause inflammation and a worsening of heart and lung diseases
smoke particles	• this gas prevents the normal transport of oxygen by the blood • this can lead to a significant reduction in the supply of oxygen to the heart, particularly in people suffering from heart disease
carbon monoxide	these gases irritate the airways of the lungs, increasing the symptoms of those suffering from lung diseases

Key words
* biological indicators
* lichens

Biological indicators: signs of pollution

Biological indicators are useful for showing levels of pollution.

1 Black spot is a mould that grows on roses. This mould cannot grow if there is sulphur dioxide in the air.
2 In Book 1 you learned about **lichens**. These are plants which are sensitive to sulphur dioxide. Each type has a different tolerance to sulphur dioxide levels. By observing the type of lichens growing locally, environmental scientists can monitor the level of pollution.
3 Mosses are also sensitive to air pollution and have disappeared from many urban and industrial areas over the last century.

Shrubby lichens are highly intolerant of pollution.

Leafy lichens show medium tolerance.

Some lichens can tolerate higher pollution levels.

39 Describe which types of lichen profile you are likely to find in:

  • a town park
  • trees along a busy main road
  • a village orchard.

40 What technique could a pupil use to estimate the population of each type of lichen? Make a list of the equipment needed and outline the method used.

Time to think

1 The data in the table below show the percentage of four different pollutants from power stations, road traffic and other sources.

	Source of pollutant (percentage)		
Pollutant	power stations	road traffic	other sources
sulphur dioxide	72	2	
nitrogen oxides	28		21
smoke particles	7	46	
carbon monoxide	1	90	9

   a) Calculate the missing percentages.

   b) Suggest why the carbon monoxide levels are much higher from road traffic sources compared to power stations. Think about the type of combustion taking place.

   c) Suggest why the sulphur dioxide levels are low from road traffic. How might the sulphur content be removed from exhaust fumes?

   d) What effect might the smoke particles level have on the growth of plants in urban areas?

   e) Suggest one other source of each pollutant. Share your answer with your partner. Team up with another pair and discuss your answer. Agree on your final list and share the answer with the whole class.

2 Imagine that the British Government wanted to make major reductions in the levels of acid rain. What should they do to achieve this aim?

3 Imagine that you are all scientists working in a laboratory. Think about a research project to investigate some aspect of acid rain – how it forms, the damage it does, etc. Write your ideas on the board. Discuss the questions you would ask and the steps you would take to do the research.

4 Role playing. Each of you should take the role of an 'interested party' (for example a coal miner, factory owner, fisherman, farmer or forester) in a group discussion on acid rain. Think how your job either produces carbon dioxide, nitrogen and sulphur oxides, or is affected by it. Present arguments for or against laws to control acid rain.

Green machine

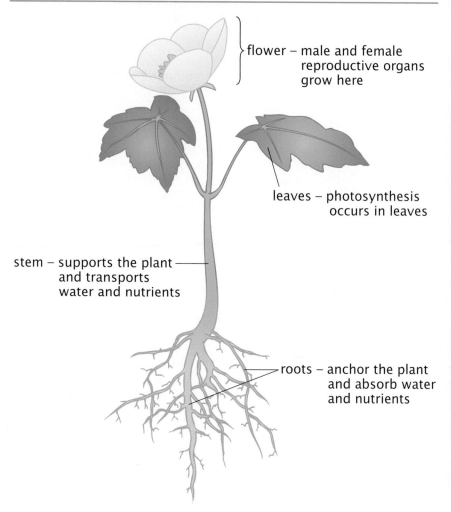

flower – male and female reproductive organs grow here

leaves – photosynthesis occurs in leaves

stem – supports the plant and transports water and nutrients

roots – anchor the plant and absorb water and nutrients

Key words
* photosynthesise
* starch

Each part of a plant has specific jobs to do.

Green plants **photosynthesise**. This is the way that these plants feed – they are able to make their own food from carbon dioxide and water.

41 Why do plants need food?
42 How is plant nutrition similar to and different from human nutrition?

The pictures at the top of the next page show the different stages for a **starch** test on a leaf.

43 Which chemical is used to test for starch?
44 What would you expect to happen if this chemical was poured onto:
  a) starch
  b) a leaf that had been kept in the light and then boiled in alcohol
  c) a leaf that had been kept in the dark and then boiled in alcohol
  d) a piece of potato?

A

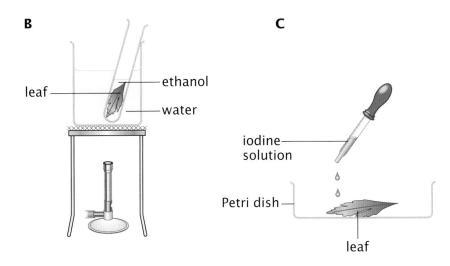

Testing a leaf for starch.

When a variegated leaf was tested for starch, it looked like this:

Variegated leaf before starch test.

After starch test.

45 a) How is a variegated leaf different from a normal leaf?
  b) What do these results show us about starch formation in a leaf?
  c) What results would you expect if a variegated plant had been kept in the dark before the starch test? Why?

Word play

¹S	T	A	R	C	H
A	R	I	E	G	²I
⁴V	A	N	O	A	O
S	H	⁶CO₂	L	T	D
E	T	⁵E	D	E	I
V	A	E	³L	E	N

In this word puzzle, the six answers spiral round to the centre. Write a clue for each answer. Check your clues with others in your group and see who has the most interesting questions.

EXTENSION Use the six words from the puzzle to write three or four sentences to summarise your ideas about photosynthesis.

What happens in the leaves?

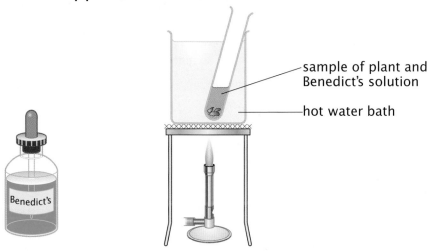

sample of plant and Benedict's solution

hot water bath

Testing leaves for sugar.

Most plants make starch when they photosynthesise. Some plants, like garlic, grass and cereal crops, make sugar. Both sugar and starch are **carbohydrates**.

Plants are very useful organisms for humans. All of the products in the photographs below come from plants. Some of them provide us with food, and others provide materials for us to use.

46 Make a table or diagram to show the different uses we make of plant products. Add two more products to each group.

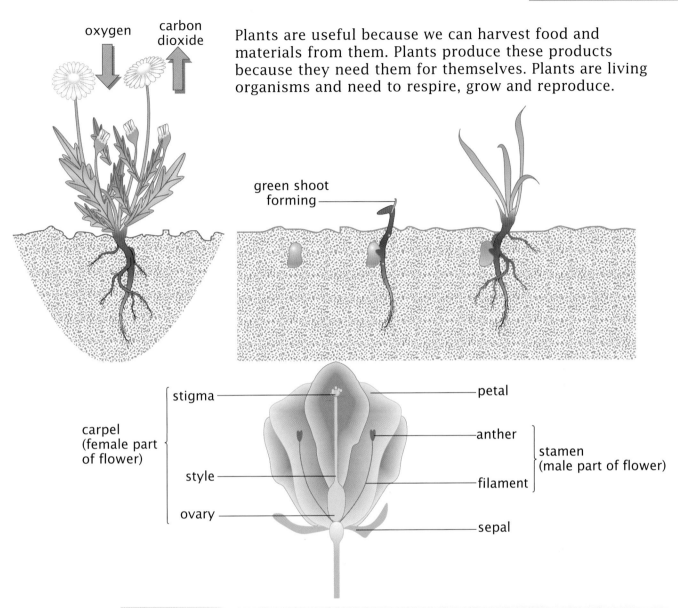

oxygen carbon dioxide

Plants are useful because we can harvest food and materials from them. Plants produce these products because they need them for themselves. Plants are living organisms and need to respire, grow and reproduce.

green shoot forming

stigma — petal

carpel (female part of flower)

— anther

stamen (male part of flower)

style — filament

ovary — sepal

Time to think

Use the information in the three diagrams above to produce a single diagram that summarises why plants need to produce glucose (sugar) in photosynthesis. Compare your summary with others in your group. 'Traffic light' each others work.

Green dot = includes ideas you had not thought of/put ideas together clearly.
Amber dot = good attempt at the level you would accept as adequate.
Red dot = some ideas missing /incorrect/muddled.

Talk to one another about your assessment, and if you got an amber or red dot, try to improve your summary.

Plants make glucose when they photosynthesise. Plants can then use this glucose when they respire. In most plants, excess glucose is converted to starch because starch stores better than glucose. In a few plants, for example, olives, the glucose is turned into oil. Glucose can also be converted into cellulose and protein, which are both important for making new cells.

The story of wheat

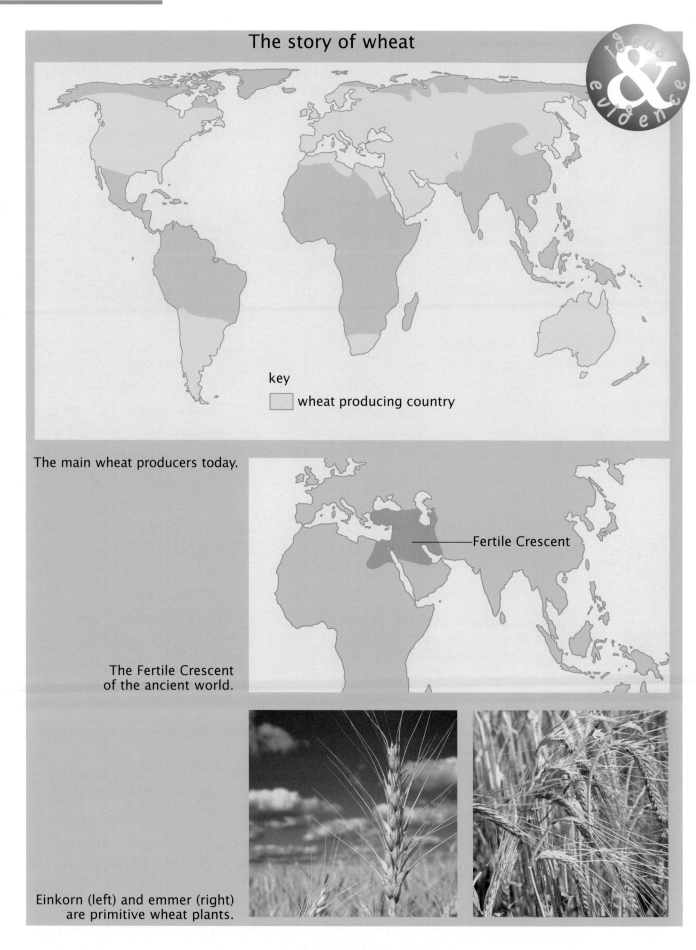

key

wheat producing country

The main wheat producers today.

Fertile Crescent

The Fertile Crescent
of the ancient world.

Einkorn (left) and emmer (right)
are primitive wheat plants.

Wheat has been cultivated by humans as a valuable food source for over 9000 years. Greek and Roman writings show that wheat was their main cereal crop. The seeds or grains of wheat were ground to make flour. Some grains of wheat have also been found preserved in Egyptian tombs.

The main advances in wheat cultivation took place in a region known as the Fertile Crescent, which today includes part of Israel, Turkey, Iraq and Iran. Much of this land is now desert, but it was once a rich farming region.

The first wheat plants were known as einkorn and emmer. These plants had long thin stalks which were easily broken in bad weather. They also had quite small seeds, so the ancient farmers needed to grow a very large crop in order to produce enough wheat for food. They began wheat breeding programs to improve both the stalk strength and the yield of the wheat plants. Today we have much better varieties of wheat, which are stronger and produce high yields. Some varieties are also resistant to drought and to disease.

Durum wheat.

Bread wheat.

One type of modern wheat is durum wheat. It has been produced by intensive breeding. Durum wheat has large grains. It is grown to provide the flour for making pasta and biscuits. In some parts of the world it is called macaroni wheat. It cannot be used to make bread because it has a low gluten content. Flour made from bread wheat has a high gluten content. Gluten makes the dough elastic and helps to trap the carbon dioxide bubbles that yeast produces. This makes the bread light and airy.

Today some countries grow wheat on a large scale with vast expanses of wheat plants. To harvest the grain, farmers use large machines called combine harvesters to collect the seeds. The wheat seeds are then stored in grain stores before they are shipped to mills and factories to make flour.

1 What evidence do we have that wheat has been cultivated for thousands of years?
2 Suggest why ancient people began to cultivate wheat.
3 How have breeding programs improved wheat plants?
4 What is meant by plant yield?
5 Why is bread wheat better than durum wheat for making bread?
6 In which parts of the world is wheat mainly cultivated today?

Research Find out about how and where cotton is grown, harvested and processed into material or thread these days. Use the internet and books to help you.

Plant drugs and poisons

In ancient times, plants were the main source of **medicines**. By trial and error, people were able to find out which plants helped with particular illnesses. The plants that worked were usually grown in special gardens and used by the local people to treat various diseases. In the Middle Ages, details of medicinal plants were recorded in books called 'Herbals'.

Ginseng has been prized in China for over 5000 years. People take its powdered root because they believe that it can help recovery from many illnesses. Today, ginseng is sold commercially all over the world.

In South America, the bark of cinchona trees is used to treat malaria. The bark produces quinine which can help control malaria. Quinine is also used to flavour tonic water.

Foxglove leaves contain the chemical digitalis, which is used to treat some heart conditions. In small doses it can help the heart beat more slowly and strongly. However, in large doses it produces heart palpitations and dizziness.

While the deadly nightshade plant is poisonous, it can be used to produce the drug atropine. This drug is used in eye surgery and to treat some stomach complaints.

Castor oil plants have been grown for health reasons since the days of the Egyptians. The oil from these plants is used to purify the digestive system. Castor oil plant beans also contain the lethal **poison** ricin. Eating just a single bean from this plant would kill an adult.

Jojoba and aloe vera plants are grown to obtain their oils. These oils keep skin soft and supple and have healing properties as they soothe the skin.

Creative thinking ## The importance of plants

Make a poster, pamphlet or PowerPoint presentation about the importance of plants to humans.

van Helmont

It was thought at one time that plants used materials from the soil to grow. We now know that plants only use a tiny amount of material from the soil to grow. Most of the plant is made using the materials from photosynthesis. One of the key pieces of research that led to this idea was carried out by van Helmont in the seventeenth century.

Jean Baptiste van Helmont was born in Brussels in 1579. He is recognised as the discoverer of carbon dioxide. Like many scientists of his time, he was interested in various aspects of science, but chemistry was his main interest. He did a lot of work on gases. The most important experiment that he did about plant nutrition was to take a young willow tree growing in a pot and weigh it and the soil in which the tree grew.

van Helmont's experiment.

Over the next 5 years he added nothing to the soil other than water. At the end of this time he found that the tree and its pot of soil had gained 164 lb (about 74.5 kg). He weighed the soil and found that it had only lost a few ounces (less than 100 g). He reasoned that the tree's food could not have come from the soil. van Helmont went on to suggest that the increase in the weight of the tree came from its taking in water. Today we know that plants take in carbon dioxide through their leaves and water through their roots. These two substances react together during photosynthesis and produce glucose.

1 Write two or three questions that would test whether someone understood the importance of van Helmont's work to our understanding about photosynthesis.

2 Check each other's questions and decide which questions are the best.

Evaluation Mung bean experiment

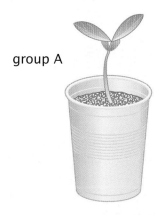

group A

Mung beans germinate and grow quite quickly. Three groups of students decided to use mung beans to carry out their own version of van Helmont's experiment.

Group A planted a mung bean in a plastic cup of moist soil. They weighed the cup of soil and bean and found that it weighed 175 g. Every day they lightly sprayed the soil surface with water. After 10 days the bean had grown, and when they weighed it again it weighed 175 g.

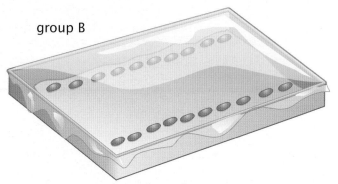

group B

Group B decided to grow 20 mung beans. They soaked their seeds and placed them on a wet paper towel in a plastic dish. They covered the top of the dish with cling film. They weighed the dish and contents and found that it weighed 50 g. They left the seeds to grow, and at the end of 10 days they reweighed the dish and contents. It now weighed 55 g.

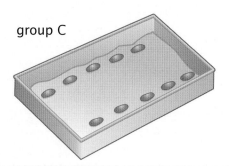

group C

Group C decided to grow ten mung bean seeds. They soaked them and then placed them on a moist paper towel in a small plastic dish. The dish and contents weighed 45 g. Every day they lightly sprayed the paper towel with water. By the tenth day, nine of the beans had germinated and grown. They reweighed the dish and contents and found that it weighed 48 g.

1 Why do you think group A did not get an increase in the weight of the pot of soil and bean after 10 days?

2 Which groups carried out a fair test? Explain what they did to make the test fair.

3 Which group's investigation had the most similar idea to van Helmont's experiment? Explain why you think this.

➡ *Looking inside leaves*

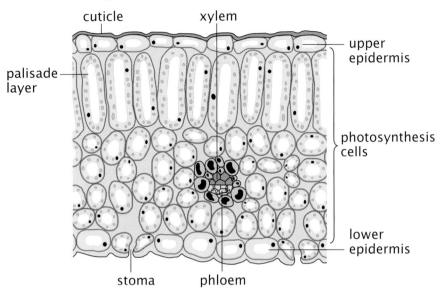

Cross-section through a leaf.

Leaves are the main site for **photosynthesis**. **Chlorophyll** is the green pigment that helps plants to make glucose. It is found in little sacs called **chloroplasts** in many of the leaf cells. Chloroplasts are energy transfer systems. They change light energy into chemical energy locked in glucose molecules. The main photosynthetic layer in the leaf is the layer just below the upper surface – this is the **palisade** layer.

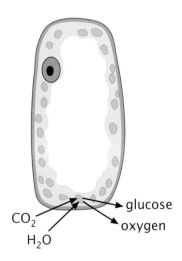

A chloroplast.

47 How are the cells in the palisade layers adapted for photosynthesis?
48 Why are chloroplasts described as energy transfer systems?
49 Which two substances do plants use to make glucose?
50 Which other product is produced in photosynthesis?

Information processing *Underwater photosynthesis*

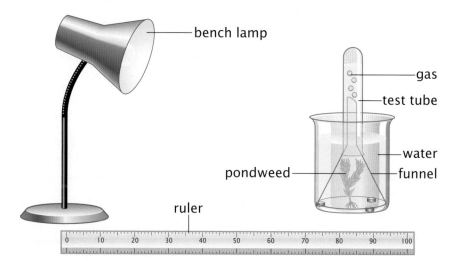

Photosynthesis results in an increase in biomass, but this takes a while to measure. Testing for glucose or starch destroys the leaf, so to see photosynthesis in action Canadian pondweed is often used in laboratories. It is used because it is an aquatic plant and the oxygen it produces in photosynthesis can actually be seen leaving the plant. The oxygen diffuses out of the chloroplasts into the leaf, pushing bubbles out of tiny pores into the water. The amount of gas or the rate that bubbles are produced gives us some indication of how quickly photosynthesis is taking place.

In one experiment, scientists looked at the relationship between rate of photosynthesis and light intensity. The graph below shows the results.

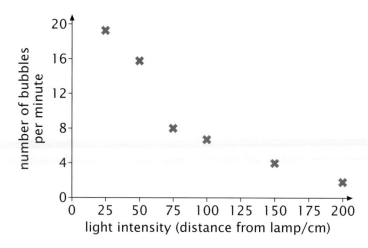

1 Which is the dependent (input) variable?

2 Which variables would be controlled (fixed variables)?

3 Why is light intensity measured in centimetres?

4 What was the photosynthesis rate when the lamp was
   a) 50 cm away
   b) 70 cm away
   c) 250 cm away?

5 How far away was the lamp if the photosynthesis rate was 8 bubbles per minute?

6 If you collected the gas produced by the photosynthesising leaves, how would you check that it contained oxygen?

The discovery of oxygen

Joseph Priestley was born near Leeds in 1733 and is recognised as the discoverer of oxygen. Priestley and other scientists of his time did not have a periodic table as we do today. They also did not know about elements and compounds in the same way that we do. In Priestley's time the phlogiston theory was the main theory that scientists used to explain their experimental findings. So when Priestley isolated oxygen and tested its properties, he called the gas 'dephlogisticated air'.

All the gases that Priestley and his fellow scientists knew about were thought to be different types of air, and the 'goodness' of air was measured depending on its 'respirability'. They carried out tests on goodness by seeing if small animals, like mice, could survive in a container of the gas.

In 1771, Priestley reported a new finding from his experiments. He had been experimenting on some 'injured air', which was air from which mice had already taken all the oxygen. Priestley found that if he put some green plants into a container of this injured air, the air's respirability returned. He tried this first with mint plants, then groundsel and then spinach. In all three experiments he found that the plants changed the air. He wrote:

'The injury which is continually done to the atmosphere by respiration of such a large number of animals ... is, in part, regulated by vegetable creation.'

1 Why did Priestley call oxygen 'dephlogisticated air'?
2 How did scientists in Priestley's time test for the 'goodness of air'?
3 Explain how you might set up Priestley's famous experiment today to show the effect that plants have on 'injured air'.
4 Write out Priestley's quote using modern language, and explain why this happens.

→ *Rooted on the spot*

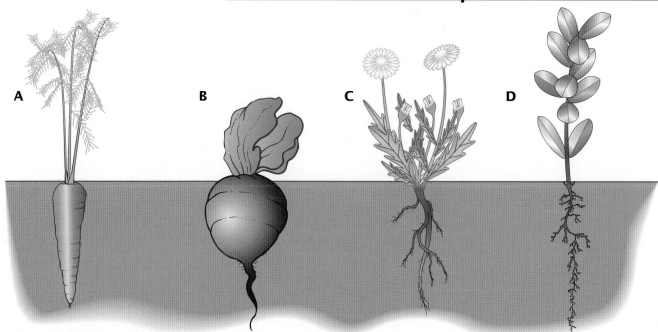

Different types of plant roots.

Roots are adapted for the jobs they do. Roots anchor the plant into the soil, and this prevents the plant from being blown away, knocked over or pulled up easily. Roots also take in water and minerals through their roots. Some roots store the starch made during photosynthesis.

51 Look at the roots pictured above. Decide which of them are are:
   a) good anchors
   b) good for exchanging materials
   c) good for storage of starch.

Adaptation also takes place at the cell level. If you look closely at the roots you can see that some of the root cells have tiny 'hairs'. These are root hair cells, and they create a larger surface area for taking up water and minerals. While plants need moist soil, they do not work well in water-logged soil. This is because the root cells need oxygen for respiration. If all the gaps between the soil particles become full of water, the root hair cells die.

Root showing root hair cells.

Reasoning *Mineral salts*

Look at this experiment which has been set up to find out which mineral salts plants need to grow healthily.

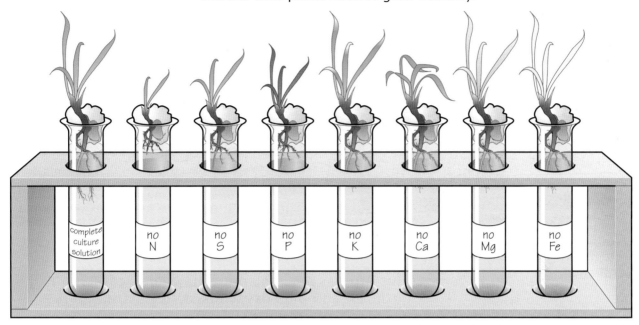

1 Construct a table to record the results of this experiment.

2 Why did the scientist use light banks and add extra carbon dioxide to the air?

3 What would be your conclusion to this experiment?

4 This shows only one plant growing in each solution. Why should the scientist grow a large number of plants in the different solutions?

Why are green plants important to the environment?

Plants make food and materials for humans and other organisms. They also regulate our atmospheric gases. The processes below take oxygen out and put carbon dioxide into the air.

Key words
* greenhouse effect
* global warming

Respiration.

This process does the opposite – takes carbon dioxide out of the air and puts oxygen back in:

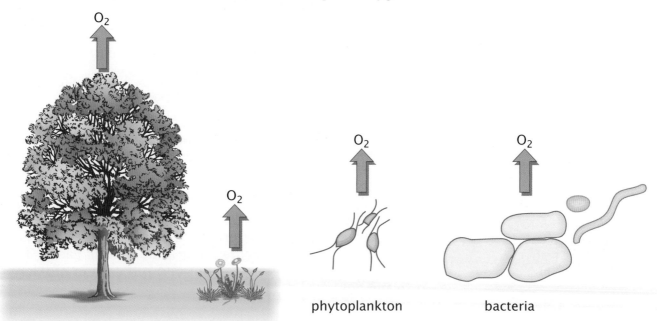

phytoplankton   bacteria

Photosynthesis.

We get very worried today when people cut down forests. Sometimes it seems necessary to do so to make way for agriculture or roads. If the proportion of the world covered by plants decreases, then less carbon dioxide will be taken out of the air and less oxygen will be put back into it. In a similar way, if we continue to burn fossil fuels in factories and power stations we will be adding to the carbon dioxide and reducing the oxygen in the atmosphere. Increasing the carbon dioxide in the atmosphere can increase the **greenhouse effect**. This is one of the factors that may be causing climate change such as **global warming**.

Reasoning *Balance of gases*

Look at the three initiatives below. How will they help to maintain the balance of gases in the atmosphere?

1 Laws have been passed to make timber companies plant new trees for every tree they cut down.

2 Some countries have asked their population to switch from coal-fired to nuclear-power stations.

3 Some councils in the UK now collect and compost garden waste.

Time to think

1 Pick a topic that you feel you need to work on. Read it through carefully, write notes on it and read it again. Highlight your notes to emphasise the important points. Write a ten mark test on the topic, and give it to another pupil to try out. Try and complete the test that they have created.

2 Write a short sentence on a card that explains some particular idea from this chapter, for example:

Photosynthesis is an energy-transfer process.

Cut the sentence into two parts.

Photosynthesis is

an energy-transfer process.

Do the same for five more sentences. In a group of four to six pupils, put all of the sentence beginnings into a pile. Share out the sentence endings between the group. In turn pull out a sentence beginning card and allow 5 seconds to see if anyone can finish the sentence. If the sentence is not completed, the card goes to the bottom of the pile. If someone answers incorrectly, they miss having a turn with the next card. The winner is the one who gets rid of his or her cards first.

7 *Genes and inheritance*

In this chapter you will learn:

➡ **that all living things contain genetic information**
➡ **how offspring inherit characteristics from their parents**
➡ **that characteristics are variables in a population**
➡ **that genes are organised into chromosomes**
➡ **that genes are made up of large molecules called DNA**
➡ **how sex in humans is determined**
➡ **the history of the development of genetics as a science**
➡ **that variation is due to both inheritance and the environment**
➡ **how knowledge of genetics is used in selective breeding and genetic engineering**

You will also develop your skills in:

➡ **decision making – deciding what measurements to make in an investigation**
➡ **sampling to get a 'picture' of a population's characteristics**
➡ **collecting, organising and using large data sets**
➡ **looking for patterns in data to determine what is due to probability and what is not**
➡ **evaluating the strength of evidence**

➡ ➡ ➡ WHAT DO YOU KNOW?

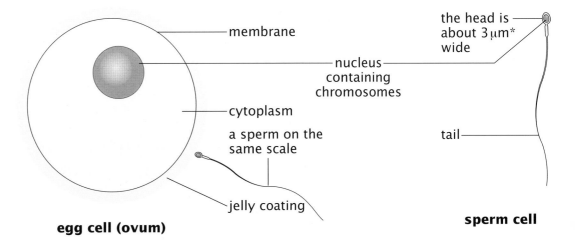

membrane

the head is about 3 μm* wide

nucleus containing chromosomes

cytoplasm

a sperm on the same scale

tail

jelly coating

egg cell (ovum)

sperm cell

*1 micrometre (μm) is one-thousandth of a millimetre (mm)

Here is quick quiz to see what your group knows about reproduction, inheritance and variation. Make one of your group the questioner and another person the 'scribe'. The scribe notes down what your group's answers are. Your teacher will tell you how long you have to do the quiz. Groups can swap and mark each other's answers.

1 What does 'inheritance' mean?

2 How is a sperm cell adapted to its function? Where are sperm cells made?

3 How is an egg cell adapted to its function? Where are egg cells made?

4 Why are brothers and sisters similar to each other and their parents in some ways?

5 Which of these diagrams shows how identical twins are formed?

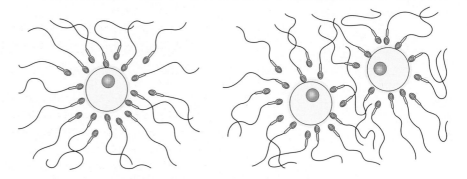

6 A farmer harvested some wheat grains from one ear of wheat and planted all the seeds in a plant pot. They germinated and he planted them out in a row in a field. When the plants grew to full size he noticed that they were all different heights. What might have caused this variation?

seeds of wheat

Inheritance

Genetics is the scientific study of **inheritance**. Inheritance is how plant and animal **offspring** get **characteristics** from their parents. Every organism on the planet has **genes**, but scientists have only discovered them within the last 100 years.

In the nineteenth century some scientists thought that the sperm cell contained a miniature model of an adult. This tiny thing was thought to have grown inside the mother until it was born. It was assumed that the mother did not pass on any of her own characteristics to the baby.

Other scientists thought that the mother contained a seed that grew into the new child and that the father did not influence how that child would look. Of course we now know that both the sperm and the ova (egg cells) are important. These sex cells are called **gametes**, and each contains half a set of coded instructions that when combined during **fertilisation**, form an **embryo**.

The beginning of the study of inheritance

In 1866 an Austrian monk called Gregor Mendel published the results of 7 years of pea breeding experiments. He was interested in looking at how characteristics (variables in organisms) are **inherited** from one **generation** to another. Mendel used pea plants in his experiments because it is easy to see how their appearance varies. Some of the characteristics he studied were:

- height of pea plants
- shape of pea seeds
- colour of pea flowers
- colour of pea pods.

He crossed parent pea plants with different characteristics and looked at the appearance of their offspring.

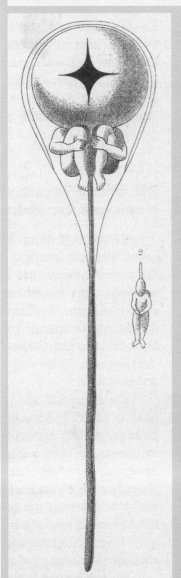

Menschliche Samenkörperchen
nach alten Darstellungen.

1) Abbildung nach der Theorie Hart=
soekers; 2) entpupptes Spermato=
zoon, welches Dalepatius (de la
Plantade) in dieser Gestalt gesehen
haben wollte.

A drawing from 1894 of a human sperm cell containing a miniature adult.

Gregor Mendel.

Information processing *Mendel's experiment*

Some pupils repeated Mendel's pea experiments. Here are the notes they made:

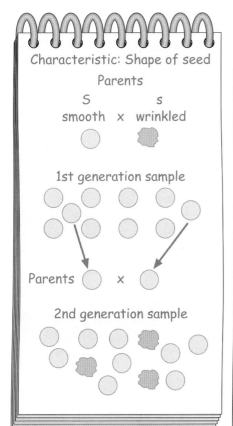

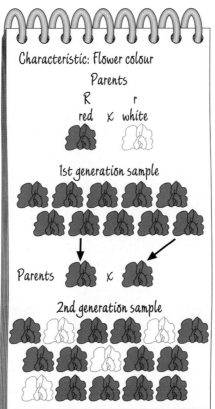

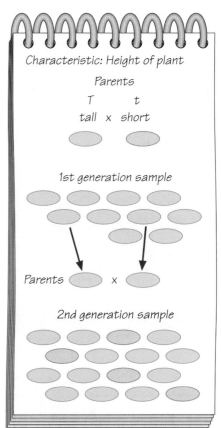

The pupils have used symbols to represent characteristics.

1 Write down what each of these symbols stand for:

T t S s R r × ↓

2 Copy this table and use information from the pupils' note books to complete it. '×' means 'crossed with'.

Characteristic	Parents crossed	First generation offspring – numbers and characteristics	Second generation offspring – numbers and characteristic
shape of seed (pea)	smooth ×	.... all smooth	.... smooth and 3 wrinkled
colour of F.........	.... × white	12 all R.........	12 red and 4 ....
height	.... ×	.... all	..... tall and ...... short

3 What do you notice about all of the offspring in the first generation?

4 Write down the ratios of the two types of offspring for each of the sets of second-generation offspring.

5 What pattern do you notice?

Chromosomes

The invention of the microscope showed that organisms are made up of cells, but it was not until the end of the nineteenth century that Thomas Hunt Morgan, a professor at Columbia University, saw down his microscope some strange thread-like strings floating around inside the cells of worms that lived inside the intestines of horses. When the cells divided (to reproduce) these threads seemed to go through a series of complicated movements, like a dance. The threads are now called **chromosomes**.

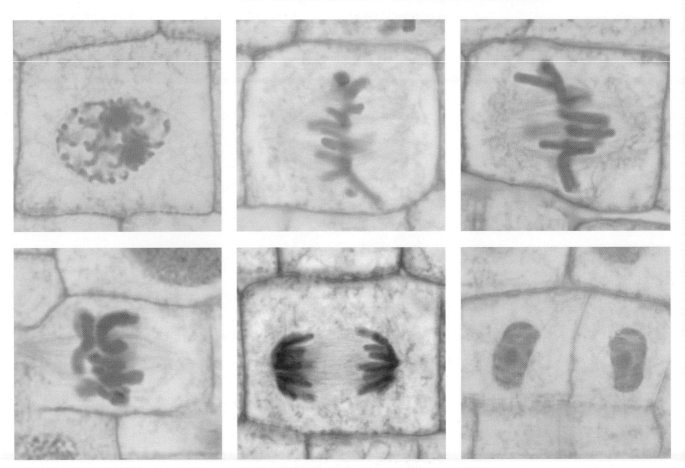

Chromosomes duplicate inside a cell, then divide up to make two new cells.

When a cell divides each chromosome makes a copy of itself so that for a short while there are two identical sets of chromosomes inside the dividing cell. When the cell finishes dividing, each of the two new cells has just one set of chromosomes inside it. This cycle is repeated over and over again to make many new cells, each containing an identical set of chromosomes to each other and to the original parent cell. Chromosomes carry information as thousands of genes. Genes are responsible for all the characteristics of organisms.

Some characteristics are not visible in the offspring of the first generation. Mendel called these **recessive** genes. The characteristics that are visible in the first-generation offspring are called **dominant** genes.

A capital letter is used to represent the dominant gene, and the recessive gene is shown with a small (lower case) letter.

1 In the table below write down the recessive and the dominant genes and how they are represented, either by a lower case or a capital letter. The first one has been done for you:

Characteristic	Dominant gene	Recessive gene
height	tall T	short t
pea shape		
flower colour		

This is a genetic diagram of one of the pupil's crosses:

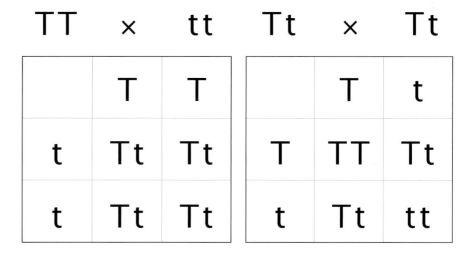

Reasoning *Gardening expert*

Imagine that you are a member of the panel on Gardener's Question Time. Mr Floribunda asks the team:

'I want to grow only red flowering pea plants to sell. No one wants to pay for the white flowering plants. Every time I cross two red flowering plants I get some white flowered plants. Why is this happening, and can I do something to make sure I only get red flowered offspring in the future?'

1 Draw a genetic diagram that explains what happens in the first and second generation offspring when you cross a pure bred red (RR) plant with a pure white short plant (rr).

2 Use your genetic diagram to write a reply to Mr Floribunda that could be read out on radio.

Genetic code

2 The gene model used in Book 1 gives an analogy for our understanding of genetics today. Write down the missing labels to remind you what each part stands for.

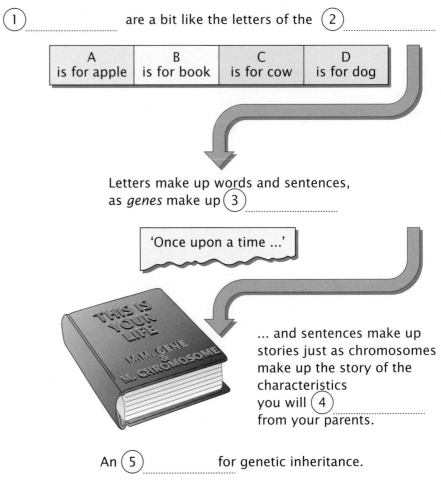

(1) .... are a bit like the letters of the (2) ....

| A is for apple | B is for book | C is for cow | D is for dog |

Letters make up words and sentences, as *genes* make up (3) ....

'Once upon a time ...'

THIS IS YOUR LIFE
M.M. GENE & M. CHROMOSOME

... and sentences make up stories just as chromosomes make up the story of the characteristics you will (4) .... from your parents.

An (5) .... for genetic inheritance.

3 What is an analogy? Why are analogies helpful in understanding scientific theories and ideas?

Genetic information (in the above figure this is the text) is organised into genes (sentences) and stored in the DNA (a book). Each gene contains instructions (words) to make one product. The individual 'words' identify the materials to be used, and the word sequence details the order in which the materials are assembled. A very simple language is used. This language is the **genetic code** and it has just 64 words. A huge number of different messages can be written with a 64-word vocabulary. Every living thing uses the same language, but different types of organisms use it to produce different sets of instructions. This is like saying that there are very different 'stories' written – a fish story, a tree story or a human story. Because all living things use this same basic vocabulary it is possible for different organisms to 'read' and understand genes for another organism. This is why **genetic engineering** is possible.

This is the process of cutting genes out of chromosomes in one organism and moving them to another chromosome in another organism. Scientists can do this by using enzymes to cut up chromosomes into pieces.

More about Mendel

→

Key words
* fertilised
* self-pollinate
* pollen
* anthers
* stigma
* ova

To do his investigations Mendel had to know how plants are **fertilised**. This was so that he could control which two parent pea plants would breed together to produce seeds that could be grown into offspring. Peas were ideal organisms to investigate because they have easily observable, contrasting characteristics, for example pea seeds are either round and smooth or wrinkled, and the plants can be either tall or short. Another advantage is that pea flowers **self-pollinate**.

Information processing *Pea cross*

Here is another example of one of Mendel's pea-crossing investigations:

First cross-pollination

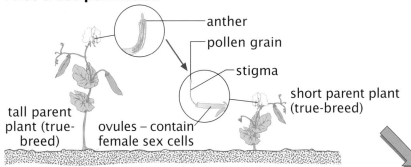

anther
pollen grain
stigma
short parent plant (true-breed)

tall parent plant (true-breed)
ovules – contain female sex cells

First generation (cross-breed)
all plants are tall

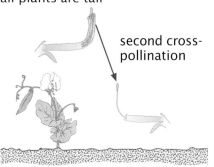

second cross-pollination

Second generation (cross-breed)

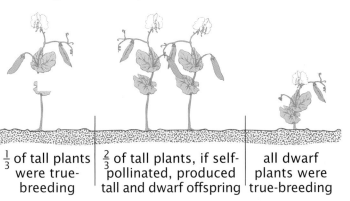

$\frac{1}{3}$ of tall plants were true-breeding

$\frac{2}{3}$ of tall plants, if self-pollinated, produced tall and dwarf offspring

all dwarf plants were true-breeding

two cross-breed first generation plants fertilise each other to give 3:1 tall to short plants

1 What do you notice about the ratio of tall to short plants in the offspring?

2 Why are the first generation plants all tall?

Pollination

This is when the male gametes, the **pollen**, are transferred to the female part of the flower. Pollen is made in the **anthers** (male part) of a flower.

In self-pollinating flowers the pollen falls onto the **stigma** (female part) of the same flower, and the flower is then self-fertilised. All the seeds in that flower contain the same genes as the parent plant. Mendel changed this process by cross-pollinating from one plant to another. This is artificial pollination. He put the pollen from a flower of a different parent plant onto the stigma of the first flower.

1 The immature stamens of a young flower are exposed.

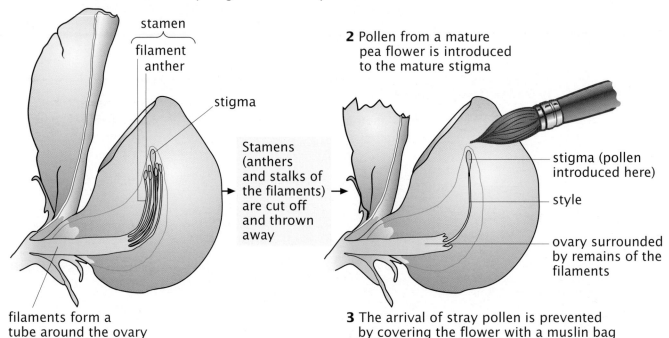

stamen
filament
anther
stigma

filaments form a tube around the ovary

Stamens (anthers and stalks of the filaments) are cut off and thrown away

2 Pollen from a mature pea flower is introduced to the mature stigma

stigma (pollen introduced here)
style
ovary surrounded by remains of the filaments

3 The arrival of stray pollen is prevented by covering the flower with a muslin bag

Cross-pollination from one flower to another flower happens naturally when the pollen is carried by either the wind or by insects.

Wind pollination.

Insect pollination.

How fertilisation occurs in plants

Flowers can be self- or cross-pollinated. This causes self- or cross-fertilisation.

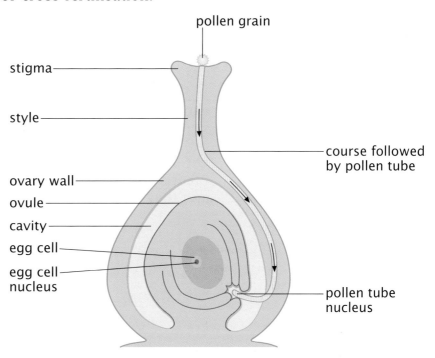

4 Look at a real flower using a hand lens. Draw its appearance and label these parts:

- petal
- sepal
- anther
- stigma
- stem.

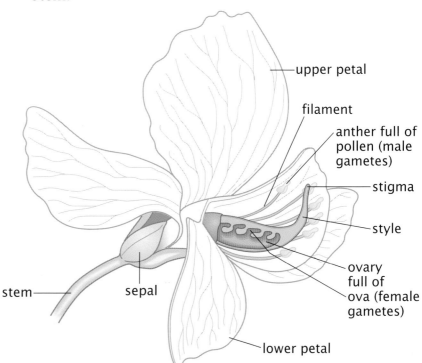

Now cut it open and separate out the sexual parts. These are where the male and female gametes are made – the pollen and **ova**. Draw or stick these into your notebook and write some notes by each part to remind you of their function and how pollination and fertilisation happens in this plant.

Cloning

This is not a sexual process. It is **asexual**, which means that it does not involve sex cells. Instead, a cell divides so that each of the two daughter cells still contain the identical number and type of chromosomes as the original cell.

Gardeners regularly **clone** organisms, for example they cut potato tubers in half to grow potato plants that are identical in their genetic make up to the original potato, and they take cuttings of plants like ivy and geraniums.

Key words
* asexual
* clone

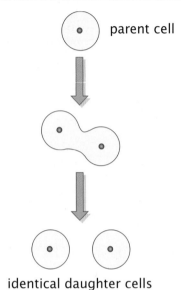

parent cell

identical daughter cells

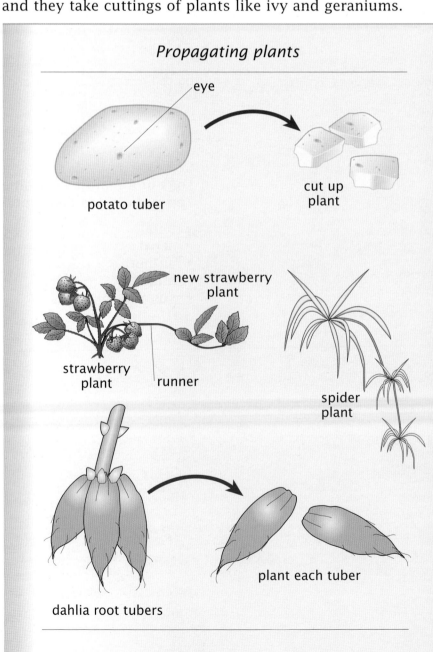

Propagating plants

eye

potato tuber

cut up plant

new strawberry plant

strawberry plant

runner

spider plant

dahlia root tubers

plant each tuber

Scientists are just starting to clone animals successfully. Dolly the sheep was the first cloned animal to survive. Many successful racehorses are gelded (neutered) if they are male to make them easier to handle and train. This means that they cannot be bred from, but as successful racehorses are worth lots of money, some horse breeders are funding research to clone horses. In August 2003 the first cloned foal was produced.

Time to think

1 Who was Mendel, and why do scientists think he is an important historical person?
2 What parts of a cell control the characteristics of an organism?
3 Why were pea plants ideal for Mendel's investigations on inheritance?
4 Write a sentence that explains the difference between cross- and self-pollination.
5 How does cross-pollination occur naturally?
6 How would you artificially cross-pollinate a flower? Why would you want to do this?
7 Write all the names for the sexual parts of a flower.
8 Make up five questions to test other peoples' knowledge of plant sexual reproduction. Do not forget to include a mark scheme. Try out your test on another group.

Sex cells

Key words
* cell division
* sperm
* ovum
* zygote
* embryo
* X chromosomes
* Y chromosome

Humans only reproduce sexually. Unlike peas, humans never self-fertilise! Each of our normal cells contains 46 chromosomes. These pair up into 23 pairs during the process of **cell division**, when the genetic material duplicates itself so that each new cell will also have 46 chromosomes. To make a sex cell (gamete) a normal cell divides into two cells. Each new cell only has 23 chromosomes, half the number in the original parent cell. During fertilisation, a male gamete (**sperm**) containing 23 chromosomes from the father, fuses with the female gamete (**ovum**) containing 23 chromosomes from the mother. The new cell (a **zygote**) has 46 chromosomes. It can replicate and grow into an **embryo** with a full set of genetic instructions, half from the mother and half from the father.

One pair of chromosomes in each cell has the special function of deciding the sex of the embryo. They are the sex chromosomes. Women's and girls' cells each contain two identical sex chromosomes – the **X chromosomes**. Boy's and men's cells contain one sex chromosome like the female one, an X chromosome, but the other in the pair is different – it is a **Y chromosome**. What we inherit from our parents is a bit of a lottery. You cannot predict which sperm cell will fertilise which egg cell. It is a matter of chance which of the two types of male sperm cell (with an X or a Y chromosome) fertilises the female's ovum.

Reasoning **Same or different?**

Cell	Same or different genetic information?	Reasons
two cheek cells from the inside of Jane's cheek	cheek cells	
a cheek cell and a brain cell from Jane's body	brain cell / cheek cell	
a cheek cell and an egg cell from Jane's body	egg cell / cheek cell	
two egg cells from Jane's body	egg cells	

Determining the sex of a baby

We can use a simple table to help us show how sex cells determine if a baby is born male or female. This table is like the genetic diagrams earlier in this chapter.

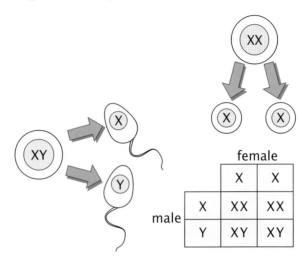

	female	
	X	X
X	XX	XX
Y	XY	XY

male

The table shows that 50% of the sperm cells contain an X chromosome and 50% contain a Y chromosome.

5 What percentage of ova contain Y chromosomes and what percentage contain X chromosomes?
6 Write down what **proportion** of babies will be female and what proportion will be male. The table gives you the answer.

Probability

We can model the inheritance of sex by spinning coins.

7 If you spin a coin what are the chances (the **probability**) of it landing heads up?
8 What are its chances of landing tails up?
9 How would you prove this?

Imagine that heads represents the female X chromosome and tails represents the male Y chromosome.

10 Work with a partner and spin pairs of coins 50 times. Record your data in a frequency table like this:

Chris's coin	Tansy's coin	Sex determined
head	head	XX female
head	tail	XY male

11 Copy the table and note down all the other possible combinations of two coins landing head up.
12 Do two tails, representing YY chromosomes represent a male or female embryo?

13 From your table what are the likely ratios of spinning two heads or two tails or one head and one tail?

14 Do you think that coin spinning is a good model to show how a baby's sex is determined? Explain your answer.

Look at these pictures and decide which word goes with which pair: identical, similar or different.

In your group, write a paragraph that includes all three words so that their meaning is clear.

Amniocentesis

A pregnant woman may have an amniocentesis test. This is recommended when she is about 16–18 weeks pregnant if there is concern that the embryo may be carrying the disorder spina bifida, or a genetic fault, for example Down's syndrome. There may be concern because the woman has a history of this disease in her family. For an amniocentesis test a doctor takes a sample of the fluid that surrounds the baby in the womb. This fluid has some of the baby's cells floating in it. The doctor puts a long needle through the wall of the abdomen into the amniotic fluid surrounding the baby in the womb. Fluid is drawn up into the syringe and then the chromosomes inside the baby's cells are looked at under a microscope to check that they are normal. The baby's sex can also be determined.

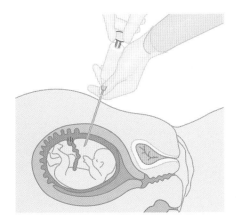

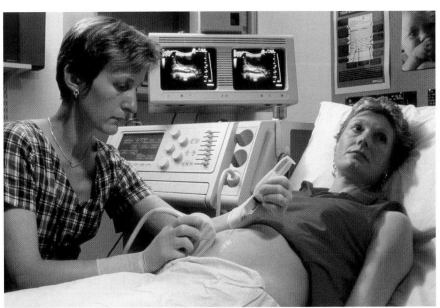

Amniocentesis.

→ *Some inherited diseases*

Cystic fibrosis
Symptoms: respiratory problems caused by overproduction of mucus which collects in the lungs. Poor digestion so nutrients are not absorbed from food.

Inheritance: from two genes, one from the mother and a similar gene from the father. Most common in people whose ancestors were from white northern European populations.

Thalassaemia
Symptoms: red blood cells are destroyed too rapidly, before new ones are made in sufficient numbers to replace them.

Inheritance: from two genes, one from the mother and a similar gene from the father. More common in people whose ancestors were from Mediterranean and Indian populations.

Huntington's disease
Symptoms: slow degeneration of the nervous system. Symptoms appear in adults aged 30–40 years old.

Inheritance: only one disease gene is needed, from the mother or the father, to cause this disease in the offspring.

Haemophilia
Symptoms: lack of blood clotting factors so wounds do not stop bleeding.

Inheritance: from two genes, one in an X chromosome from the mother and the other in the father's X chromosome.

Sickle cell anaemia

Symptoms: red blood cells are not round but crescent-moon (sickle) shaped. This means that each cell can carry less oxygen.

Inheritance: inheriting one gene from the mother and one from the father causes the serious form of the disease, but there are mild symptoms where the children inherit only one disease gene from either of the parents, and the other parent passes on a healthy gene. More common in people whose ancestors were from African and West Indian populations.

Information processing   *Genetic diseases*

Make a table of genetic diseases. Use these headings for your table: Name of disease, Symptoms, Genetic inheritance

---

Key words
* carriers
* genetic screening

Genetic carriers

People who carry a gene that causes an inherited disease, but who do not suffer from the disease themselves, are called **carriers**. **Genetic screening** and counselling is offered to people who have a family history of a particular disease and they may be advised about the chances of passing the gene on to their children.

Science and society

15 Think of one advantage and one disadvantage of allowing parents to choose the sex of their baby. Now ask other people in your group what they think are advantages and disadvantages. Are your views similar, identical or different?

16 Your teacher may compile a whole class list of advantages and disadvantages and use this to ask everyone to vote 'YES' or 'NO' to giving parents the right to choose their baby's sex. What did the majority vote in your class?

> ## 'Designer baby' is perfect match
>
> A 'designer baby' has been confirmed as a perfect genetic match with the brother his stem cells could save.
>
> Baby Jamie Whitaker was born in June after his embryo was genetically selected in the hope that it would be a match for his four-year-old brother Charlie.
>
> Charlie has the life-threatening blood disorder Diamond Blackfan Anaemia. A stem cell transplant is his only hope of a cure.
>
> Blood tests have now shown that month-old Jamie is a match, so stem cells from his umbilical cord can be used to treat Charlie.
>
> The boys' parents, Michelle and Jayson Whitaker, say they are delighted by the news.
>
> The family, from Derbyshire, must now wait until Jamie is around six months old to ensure he does not have the blood disorder before a stem cell transplant can go ahead.
>
> BBC News, 27 July 2003

Reasoning   *Twins and siblings*

1 Copy these diagrams showing fertilisation. Decide which diagram shows siblings being created, which shows identical twins and which shows non-identical twins being created.

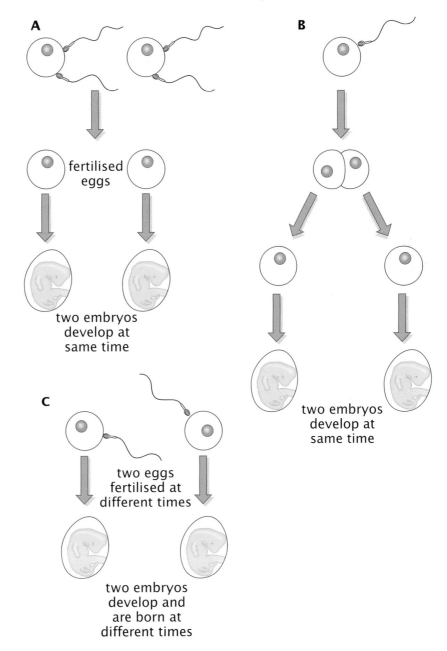

2 Why are identical twins more similar than brothers and sisters or non-identical twins?

3 Can a boy and a girl born at the same time, to the same mother, be identical twins?

4 Do you think multiple births from eggs fertilised outside the body '*in vitro*' (in the test tube) and then implanted produce identical or similar offspring?

Creative thinking ## Boy or girl?

Imagine that your team have been asked to design a poster for Year 6 pupils to explain how we are born male or female. Make a poster that is large, bright and easy to understand.

→ # Variation

Key words
* unique
* variation
* variable
* range
* continuous
* discontinuous
* sample

All organisms are **unique**, even when they belong to the same species. Look around your class. You can recognise each individual by their unique characteristics, but you also know that they are all human because of the features they share.

17 Write down the characteristics that make up the human species.
18 What characteristics do you notice most in your best friend?

Reasoning ## Variation in populations

Here are some drawings of a human population and a population of pea plants. The drawings show **variation** in heights of both populations. Height is a **variable**.

scale 1:40

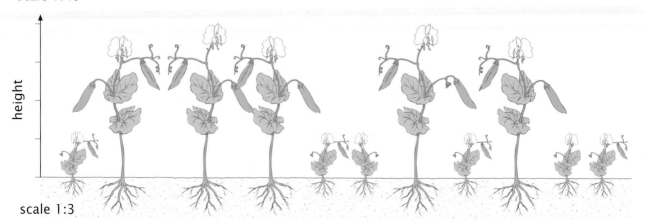

scale 1:3

1 Make a table for each of these species so that you can record the height of each individual.

2 What is the **range** of the human population's height?

3 What is the range of the pea population height?

Height in humans is a **continuous** variable; height in peas is a **discontinuous** variable.

4 If you were plotting a graph to show the range of heights for a human population and for a pea population, which type of graph would you create for each and why?

It is not always easy to tell if a characteristic (variable) is discontinuous or continuous. You would need to look at large numbers of individuals in a population to be sure.

Word play

1 Which of these lines is discontinuous and which is continuous?

_____   -

2 If a manager of a supermarket told you that the manufacturer had discontinued your favourite brand of biscuit, what would she mean?

3 If a biologist told you that the height of pea plants is a discontinuous variable, how many different heights of plants would you expect to grow from a packet of seeds?

Surveying human characteristics

Here are some easily observed human characteristics, or variables:

- height
- eye colour
- tongue rolling
- hair colour
- weight
- ear lobe attachment
- skin colour
- pulse rate
- finger prints

Some of these variables are continuous, and some are discontinuous.

19 Copy the characteristics out under the correct heading: Continuous or Discontinuous.

20 Why is it best to **sample** a large population to see if a particular variable is discontinuous or continuous?

Enquiry Eye colour

One gene can exist in several different forms, for example the human eye colour characteristic.

1 List all the eye colours that your group can think of.

2 Is eye colour a discontinuous or a continuous variable?

3 Make a table like the one below and add your list of eye colours to the second column. Complete the third and fourth columns by doing a survey and collecting data from people in your class.

Characteristic (variable)	Variation	Number of pupils in your class showing this variation (total number in class = ...)	Percentage of pupils showing this variation
eye colour	brown		

4 Add two rows to your table and collect data to complete these rows for another two discontinuous human characteristics.

Evaluation Characteristics

1 Which of these characteristics do you think might be continuous and which discontinuous variables?

- length of a human hand
- length of a worm
- number of peas in a pod
- length of pine cones
- number of flowers on a bluebell stem

2 In groups, choose three non-human characteristics from the list and decide how many individuals from a population of organisms with that characteristic you would need to sample to decide if the characteristic was continuous or discontinuous. Choose one of the characteristics to measure.

3 How would you measure that characteristic?

4 How big would you make your sample to give you a representative sample of the population?

5 How would you record your data?

6 Listen to what other groups chose and discussed. Did their views change your decisions?

Looking for patterns in data

A frequency table is a good way to collect data about variations in characteristics. We call this a **data set**. The larger the data set the more reliable it is in representing all the possible variations that individual organisms in that population have.

Here is a frequency table for the number of petals in a daisy head. Strictly speaking, a daisy head is not one flower, but made up of many little part-flowers. Each of these is called a 'ray floret'.

petals

a single ray floret

A daisy head.

Number of daisies with this number of florets

Number of ray florets	Score (tallies)	Total
34	ⅢⅠ II	7
35	ⅢⅠ II	7
36	ⅢⅠ ⅢⅠ	10
37	ⅢⅠ ⅢⅠ ⅢⅠ IIII	19
38	ⅢⅠ ⅢⅠ III	13
39	ⅢⅠ ⅢⅠ I	11
40	ⅢⅠ III	8
41	ⅢⅠ II	7
42	ⅢⅠ II	7
43	IIII	4
44	IIII	4
45	III	3
Total in sample		100

21 Plot a graph of the results. Is it going to be a line or a bar graph?

22 What is the smallest number of ray florets?

23 What is the largest number of ray florets? What is the range?

24 What is the median?

25 What is the average number of ray florets?

26 Why do you think that there are 100 daisies in this sample and not 50 or 10?

Enquiry # Flower survey

In a group of four carry out your own investigation into the variation in the number of ray florets or petals of flowers that grow in sunlight and those that grow in shade.

Flowers with ray florets that you could sample include dandelions, daisies, camomile, yarrow, and thistle.

Flowers with petals that you could sample include bedstraw, dog rose, buttercup, and mallow.

Daisy.

Thistle.

Buttercup.

Mallow.

Your groups' work will be assessed on your ability to:

- decide what flowers to sample and why
- sample and count ray florets or petals in an efficient way, taking into account how long your team have to do this task
- collect and record data in a frequency table
- identify and describe any patterns in your data.

Evaluation # Good investigation

Scientists say that a good investigation compares 'like with like' to make it fair.

1 Which of these investigations would give the best data for making scientific deductions?

Investigation 1
Mr Boffin grows 70 daisy plants in the shade of a wood and 70 buttercups in the middle of a field with no shade, so that he can compare the effect of light on plant growth.

Investigation 2
Ms Brains grows 47 daisies in her greenhouse and 45 daisies in her garden, so that she can compare the effect of different environmental factors on daisy growth.

2 Looking back at your flower survey investigation, is there any way that you could improve it if you were asked to do something like this again?

3 Use ICT to add your results to the rest of the class data.

4 Evaluate whether or not this bigger data set confirms your group's data set.

5 Why do you think that there is variation in the number of ray florets in daisies?

→ # *Environmental factors*

Key words
* environment
* factors
* influences

The **environment** is the place in which an organism lives. **Factors** are the variables in the environment, for example, temperature, light, other organisms that might be predators or prey for that organism, and availability of water.

The environment, as well as genetic make-up, **influences** the way an organism looks and functions.

27 List three environmental factors that surround you.
28 What conditions would affect the height of an oak tree, other than its genetic make-up?
29 What environmental factors influence a human baby to grow up with good physical and mental health?

Variations of characteristics in a population can be caused by:

* the environment the organism lives in
* inheritance (the genetic make-up of the organism from its parents)
* a mixture of both genetic make-up and environmental factors.

30 Work in pairs to talk about these organisms and their variations, and decide which cause is most likely to have created the variations:

   * Leaves of a beech tree growing in a wood are larger and thinner than leaves of a beech tree growing in a garden with no shade.
   * The banded snail shell can be pink, yellow or brown, wherever the snails live.
   * Seedlings of beans grown in a dark cupboard are white and seedlings of beans grown on the windowsill are green.
   * Supermarkets ask farmers to plant their dwarf carrot varieties very close together so that they are small.
   * Sheep that live in the highlands of Scotland have shorter legs than sheep that live on the fens in Cambridgeshire.
   * Breast-fed babies are larger on average than bottle-fed babies when they are about 6 months old.
   * People today are taller on average than their grandparents.

DNA – life's spiral staircase

In 1870 a scientist called Johann Friedrich Miesher realised that pus leaked out of damaged cells. It could be collected from the bandages of patients in his hospital. By analysing the pus, Miesher found out what cells contain. He isolated the chemicals found in the cell **nucleus** and called these **nucleic acids**. In 1944 Oswald Theodore Avery, an American doctor, proved that genes were made of nucleic acids. In the late 1950s James Watson, Francis Crick and Rosalind Franklin, British and American scientists, used X-rays to find out the chemical structure of one particular nucleic acid, deoxyribonucleic acid, **DNA** for short. Franklin fired X-rays at crystals of DNA and took photographs of the way the X-rays bounced off DNA molecules. From these photographs, Watson and Crick were able to build a model of DNA and worked out that to give the kind of pictures that Franklin was recording, the molecule had to be a **double helix**. Franklin died at an early age in 1958, without being recognised for her work, but Watson and Crick received a Nobel Prize in 1962.

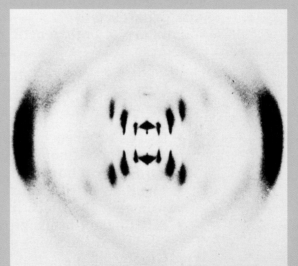

An X-ray photograph of DNA taken by Rosalind Franklin.

James Watson.

Francis Crick.

Rosalind Franklin.

DNA molecules are crammed tightly inside the cells that hold them because they are so long. If they were completely unwound they would be several thousand times the length of the cell. DNA consists of two long thin **strands** that are wound around each other to form a **spiral**. This is called a double helix. The strands contain lots of nucleic acids called **bases**, and there are four different types of bases. Every strand of DNA contains about 12 billion individual bases.

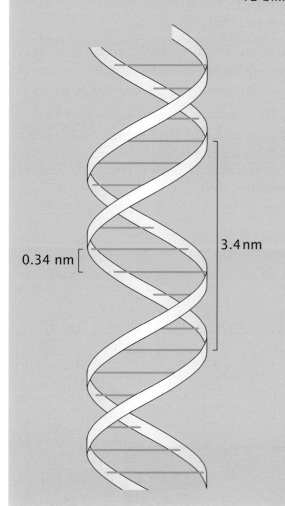

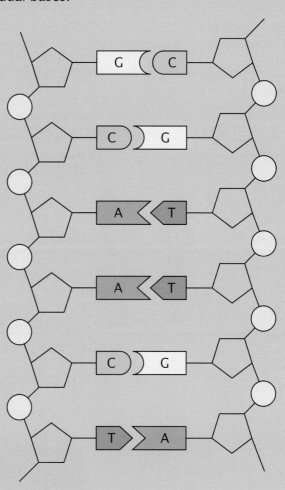

The double helix.

DNA base pairs on two strands of DNA.

1 Write down the names of these people in order of the earliest scientist first, and say what they discovered:
Oswald Avery
Johann Miesher
Francis Crick
James Watson
Rosalind Franklin

2 Some people call the DNA molecule 'life's spiral staircase'. Why is this?

3 Draw a spiral in your notebook. Now add a second spiral in a different colour to make a double spiral or double helix, like the picture of DNA here.

DID YOU KNOW?

DNA is one of the largest known molecules. A DNA molecule weighs 100 000 times more than one sugar molecule.

The Human Genome Project

Begun in 1990, the Human Genome Project has the following goals:

- to identify all the approximately 30 000 genes in human DNA ('the human genome')
- to determine the sequences of the 3 billion chemical base pairs that make up human DNA
- to store this information in databases
- to improve tools for data analysis
- to transfer related technologies to the private sector
- to address the ethical, legal, and social issues (ELSI) that may arise from the project.

Source: *the Human Genome Project website*

The project was originally planned to last 15 years, but technological advances have meant that sequencing of the human genome was completed in 2003.

If you want to know more about this exciting science you can look it up on the Human Genome Project website – www.ornl.gov/hgmis/

Cell division

When a cell starts to divide, the DNA inside the nucleus coils up very tightly into chromosomes which are visible under a microscope.

Every living organism has a certain number of chromosomes. A mosquito has 6, and a cabbage has 18. Humans have 46.

Your father passed on the DNA that is contained in 23 of your chromosomes to you before you were born. Your mother passed on the DNA contained in another 23 chromosomes to you.

Research

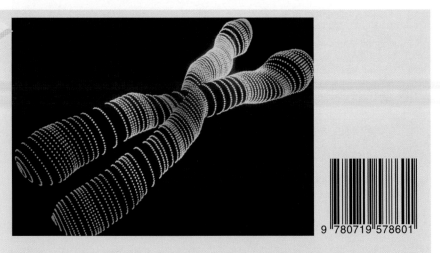

This close-up of a chromosome, made using a microscope camera, looks a bit like a bar code on something you might buy. A bar code is a good analogy (model) for thinking about chromosomes.

Find out what bar codes are for. In what ways is a bar code like a chromosome, and in what ways is it different?

Gene mapping

→

Key words
* genome
* gene mapping

It is possible that within the next 10 years each person could have a personal 'map' of his or her **genome**. A genome is the whole set of genes in an organism's normal cells. It is probable that this will be an expensive process so would not be available for everyone. **Gene mapping** would show people if they carried any genes for a disease such as cystic fibrosis, Huntington's disease, or an increased risk of breast cancer. However, depending on the disease, carrying the gene does not always mean a person will get the disease.

Creative thinking

Gene map

Imagine you are making an application form for the health service to give to people who want to request a personal gene map. Use ICT to design your form.

First decide what diseases are likely to be inherited, and then think what questions you would ask someone to find out his or her family's medical history. It is useful to find out what caused the deaths of close relatives.

1 Think of one advantage and one disadvantage to knowing what genes you have.

2 Would you want to have a personal gene map?

3 What opinions do other people in your class have?

Time to think

1 List these in order of size, starting with the smallest: cell, chromosome, gene, DNA, nucleus, genome.

2 Which of these statements are true and which are false?

- Genes are grouped together on chromosomes.
- Chromosomes are grouped together into genes.
- DNA is a larger molecule than sugar.
- A genome is a large gene.
- All living things contain genetic information.
- A double helix is shaped like a string of beads.
- DNA is found in the cytoplasm of a cell.
- A gene map would show what a genome contained.

→ The invention of biotechnology

Scientists can now change the genetic code by moving genes about along chromosomes. This became possible in 1968 when the Swiss scientist Werner Arber discovered enzymes that could chop DNA into pieces which could be rejoined in different sequences. These genes can be moved from one place to another and still function. Once it was realised that **biotechnologists** could use this technique commercially, **bioengineering** and **genetic engineering** industries were created.

Some bacteria have genes that cause them to produce a substance that kills insects. These bacterial genes can now be put into crops so that if the insects eat the crop, they die. Human genes that control the immune response have been put into pigs. These pigs become **genetically modified** organisms, **GMOs**. In future it might be possible to transplant pig hearts into humans because the human body would not reject the pig tissue as alien.

Creative thinking ## Company identity

Imagine that you have been asked to design a name and a logo for a new biotechnology company that specialises in genetic engineering. Use a computer graphics or design package to make a sample letterhead of the name and logo that the company could use.

Genetically modified crops

These are known as GM crops. GM tomato and wheat crops are widely grown in China, America and Canada, but are not yet grown in the UK by farmers. Most common crops can be genetically modified to be **herbicide** tolerant or to produce their own **insecticides**. In Europe crops have to go through safety testing before they can be planted outside plant research institutions.

The government has carried out a consultation process with the public to find out what we think about GM crops being grown. The risks that concern scientists are:

- the crops may spread their seeds into the wild plant populations and become strong weeds, competing with the natural vegetation
- insects such as bees and butterflies may be affected in unpredictable ways because their food source has been changed
- the foods from GM crops may have long-term harmful effects on human health or on the domesticated animals that are fed on them
- GM plants might breed with wild plants and produce 'super weeds' (weeds are defined as any plant growing in the wrong place).

The first two risks also apply to any new organisms we may introduce from one environment into another. For example, the Romans introduced rabbits to the UK. They bred the rabbits for food, but some escaped and they are now widespread and very destructive.

Genes could spread via pollen from GM crops to wild plants and this might be a bad thing, for example, if wild plants became herbicide resistant from cross-fertilising with GM plants that had the herbicide resistant gene in their cells. Making GM crops **sterile** (unable to reproduce) through genetic engineering or harvesting them before flowering can reduce the risk of the spread of genes from GM to wild crops. Most domestic crops are unable to breed with the wild forms and many cannot survive in natural, unfarmed conditions. It is very unlikely that eating GM food will transfer modified genes into our bodies. When we digest food the DNA is broken down. We eat miles of DNA daily, and swallow whole genomes of many organisms such as oranges, apples and all the microbes we ingest. Our bodies chemically treat modified DNA in the same way as other foods.

There is the potential to use GM crops to benefit people. GM rice can have a 35% bigger yield than existing rice varieties, and this could help particularly in less economically developed countries to produce more food on the same amount of land.

Information processing   *Genetic engineering*

Write a short article for a popular teenage magazine about genetic engineering. Make sure that you explain the possible benefits and the concerns people have about this new technology.

Key words
* evolution
* natural selection
* adaptations

Evolution

ON

THE ORIGIN OF SPECIES

BY MEANS OF NATURAL SELECTION,

OR THE

PRESERVATION OF FAVOURED RACES IN THE STRUGGLE
FOR LIFE.

By CHARLES DARWIN, M.A.,

FELLOW OF THE ROYAL, GEOLOGICAL, LINNÆAN, ETC., SOCIETIES;
AUTHOR OF 'JOURNAL OF RESEARCHES DURING H. M. S. BEAGLE'S VOYAGE
ROUND THE WORLD.'

LONDON:
JOHN MURRAY, ALBEMARLE STREET.
1859.

The right of Translation is reserved.

Today geologists estimate the world is 4500 million years old and that life originated 3500 million years ago. Evolution takes time. Up until the eighteenth century, most people in the western world believed that the world and all the animals and plants in it had been created in seven days, as described in the Bible. By the 1800s geologists such as Charles Lyell began to realise that the Earth was very old. This thinking influenced Charles Darwin's famous book *The origin of species by natural selection*, published in 1859.

Natural selection

Darwin made some very important observations that still influence the study of genetics and **evolution** today. These are:

1 Most organisms have the potential to produce very large numbers of offspring, but these do not all survive to become parents themselves. Competing for resources like food or space means that some organisms survive to go on to breed and some do not.

2 All organisms vary, even members of the same species and in the same population.
3 The offspring that survive are those that have the best characteristics for survival in their environment. This is called the survival of the fittest by **natural selection**.
4 The fittest offspring pass on their favourable survival characteristics to their offspring when they breed. These characteristics are inherited.

Adaptation

Over many generations organisms of a population will develop **adaptations** that make them well-suited to their environment. One type of organism may evolve into several different species.

These finches were studied by Darwin when he visited the Galapagos Islands in South America. They show adaptation – all of the different types of finches found on the Galapagos Islands originated from the large ground finch.

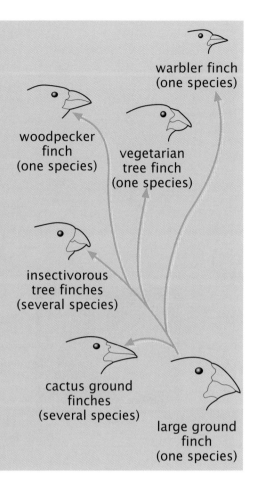

warbler finch
(one species)

woodpecker finch
(one species)

vegetarian tree finch
(one species)

insectivorous tree finches
(several species)

cactus ground finches
(several species)

large ground finch
(one species)

Word play

Here are some sentences using the word 'adapt(ed)':

- The leaves of a cactus plant are adapted to reduce water loss in the desert.
- Shakespeare's plays have been adapted for television.
- People who climb mountains at high altitudes for several weeks adapt to the lower oxygen content in the air they breathe by producing more red blood cells.
- On leaving a dark room your eyes take a few seconds to adapt to bright sunshine.
- Fish are adapted to live in water.
- Old tractor tyres can be adapted to grow potatoes in.

These sentences show three different ways of using the word 'adapt(ed)'. In some of them 'adapt(ed)' is used biologically to mean a process of short-term change that is reversible. In others the use is still biological but the changes are long term and permanent, and they have been caused by natural selection. Some statements use adapt(ed) in a non-scientific way.

Talk to a partner and decide which statements belong in which category.

Artificial selection

This is the process of deliberately modifying plants and animals so that they are more useful to humans than the wild form. It is a kind of artificial, speeded-up evolution. Over hundreds and perhaps thousands of years humans have controlled which wild plants and animals to breed. By mating the best males and females together, we can look at the offspring and select the best characteristics for our purposes. We can **cull** (kill) offspring that are not suitable or are weak. If this is done over lots of generations then there is deliberate genetic change in the population.

Darwin bred pigeons to show how **selective breeding** could lead to greater variety. All varieties of pigeons come from the rock dove (below centre).

The dog was probably the first animal to be domesticated by humans. It was domesticated from the wolf about 13 000 years ago, by selective breeding.

31 What features do all the dogs in the photographs and their wolf ancestor share?

32 Which features are unique to the collie (sheep dog), and which are unique to the greyhound?

33 Why do you think these features have been selectively bred into each of these dog varieties?

34 How do breeders make sure the right kind of puppies grow to adults and are used for reproduction?

Reasoning *Better breeds*

Friesian cow.

Hereford bull.

The offspring of the Friesian–Hereford cross.

1 From the photographs, list the features that the offspring has inherited from the Hereford parent and the features it has from the Friesian parent.

Friesian cows are good milk producers but Herefords are known for their beef. What do you think the cattle breeder is looking for in a good cross?

2 In your group, imagine you are responsible for some plant- and animal-breeding programmes. Draw up a table like this:

Organism	Characteristic	Why desirable/useful

Decide which characteristics you would try to selectively breed for and why you think those characteristics might be desirable in these plants and animals:

- pig
- sheep
- cow
- dog
- wheat
- tomato
- daffodil
- lettuce.

Some characteristics or variables will be easily observable, but others may be 'invisible', for example resistance to mildew, good flavour, different ripening time or resistance to cold.

Different types of lettuce.

Different types of tomato.

Enquiry *Peas*

Here is a range of supermarket products. For each product specific characteristics have been bred into the peas.

Design an investigation to compare the characteristics of the different varities (frozen peas, tinned mushy peas and fresh peas), for example taste, colour, size, and cooking time.

1 How will you make sure the sampling method is representative?

2 Decide on your method and apparatus.

3 How will you evaluate what the data indicate and your investigation process?

→ *Mutations*

Key words
* mutate
* mutation
* mutant
* gene pool
* gene therapy
* hybrid

Genes can **mutate**. A **mutation** is a spontaneous and sudden change in a gene which may produce a difference in the organism. Some mutations may be caused by environmental factors such as nuclear radiation; others seem to happen without any apparent external cause.

A **mutant** is an organism that carries a mutation. Most people think that a mutation is a bad thing, but mutations may be bad, good or may make no difference. If a mutation gives an organism an advantage over the rest of the population when it comes to reproducing then the mutation may be passed on to the offspring and, over time, may become a common characteristic through the process of natural selection. The resistance of some bacteria to antibiotics is an example of this. The genomes of all the individuals in a population make up the **gene pool** for that population.

Many mutations do not give any particular advantages or disadvantages; they are variations of that characteristic in the population.

If a mutation is a disadvantage for an organism then it is highly likely that the organism will die before reproducing or be infertile, so that the mutation is likely to 'die out' of the population.

Many human diseases are caused by gene mutation. It may be possible to treat these by using human **gene therapy**. Cells are taken from the patient and the mutant gene is transformed into normal non-mutant copies of the gene. These are reintroduced to the patient's body so that normal cells will start to multiply to make the required protein coded from their corrected DNA.

In 1990 French Anderson and Michael Blaese treated four-year-old Ashanti DiSilva using genetic engineering methods. She suffered from a genetic disease that kills T-lymphocytes. This disease meant that minor infections could be fatal. Ashanti had to live totally isolated from other people, in sterile conditions. After genetic manipulation, Ashanti now goes to a normal school and can be hugged by her parents without any sterile barriers in the way.

Research Find out about rare breed centres and national plant collections. Why do you think people put time, money and effort into creating them?

Rare breed centre.

A national plant collection.

Time to think

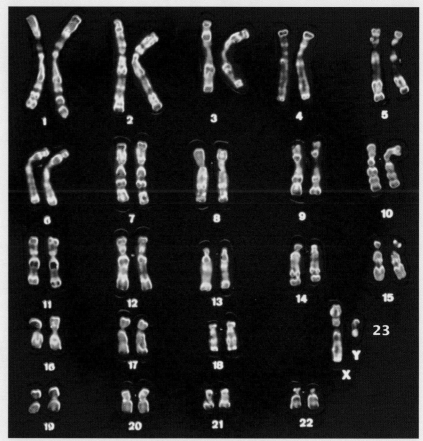

The photograph shows the chromosomes from a human embryo. They have been arranged in pairs.

1 What is special about the 23rd pair?
2 Is this embryo going to be a baby boy or a baby girl? How do you know?
3 Can you tell which chromosome in each pair came from the sperm cell and which from the egg cell?

STOP PRESS!

• •

An American clinic is advertising a 'designer baby' service. For just $100 000 you can make sure your baby will look the way you want it to. All designer babies will be guaranteed free of inherited diseases.

4 Do you think this report is true?

5 If it is true, why do you think some people would want to close the clinic down? Do you think designer babies should be allowed?

6 If this was about 'designer wheat' or 'designer rice', would you have a different opinion? Would those same people have a different opinion?

7 Make an animated PowerPoint presentation that your group could use to explain why Mendel's work with pea populations was so important for us in understanding more about the way inheritance works.

8 Evaluate each group's presentation using the 'traffic light' system:

Green dot = excellent use of animations to show how pea characteristics are inherited, clear explanation.

Amber dot = a good explanation but a bit boring.

Red dot   = confusing and not very helpful in explaining Mendel's work.

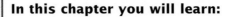

8 Pressure and moments

In this chapter you will learn:

→ how scientists define pressure and density and how they are calculated
→ how pressure differs in liquids, gases and solids and how this relates to the particle theory
→ to explain the action of levers, including examples in the human skeleton
→ what momentum and force are
→ the principle of moments
→ to use the principle of moments to explain balance and know examples of its application

You will also develop your skills in:

→ planning an investigation about balancing
→ making careful observations with precision
→ identifying patterns in results
→ accounting for anomalies in the observations of balance

→ → → WHAT DO YOU KNOW?

You have learnt that there are many different types of force. These include:

- gravitational force
- forces that stretch or pull
- forces that push or squash
- forces that twist.

When forces act on an object they may:

- start it moving
- make it move faster
- slow it down
- make it stop
- change its shape
- change the direction in which it is travelling.

1 We can see some of the effects of forces in the pictures at the top of page 229. What sort of force are the children providing? Is it gravity, stretching, pulling, pushing or twisting? What effect is this force producing?

2 What sort of force acted on the car? What effect did this force have?

3 What force is acting on the bungee jumper in the first picture?

4 What forces are acting on the bungee jumper in the second picture? What effect do they have?

5 What type of force is being applied to the tap?

Mass and weight

Mass and **weight** are different. Here are two definitions:

A measure of the amount of 'stuff' that makes up an object.

A **force**. It tells us about the pull of gravity on an object.

1 Which is about mass and which is about weight? Which is measured in newtons and which in kilograms? Does everyone else in your group agree with you?

Key words
* mass
* weight
* force

2 Read the following speech bubbles and rewrite them if you think you can use the word mass instead of weight to make them scientifically correct.

I have put on loads of weight over Christmas, so I need to go on a diet.

I'd rather buy the larger jar of jam as it weighs more so it is better value.

I cannot carry this bag of shopping home. It weighs 25 kg. That is far too heavy for me. I'd rather carry it on the Moon as it would weigh less!

3 Now swap your rewritten statements with another person and together decide if your new statements are correct. Help each other rewrite any you think are wrong.

4 Some Year 6 children said the following:

'Weight is a type of mass.'
'Weight is a pull.'
'Weight is not affected by gravity.'
'An object has a mass whether or not there is gravity.'
'A falling mass has weight because of gravity.'
'Weight is a force.'
'An increase in gravity increases an object's mass and weight.'
'There is tremendous weight pushing down on the centre of the Earth because of so many people and things pressing down these days.'

Discuss in your groups if each of these statements is correct.

→ # *Forceful things to remember*

Key words
* direction
* balanced
* upthrust

The strength of a force can be represented or modelled by the length of the arrow. The head of the arrow indicates the **direction** of the force. Remember that forces act in pairs. **Balanced** forces mean that all the forces acting on an object act against each other so that overall there is no change in motion, direction or shape.

5 Think of a way to help your group to learn and assess if you remember these points.

Reasoning ## Floating and sinking

If you walk down the steps into a swimming pool you begin to float when nearly all your body is in the water. You feel lighter. This is because the water has **upthrust**. This sequence of drawings shows the effect of upthrust on Peter as he walks into a pool full of water.

→ weaker pressure
⇨ stronger pressure

1 In pairs discuss what is happening in each of the three drawings, and why Peter can float on his back.

2 If Peter weighs 500 N, what weight of water is **displaced** when he floats? Is it 50 kg, 50 N, 500 kg or 500 N?

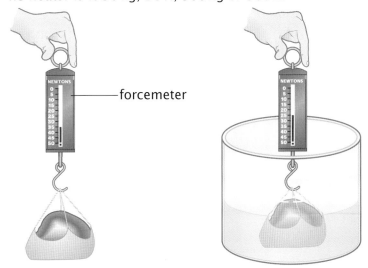

forcemeter

3 Why does the lump of rock have a different weight in the beaker of water?

Word play In everyday speech the word force may be used in a sentence such as: 'When I go to visit my gran, I'm always forced to eat cabbage'. Pressure is another word that has a special scientific meaning as well as an everyday meaning. In groups, write down three or four sentences using everyday meanings for pressure and force, and two or three using the same words scientifically.

Pressure

Key words
* area
* pressure
* newtons
* pascal
* isobars
* millibars

Look at the picture showing a man lying on a bed of nails. His weight is spread over the whole **area** of his body. This means that the area over which the force (his weight) acts is quite large.

There is a relationship between force and area. It is called **pressure**. The pressure depends on not only the size of the force but the area over which the force is acting.

$$\text{pressure} = \frac{\text{force}}{\text{area}}$$

If the force is measured in **newtons**, and the area is measured in square metres, the pressure is measured in newtons per square metre (N/m^2). This unit is given a special name, the **pascal** (Pa). It is often more convenient to use a smaller unit, the newton per square cm. You may also find pressure measured in psi (pounds per square inch) or bars (1 bar = 100 000 N/m^2 which is approximately one atmosphere).

6 Would the man lying on the bed of nails find it more or less painful if he got up and stood upright on the bed of nails? Why?

Weather maps show yet another way of measuring air pressure. The picture shows a typical weather map for Great Britain. Air pressure changes are shown using lines called **isobars**. An isobar is a line joining areas with the same pressure. The units of pressure are called **millibars**.

Research

Why do you think the unit of pressure is called a pascal? How would you find out if you are right?

Blaise Pascal.
Born: 19th June 1623 in Clermont-Ferrand, Auvergne, France.
Died: 19th August 1662 in Paris, France.

Reasoning ## More pressure

Look at the following pictures.

1 Sam wants a new bag to carry his school books in. Which of these would your group advise him to buy and why? Make a list of the variables that he should consider before he makes his purchase, and put them in order of importance. How does your group's list compare with other groups in your class?

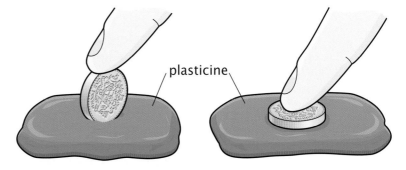

plasticine

2 In which picture would it take the most effort to make an impression in the plasticine?

3 What would you need to measure and compare to see if skis or snow shoes puts more pressure on the snow?

Enquiry ## Planning an investigation

Plan a quick investigation that would test out which bag would reduce the effort Sam needs to use to carry his school books.

1 How would you make sure this is a fair test?

2 What are the input variables and what are the outcome variables in your investigation?

3 What measuring instruments or methods would you use to record your results?

4 How would you present your results?

Creative thinking ## Car safety

Design an eye-catching poster for the school staffroom to remind teachers of the important safety points about car tyres.

➡ *Calculating pressure*

As we have already seen, pressure is related to two variables – force and area. It is the ratio of force to area.

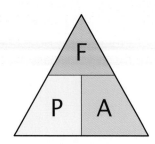

A clever trick is to show a ratio relationship using a triangle diagram. You have now got a kind of 'calculator'. The ratio is useful when doing problems when you need to work out pressure and you know about the force being applied and the area it is being applied to. However, if you need to calculate force and you know the pressure and area, cover the letter F in the triangle and you see that:

Force = **P**ressure × **A**rea

7 Using the triangle, write down how to find area.

8 Using the triangle, write down how to find pressure.

9 a) The picture at the top of the following page shows a block. It weighs 25 kg. (25 000 g). Calculate the area of each of the surfaces.

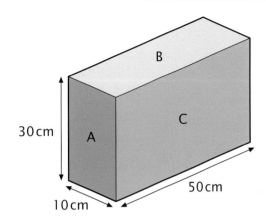

The block is placed on some sand.

b) Redraw the block to show which surface it should stand on to reduce how far it sinks into the sand.

c) Draw the block standing on the surface that would make it sink furthest into the sand.

d) On which surfaces would the sand exert the most pressure?

e) Calculate the greatest pressure and the least pressure.

The picture shows a shoe with a stiletto heel. The area of the heel is 1 cm^2. Suppose a girl with mass 500 N wears it. To calculate the pressure she would exert let us say that she is standing with just her heels on the ground. This is an area of 2 cm^2. Remember that pressure is given by:

$$\text{pressure} = \frac{\text{force}}{\text{area}}$$

so the pressure on the ground will be:

$$\text{pressure} = \frac{500}{2}$$
$$= 250 \text{ N/cm}^2$$

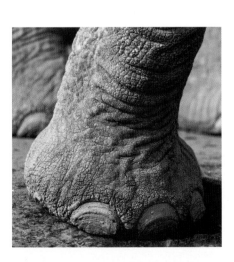

Imagine an elephant. The estimated size of an elephant's foot is 400 cm^2. With all four feet on the ground the area in contact with the ground will be:

$$4 \times 400 = 1600 \text{ cm}^2$$

An elephant will typcally have a mass of 2 tonnes. (This is 2000 kg). It would exert a downward force on the ground of 20 000 N. So the pressure is given by:

$$\text{pressure} = \frac{\text{force}}{\text{area}} = \frac{20000}{1600}$$

$$= 12.5 \text{ N/cm}^2$$

10 Who is pressing down with the most pressure – the girl or the elephant?

11 If you had laid an expensive carpet or wooden floor in your house, who would you let walk across it – the elephant (assuming the room and door is big enough!) or the girl? Why?

Enquiry ## Effect of force and surface area

Look at the equipment shown in the diagram. It can be used to design an experiment to look at the effect of force and surface area.

Equipment list
newton balance
scale bowl
soft plasticine or modelling clay
a selection of dowel rods of different cross-sectional area.

1 What variables do you think will affect the depth of the impression (mark) in the plasticine?

2 In your groups plan an experiment that you could carry out using the equipment listed. Draw out your instructions as a series of diagrams, with a sentence under each diagram to explain what you would do. Here is an example of a possible first sentence: Cover the bottom of the scale bowl with a layer of plasticine about 3 cm thick.

Here are the results obtained by a group doing an experiment using similar equipment. In their experiment they chose to push each rod down until it made the same impression in the plasticine as the previous rod. They did this by changing the force pressing down on the rods.

Area of rod (cm²)	Force (N)
0.5	20
1	40
2	80
4	160
6	240

3 Is there any relationship between the area of the rod and the force?

4 Plot these results on a graph.

5 If a rod with a cross-sectional area of 3 cm² was used, what force would need to be applied to produce the same indentation in the plasticine? How did you work this out?

Using your graph, make up three more questions for someone else to answer. Mark their answers and explain where they might have gone wrong if they could not answer any of your questions.

Under pressure

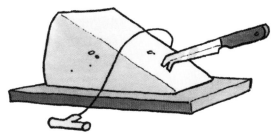

12 Look at the picture above. It shows a cheese cutter and a cheese knife. Which do you think will cut through cheese more easily? Why?

13 Which would you rather walk across – the sand or the pebbles? Why? Explain your answers to a friend. Make sure that you include the words pressure, force and area in your explanation.

Creative thinking *Sports products*

Expansion of sports manufacturer

ROLIF **LOPA**, the well known Italian sports manufacturer, has announced its expansion into the winter sports market with its new range announced today in Cortina. The initial range of products will include new cutting-edge technology snow shoes. These are constructed from high density copper and steel alloy with a smaller surface area than those produced by any other manufacturer. They guarantee faster sinking through snow and even mud and sand or your money back.

The company are also producing a range of ice skates with an innovative new base consisting of no less than three parallel blades per shoe, each constructed from flexible wide contact area plastic.

Financial Review, 1ˢᵗ April 2003

1 Read this article from a financial newspaper, and discuss it with your partner.

2 What do you think about the company's new products? Would you invest your money in this company?

3 What properties would you want snow shoes to have, and why?

4 What properties would you want ice skates to have, and why?

5 Rewrite the article and rename the company so that their products stand a bigger chance of success.

Time to think

Put these three states of matter into a sequence starting with the most dense and ending with the least dense:
solid, gas, liquid.
Which is the most difficult to compress? Why? (HINT – Think about the particle model.)

➡ *The particle theory and pressure*

This was first discussed in Book 1. Think back to your earlier work to explain the ideas of air pressure in terms of moving particles and the relative distance between them in different substances.

14 Look at the sentences below and match the first half to the correct ending. Write the full sentences in your exercise book.

Air consists of	with each other and everything around them.
These particles collide	different speeds.
Different particles move at	they bounce back with the same average motion energy.
When the particles hit the side of a container	a mixture of particles moving all the time.

Now think about the particles of air contained in a can with a tightly fitting lid, which is being heated.

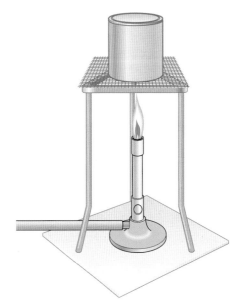

15 Look at the sentences below and match the first half to the correct ending. Write out the full sentences in your exercise book.

The air particles moving around inside the can will	they gain energy and move faster.
As the particles get hotter	the pressure inside the can increases.
They hit the sides of the container harder and	hit each other and the sides of the can.

16 a) If your teacher asked you to explain what happened in the collapsing can experiment would you expect to do this:

- clearly and accurately
- quite well but you would need some help
- not well at all – you would like someone to explain this to you again?

   b) Who in your groups selected the first option? Ask them to explain the experiment to the whole group.

c) Now check your understanding by using the sentences below to match the first half to the correct ending. Write the completed sentences in your exercise book.

In the collapsing can experiment, at the start,	there are no air particles hitting the inside of the can.
As the air is removed,	there is air inside the can exerting the same pressure as the air outside.
The pressure inside the can falls to zero because	there are more air particles hitting the outside of the can.
The pressure on the outside of the can	makes the can collapse.

→ *Going down deep*

The further a diver descends into the sea, the greater is the pressure that he experiences. Pressure increases with depth. Because water is much more dense than air, the pressure increases rapidly as you go down through the water. At 10 m below the surface the pressure has increased from normal atmospheric pressure to about twice as much. At 20 m below the surface the pressure is about three times the normal pressure at the surface. Some watches are guaranteed to 5 atmospheres pressure. This means that they will work under water at a depth where the pressure is five times greater than at the surface.

The picture on left shows a simple demonstration of this effect using a large plastic cola bottle with holes drilled in the side.

The pressure depends not only on the depth, but also on the density of the liquid.

Another thing you should note is that the pressure of the water in the bottle is acting both down and on the sides. We can see this because the water is squirting out sideways from the holes.

About 80% of the air we breathe is nitrogen, and so our blood contains a small amount of dissolved nitrogen. Deep sea divers take tanks of air with them to breathe from. The further down they dive, the greater the pressure gets and more nitrogen is able to dissolve in the blood.

If a diver comes to the surface too quickly the pressure of the water on him or her gets less very quickly, and the dissolved nitrogen gas is released as bubbles. When this happens the bubbles can block small arteries and it is very painful. This is called 'the bends', and it can be fatal. To avoid getting this decompression sickness, the diver must rise to the surface of the water slowly, or make stops on the way up to allow the gas to come out of solution.

The Titanic.

When the 'unsinkable' Titanic hit an iceberg in the North Atlantic Sea in 1912 it sank quickly to the seabed, which was about 4000 m down. The pressure this deep was about 400 times the normal atmospheric pressure, which made it very difficult to recover the ship. It was not until 1985 that a joint French and American scientific expedition, led by Dr Robert Ballard, discovered the wreck of the Titanic.

17 Think of three questions to check whether someone has understood this piece about underwater pressure. Try out each other's questions and decide which are the best.

→ *Liquid levels*

There is an expression 'a liquid always finds its own level'. From our knowledge of pressure we can see why this must be so. In the diagram below the tap is initially closed. Water is then added into the left hand side. When the tap is opened the water will flow into the right hand side. The pressure depends on the height of the water. The pressure at X due to the column of water on the left will be the same as the pressure at Y due to the column of water on the right.

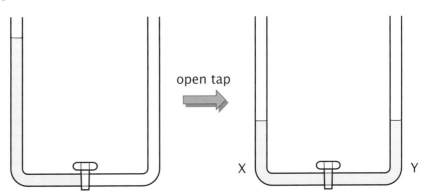

Look at the diagram below. If some water is poured into the right hand side to the height shown, where will the water rise to in the connecting parts of the container?

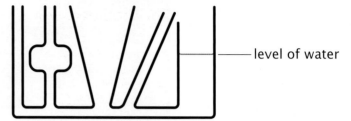

level of water

Builders often use the levelling effect of water during construction to check if the heights of walls and other sites are level. A length of plastic tubing is filled with water and the two ends are placed apart at the two places where the heights need to be the same. The height of the water at the two ends is the same if the heights are the same, so looking at the picture below it follows that the heights on each side are different.

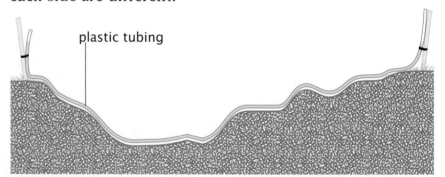

plastic tubing

Pressure at work

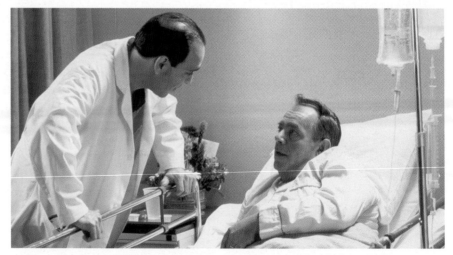

In hospital a patient might be given a saline drip. The saline solution is put into the body through a vein in the patient's arm. The purpose of a saline drip is to replace fluid in the circulatory system. The higher the plastic container, the faster the saline flows into the body, unless it is regulated.

18 If the tube didn't have a one-way valve in it, what would happen if the drip bag was stored underneath the patient?

The drawing below shows how an artesian well is made.

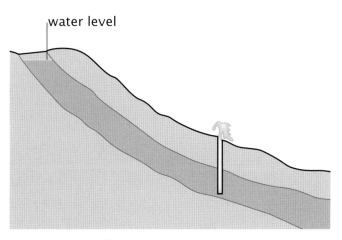

An artesian well.

19 How many layers of rock can you see?
One layer soaks up the ground water – this is called an aquifer. The bottom layer is clay, which is impermeable. The top layer is also clay. If a hole is drilled down to the aquifer the pressure of the water above causes the water to rise up through the well.

20 Copy the diagram of the artesian well and the information from the passage to label the diagram.

Look at the picture of the fountain at Witley Court in Worcestershire. To keep water going to the fountain a reservoir was built and pipes were laid to bring the water through tunnels to the fountain. Pressure in the fountain head (reservoir) is so great that the main jet is able to reach a height of about 35 metres.

Fountain at Witley Court.

Research

A famous fountain is to be found at Chatsworth House. This was built around 1843. Use the internet or other sources to find out about the construction of the fountain at Chatsworth.
(HINT – Useful key words in a search could include Chatsworth, fountain and construction.)

When reservoirs are constructed, the walls of the dam need to be very strong because of the large pressure exerted by water at the base. Reservoirs provide a source of water for drinking and irrigation, and the water from the dams is used to generate electricity.

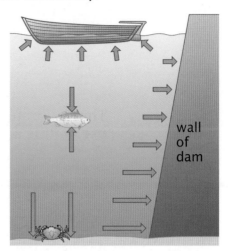

wall of dam

→ *Pressure through a liquid*

Key words
∗ compress
∗ hydraulic press

Look back to Question 1 on page 231. If you answered this correctly, you will know that the force acting upwards is the upthrust. Our ideas of pressure can be used to explain the term upthrust. Look at the drawing below. The size of the arrows represents the size of the forces acting.

21 Do the forces on the sides balance out?
22 Are the forces on the bottom bigger or smaller than at the top?
23 In which direction is the resultant force acting?

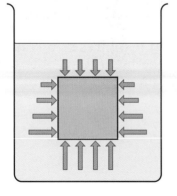

In earlier work you learnt that compared to a gas, a liquid is very difficult to **compress**. This is because the particles are much more tightly bound together in a liquid than in a gas. If you try to put a cork into a bottle containing air it is quite easy. If you try to push it into a bottle completely full of water it is impossible because you cannot compress the water.

Look at the drawing showing two syringes joined together. One syringe is large; the other is small. They are both filled with water. If you place your thumbs on the plunger of the syringes and press the plunger of the small syringe you can feel the forces. Water goes through the connecting tube into the large syringe. The pressure in the water is the same throughout, but the forces are different because of the different areas of cross-section of the syringes.

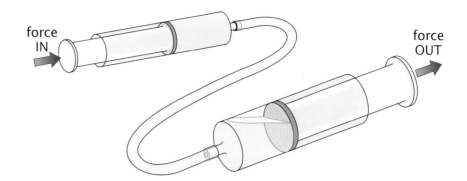

This apparatus demonstrates the principle of the **hydraulic press**. It is also the basis of the robotic arms that are used extensively in the motor construction industry.

➡ *Some applications of pressure*

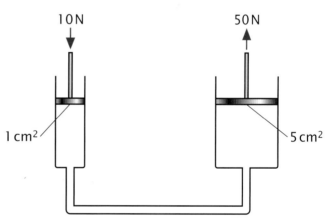

The principle of the hydraulic press.

Key words
* piston
* hydraulic jack
* load
* effort

Joseph Bramah invented the hydraulic press around 1795. The principle is shown in the diagram above. The force on the left hand side is 10 N, so the pressure exerted on the water by this **piston** is given using the formula:

$$\text{pressure} = \frac{\text{force}}{\text{area}}$$

$$\text{pressure} = \frac{10}{1} = 10 \, \text{N/cm}^2$$

As the pressure is the same throughout the liquid, the pressure exerted on the other piston is the same, namely $10 \, \text{N/cm}^2$. Therefore, pressure out $= 10 \, \text{N/cm}^2$.

As pressure out $= \dfrac{\text{force}}{\text{area}}$

$10 = \dfrac{\text{force}}{\text{area}}$

As the pressure is constant, the greater the area of the piston, the greater is the size of the force.

pressure out $= 10\,\text{N/cm}^2 = \dfrac{\text{force}}{5\,\text{cm}^2}$

The area on the right is five times as big, so the force on the right must be five times as big. The force is 50 N.

The hydraulic press is used a lot in industry, and a similar device, the **hydraulic jack**, is used in garages. Here the force that is exerted is much less than the **load** (the car). Note, however, that the distance moved by the load is less than the distance moved by the person's force.

24 In the above example, the **effort** is 10 N and the load is 50 N. If the load moved up through 3 cm, how far would the effort have to move?

Hydraulic jack holding up a car.

25 What is the main idea behind how a hydraulic lift and jack work?

Joseph Bramah, inventor of the hydraulic press, also patented the Bramah safety lock, in 1784. His lock was considered unpickable until it was finally picked in 1851. He also invented a beer pump, a quill sharpener, methods of paper-making, improved fire engines and printing machines. In 1806 Bramah patented a machine for printing banknotes that was used by the Bank of England.

Another example where the principle of hydraulics is used is in the brakes of a car.

Joseph Bramah.

Above the stage in most large modern theatres is a space called the 'fly tower', which provides walkways and working platforms above the stage, and storage space for scenery not required on stage. Technicians called 'fly men' operate each individual fly bar. Flying scenery can be moved by electrical or hydraulic systems. Originally nothing more than simple painted backcloths or curtains were flown, but it is now common to hang large three dimensional items of scenery, each weighing several tons.

Power to move stage machinery has changed over the years. Originally human muscle power drove all the equipment, by means of ropes and various simple machines. Hydraulic motors and pistons however are ideal for use in theatres, because they are powerful and they run quietly. In London, several theatres had their hydraulic power provided by the London Hydraulic Power Company while it existed.

Electric motors are now the most common form of method to power stage machinery, and computers are extensively used to control all the stage machinery.

→ *Pneumatic systems*

Key words
* pneumatic
* vacuum

Differences in air pressure, just like differences in liquid pressure, can be used to do work. Air-driven systems are **pneumatic**.

Word play

1 The French word *pneumatique* means relating to air or gas. So in French *pneu* is a tyre.
The French word for a mattress is *matelas*. What do you think *matelas pneumatique* means?
2 In medicine, *pneumonia* refers to the air passages (lungs) being infected. What do you think *pneumothorax* means?

Steam pressure

Thomas Newcomen invented the first steam engine, in 1712. The invention was patented as a way to pump water from mines. The next major development came when James Watt invented a far more efficient steam engine with a separate condenser. He greatly improved Newcomen's steam engine.

Many ideas led to the development of the steam engine: the concept of a **vacuum** and how to make one; an understanding of pressure; methods for generating steam; and the invention of the piston and cylinder.

Various scientists in Europe made many discoveries about air pressure in the seventeenth century. In France, work was done by Pascal. In Italy, Torricelli suggested ideas about a vacuum. In Germany, Otto von Guericke performed his famous vacuum experiment, and in England work on gases was being done by Robert Boyle. The idea of using steam under pressure to do work had been around for some time before Newcomen got to work, and one of the earliest records is of Hero of Alexandria, in about 100 AD.

→ # *Vacuums*

You can blow up a balloon without blowing into it by removing air from around it. Imagine that a balloon is partially blown up, tied, and then placed inside a bell jar. If all of the air is then pumped out of the bell jar, the balloon inflates.

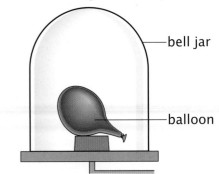

bell jar

balloon

26 Explain why the balloon inflates as the air in the bell jar is removed. Draw a balloon in a bell jar with the air removed and use arrows of different lengths and sizes to compare the pressure inside the inflating balloon and the pressure outside the balloon.

A vacuum is created when all the particles of matter have been removed from an area. There are no gas particles present to exert a pressure.

Key words
* hemispheres
* atmospheric pressure

Vacuum pump

Otto von Guericke built the first vacuum pump and used it to create vacuums in various containers. On 8th May 1654 Guericke carried out his famous 'Magdeburg **hemispheres**' demonstration. This used two joined hemispheres from which the air had been removed. Two teams of eight horses could not pull them apart because the pressure of the Earth's atmosphere was acting on the outside to hold them together.

Guericke's Magdeburg hemispheres demonstration.

You may have seen a version of this experiment in school. The apparatus used in schools is shown here.

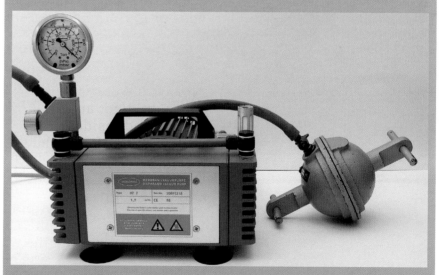

1 What shape is a hemisphere?
2 Draw the school apparatus and show with arrows where **atmospheric pressure** is pressing.
3 What do you think is inside the hemisphere once the air has been removed?
4 Here is a philosophical question: what is nothing made of?

The rubber sucker

Rubber suckers work because of the action of air pressure. The picture shows a sucker pressed onto a surface. It is hanging upside down but stays in place.

27 Explain why the rubber sucker stays in place.

Enquiry **Rubber suckers**

Design an experiment to investigate the action of rubber suckers. Think about a question you want to answer, for example:

- What is the biggest load needed to dislodge the rubber sucker?
- Do differently shaped suckers stick for different lengths of time?
- Does it make a difference if the surface the sucker is attached to is wet or dry?

Decide on what you are going to find out. Write down a prediction of what you think the answer to your question might be.
List all the variables that you could change. What will be the dependent and independent variables?

→ *Measuring gas pressure*

There are many different ways in which gas pressure can be measured. Different equipment is used for different types of pressure measurement.

Key words
* barometer
* mercury
* aneroid
* manometer

The barometer

A device that measures air pressure is called a **barometer**. Evangelista Torricelli (1608–1647) invented the first **mercury** barometer in 1643. It consisted of a 1 m long glass tube, sealed at one end. The tube was filled with mercury and then turned upside down, with the open end dipping into a bowl of mercury. The mercury level fell a little but not all the way. It dropped until the height was about 76 cm. Air is pressing down on the surface of the mercury in the bowl. As no air was allowed into the tube, there is no air in the region labelled A in the picture opposite. It is a vacuum. The column of mercury is exerting a pressure at the bottom of the tube. This pressure must exactly balance the atmospheric pressure on the surface of the mercury.

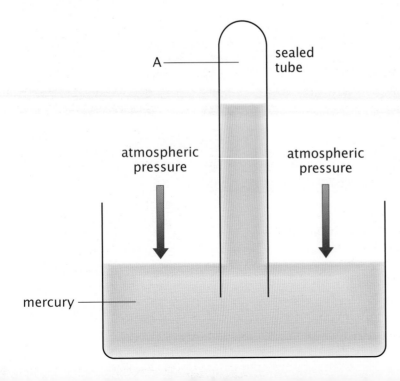

A — sealed tube

atmospheric pressure

atmospheric pressure

mercury

The aneroid barometer

The **aneroid** barometer works rather like the collapsing can. It is a metal box with strong sides and a spring lid, and it has had some air removed. A strong spring holds the lid to stop it being totally crushed. The middle of the lid is connected via levers to the pointer. As the air pressure alters, the lid flexes up and down. The levers magnify this movement and the pointer moves across the scale.

An aneroid barometer.

The manometer

The **manometer** is a another useful device for measuring pressure differences. It contains water. When there is a pressure difference on the opposite ends of the tube, the water is forced to move between the two ends of the tube. The difference between the two water levels is a measure of the gas pressure. You may have used a manometer similar to this to measure the gas pressure at the taps in the laboratory. The difference in heights between the water levels gives a measure of the gas pressure.

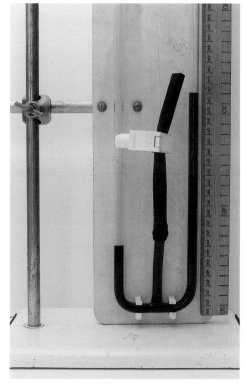

Manometer.

The Bourdon tube pressure gauge

This is another piece of equipment that is used to measure gas pressure. It works in a similar way to a party blowout. The harder you blow, the more it uncurls.

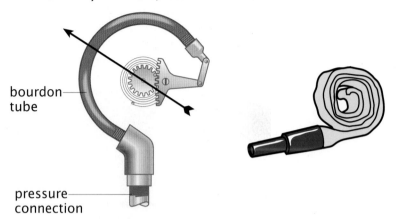

bourdon tube

pressure connection

→ *The pressure exerted by the Earth's atmosphere*

The Frenchman Blaise Pascal suggested that the air pressure decreases as we go higher. He and his father investigated this by measuring the pressure at the foot of the Puy-de-Dôme (a mountain in the Auvergne region of France) and then the pressure at the summit. They found that the air pressure was less at the summit.

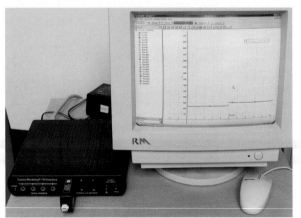

Digital pressure sensor

A digital pressure sensor will help you to compare the pressure at the foot and at the top of a tall building. Note the reading on the ground floor and then walk (or take the lift!) to the top floor of the building and note the pressure reading. As you climb, the pressure reading decreases.

You may have seen the collapsing can experiment. This shows the large pressure that the Earth's atmosphere exerts. You could say that we live at the bottom of an ocean of air. At sea level, there is the maximum amount of air above us, so the air pressure is greatest. We know that the pressure exerted by the air at sea level is about 100 000 Pa. The air pressure gets less as we go up. This is because the air particles are packed in less tightly the higher we go. In everyday language we say that the air is 'thinner' higher up. The atmosphere extends to a height of several kilometres but it doesn't suddenly end, it just becomes less and less. Mountaineers carry oxygen supplies with them to help them to breathe at high altitudes.

New Zealander Sir Edmund Hillary and Nepalese Sherpa Tenzing Norgay scaled 8848 m high Mount Everest on 29th May, 1953. They are credited with being the first people to do so.

The photograph shows Sir Edmund Hillary wearing full climbing gear and carrying oxygen apparatus.

Peter Habeler, an Austrian, and Reinhold Messner, an Italian, were the first to reach the summit of Mount Everest without the aid of bottled oxygen, in 1978.

Sir Edmund Hillary, 1953.

Information processing *Air pressure*

The results obtained from an experiment to investigate the variation of air pressure with height are shown in the table below.

Altitude (m)	Pressure (kPa)
10	101 130
101	100 090
500	95 650
1005	90 290
2503	75 760
4002	63 240
5002	55 890
8001	37 890
10 003	28 730
12 502	19 800
15 967	11 100

1 Plot a graph of this data, and use it to answer the following questions.

2 Ben Nevis is 1342 m high. What would be the pressure at the top of Ben Nevis?

3 Mont Blanc on the French–Italian border is 4808 m high. What is the air pressure at the top?

4 Everest is 8848 m high. What is the air pressure at the top? What does this suggest about some of the equipment needed by mountaineers?

5 What is the air pressure at the top of the troposphere (16 000 m)?

6 A Boeing 747 aircraft cruises at a height of 12 000 m. What is the air pressure at this height?

Time to think

1 Write a list of all the different ways in which pressure can be measured. What are the different units that are used?

2 In an experiment to see how the air pressure varied with altitude, a remote datalogger with a pressure sensor attached was taken on a flight in a hot air balloon. These are the readings. Use them to plot a graph and answer the questions.

Altitude (m)	Pressure (kPa)
149	99.6
500	95.7
800	92.4
1140	88.9
1300	87.2
1500	85.3

a) At what altitude would the air pressure have been 90 kPa?

b) Besides the pressure and height, what other measurements would it have been useful to take?

The turning effect of a force

Key words
* moment
* pivot

When a force is applied to an object it may cause it to turn or twist. The turning effect of a force is called a **moment**. The size of a moment depends on two variables acting together – these are the size of the force and where it is applied (distance from **pivot**).

For example, the longer the spanner, the easier it is to undo the nut. We say the moment of the force is greater.

It is important to know the direction and position in which a force acts as well as to know the size of the force.

When you put a force on one end of a bar, it produces a turning effect. The picture below shows someone pushing open a heavy door. To open the door you would push as far away from the hinge as possible. Pushing in the middle of the door is much harder. Try it for yourself.

The drawing of the see-saw shows three people. One is large and the other two are much smaller, however the see-saw is still balanced.

28 What would happen if the large person sat on the end?

In diagram A on the left the moment is given by:

A

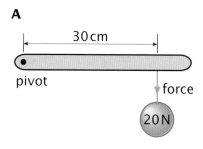

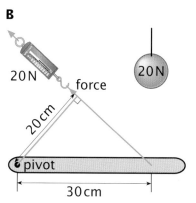

moment = force × distance

moment = 20 N × 30 cm

= 600 N cm

29 If the force was acting at a distance of 15 cm what would the moment be?

In diagram B, someone pulling on the thread with a force of 20 N provides the force. The thread is attached at a distance of 30 cm from the pivot, but the distance from the direction of the force at right angles is 20 cm. So in this case the moment of the force is given by:

moment = force × distance

moment = 20 N × 20 cm

= 400 N cm

Look at the picture of the see-saw below. When someone sits on the left hand side it goes down, turning around the pivot, as shown in the second diagram. To return the see-saw to balance, someone would have to sit on the right hand side. This person would also produce a turning effect or moment.

When the see-saw is balanced, the turning effect in the clockwise direction is the same as that in the anti-clockwise direction.

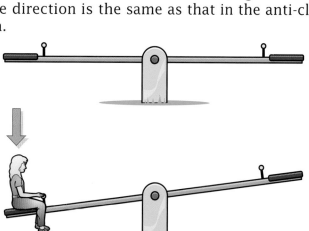

→ *Simple machines*

Key words
* lever
* fulcrum
* effort
* load

Look at the pictures. All these are examples of what we call a **lever**. A lever is a simple machine.

30 A screwdriver is being used to open the lid on the tin of paint. If the tin were very tightly sealed, what sort of screwdriver would be better to lever the lid off?

31 Where would you apply the force to lift this slab? In this example, the iron bar (crowbar) pivots around the point where it is in contact with the ground. (This pivot point is sometimes called the **fulcrum**.)

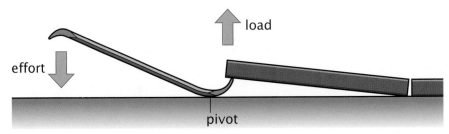

32 Look back at the pictures. In each case can you identify where to apply the force? (This force is called the **effort**). Where is the pivot point? Where is the **load**?

In the examples of the crowbar, the tin of paint, the claw hammer and the scissors, the effort is at one end, the load is at the other and the pivot is between the load and the effort (but closer to the load than the effort).

33 Look at the examples of the bottle opener, the wheelbarrow and the nutcrackers. In each case, where are the load, effort and pivot?

There is a third group of examples, shown in the diagrams below. Here the effort is greater than the load. The pivot is at the opposite end to the load.

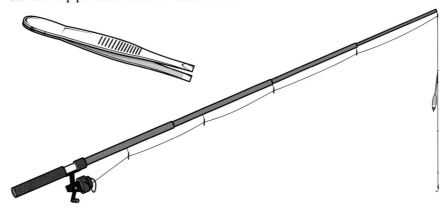

→ *Levers and joints*

Key words
* contraction
* flexors
* extensors

Levers a little bit like the tweezers and fishing rod are found in the human body. One example is the biceps muscle in the forearm. Here, although the effort is more than the load, there is an advantage in the fact that a small **contraction** in the biceps moves the hand through a large distance.

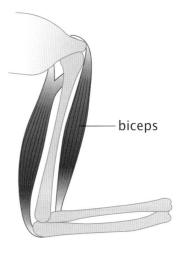

biceps

DID YOU KNOW?

The muscles in the thigh are the most powerful in the body.

EXTENSION We can walk, run, lift objects, nod our heads and arm wrestle because we can move our bones against each other. Our bones and muscles make up a living system of levers. Muscles always work in pairs. **Flexors** bend limbs, and **extensors** straighten them.

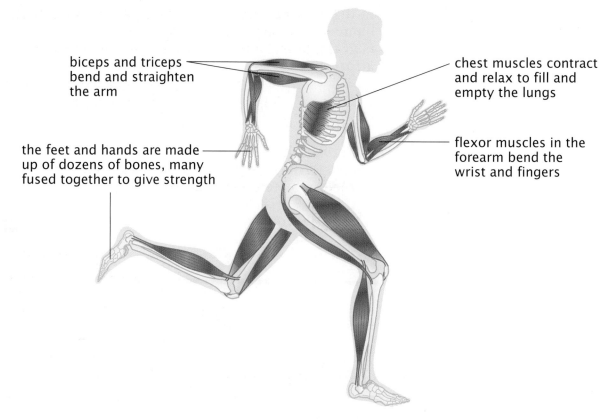

biceps and triceps bend and straighten the arm

the feet and hands are made up of dozens of bones, many fused together to give strength

chest muscles contract and relax to fill and empty the lungs

flexor muscles in the forearm bend the wrist and fingers

Machines can be made to copy human systems. This mechanical digger has pneumatic pistons and wires operating like a hinge-jointed elbow and claws. Artificial limbs are built to the same design.

Enquiry *Data analysis*

Look at the apparatus shown in the picture below. You may have used similar equipment yourself. It can be used to investigate the rules of balancing about a pivot.

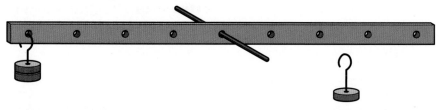

A load is placed on the left hand side, and a different load is placed on the right hand side at a different place so that the beam balances. Groups of pupils used this equipment using different loads and distances.

Baljit used a load of 3 N and placed it as shown 40 cm from the pivot on the left hand side. She found that it was balanced when she placed the 4 N load as shown.

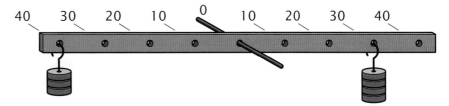

Look at the drawings of the results obtained by other pupils. From the diagrams produce a table of the results they obtained. One of them did not get their beam to balance. Can you say which one did not balance? Can you find a rule to tell us whether or not the beam will balance?

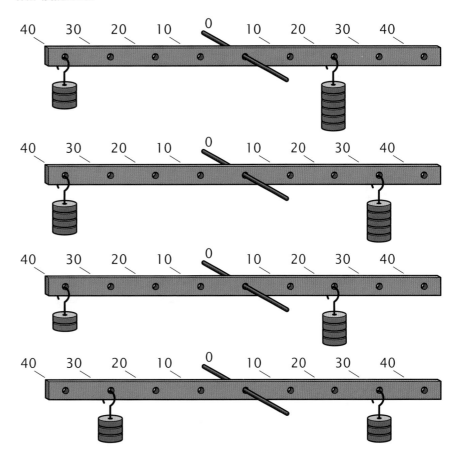

→ *Balance*

For an object to stay in **equilibrium** (balanced) there must be no resultant force acting on it, and there must not be any resultant moment.

34 Look at the two pictures showing objects balanced. Can you think of any other examples?

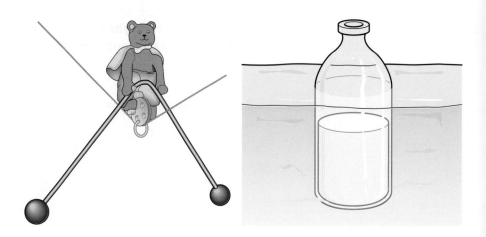

Reasoning   *In balance*

Michael has made a toy butterfly on a spring to give to his mother as a present.

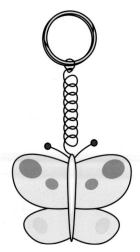

1 Copy the diagram into your book and draw in an arrow to show the force of gravity.

2 His mum hangs the toy up and pulls the butterfly down. Add a sketch of her hand to your drawing and show with an arrow where she is putting the force of her pull.

3 Use a different coloured pencil to show how the butterfly begins to move when she lets it go. What makes the butterfly move in this direction?

4 The butterfly bounces up and down for about 20 seconds, then stops. Why does it stop moving? Discuss each of these possible answers in your group then vote on the most likely answer:

- Air resistance slows it down
- It gets heavier
- It gets lighter
- Gravity decreases
- The spring stretches
- The spring tightens.

This photograph shows a crane lifting a load. The load is balanced by a **counterweight** that the crane driver can move along the short arm to counterbalance the load.

5 Where is the pivot?

6 Why is the counterweight on the short arm and not the long arm?

7 If the crane driver starts to move the load out towards the end of the arm, what must he or she do to the counterweight to stop the crane tipping over?

8 Imagine the load is 5000 N and it is moved 8 metres out from the pivot. The counterweight is 11 000 N. What is the turning moment of the load?

9 How far from the pivot must the counterweight go to keep the crane balanced?

10 If the counterweight was placed at 3 metres from the pivot what would happen?

Time to think

Professor Swot is in the process of making a helpful dictionary for physics students on her course. She keeps the key words and their definitions on separate cards. Unfortunately she dropped all the cards, and the key words and their definitions are now muddled up. Here is a list of all her information. Put the key words into alphabetical order then match each with its correct definition You might want to divide up the key words between the members of your group and the put the list back together when you have all finished your set of words.

Key words

a) mass
b) barometer
c) lever
d) manometer
e) inertia
f) momentum
g) pivot
h) newton
i) pressure
j) density

k) floating
l) balance
m) force
n) air resistance
o) free fall
p) upthrust
q) weight
r) hydraulics
s) pneumatics

Definitions

1 The SI unit used to measure force.
2 The science of gases doing work by using pressure changes.
3 A simple machine that helps us do work with less force because the force is applied around a pivot.
4 A property of an object that relates to its mass. The greater the mass of an object, the harder it is to get it moving or to stop it due to this property.
5 This is an indication of how much force is need to stop a moving object. It is related to the object's mass and how fast it is moving.
6 The downward force on an object caused by gravitational force. It is measured in newtons.
7 The science of water doing work under pressure.
8 This is the relationship between a force and the area to which it is applied. It is the ratio of force to area. It can be measured in psi.
9 This happens when an object placed in a fluid displaces its own weight with an equal weight of the fluid. The upthrust of the fluid equals the downthrust of the object so that the forces are balanced.
10 This is the friction force on bodies moving through the air. It is related to both the speed and the shape of the object.
11 This is the relationship of the mass of an object and its volume.
12 This is a push or pull. It acts to change the shape or movement of an object. Every one of these has its own equal and opposite.
13 Objects do this when they fall towards Earth under the effects of gravity.

14 This is an instrument that measures air pressure.

15 The point where a lever is joined to its support. It is sometimes called the fulcrum.

16 When all the forces acting on an object equal each other, and the object does not speed up or slow down, it does not start or stop and it does not change shape. It is in this state because there is no change.

17 The force of a fluid pushing up against an object due to its density.

18 It is the amount of 'stuff' in an object.

19 A useful device for measuring pressure differences.

9 Using chemistry

In this chapter you will learn:

→ about the chemical reaction which takes place when a fuel burns
→ how chemical reactions are used as energy resources
→ how new materials are made through chemical reactions
→ what happens to atoms and molecules when new materials are made
→ to represent chemical reactions by word equations
→ how accurate measurements have played a key role in scientific research
→ to recognise that mass is conserved during chemical reactions
→ the different stages of development of a new product

You will also develop your skills in:

→ making measurements of temperature and mass with sufficient accuracy
→ identifying questions that are suitable for a scientific enquiry
→ comparing the work of scientists
→ following the reasoning behind different scientific theories
→ investigating how you can compare new materials with existing ones

➜ ➜ ➜ WHAT DO YOU KNOW?

1 This information was collected by a group of pupils investigating fuels.

Fuel burnt	Limewater test	Cobalt chloride paper test	Observations
wood spill	✓	✓	yellow flame, some soot
Methylated spirit	✓	✓	blue flame, no soot
hydrogen	✗	✓	blue/clear flame, some condensation
firelighter	✓	✓	yellow flame, soot
candle wax	✓	✓	yellow flame, lots of soot
powdered charcoal	✓	✗	slow burning, glows red, yellow flame

a) Which gas does limewater test for?
b) What would you see happening to the limewater if the gas were present?
c) Which liquid/vapour does cobalt chloride paper detect?
d) What would you see happening to the cobalt chloride paper if that liquid/vapour was present?
e) What are the two main products of a fuel burning?
f) Which of the fuels above are the odd ones out?

2 Look carefully at the illustration of the apparatus used by the class.
a) What might the liquid in the U tube be?
b) Why is the U tube surrounded by a beaker of ice?

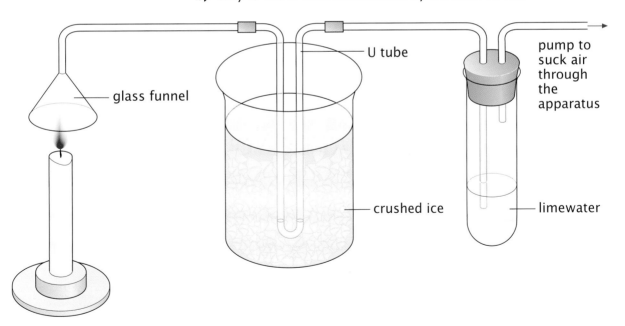

3 a) What energy transfer takes place when natural gas burns in each of these Bunsen burners?

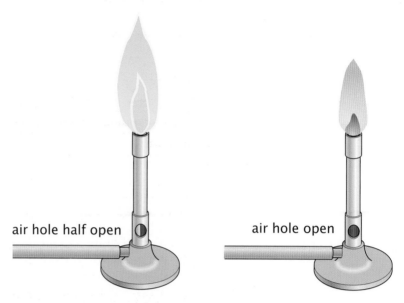

air hole half open

air hole open

b) Copy and complete this Sankey diagram to show what energy transfer takes place in a Bunsen burner.

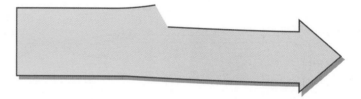

c) Look carefully at the examples in the photographs on page 264 and state what energy changes are taking place.

4 a) What are the main differences between physical and chemical changes?

b) Give an example of a physical change and one of a chemical change.

c) Compare and check your examples with three other pupils.

5 Match the key words in the table with the most helpful definitions.

Key word	Definition
1 Atom	**A** At least two different types of atoms bonded together
2 Molecule	**B** Two or more substances together, not chemically combined
3 Compound	**C** The smallest part of an element which can exist
4 Element	**D** This is formed when atoms are joined by a bond
5 Mixture	**E** Pure substance made of one type of atom

6 In the following table the answers are provided but not the questions! In pairs, write out a suitable question to fit each answer. Try them out on each other and decide which are the best questions.

The answer is...	What was the question?
atoms	
easily separated	
the particles are moving more quickly	
the burning candle is extinguished	
a mixture	

7 Divide a page into four sections and write one of the following headings in each section: atom, element, compound, molecule. Add three examples of each, and write a sentence to explain what they are. Check your ideas with those of three other pupils.

➡ *What happens when we burn a fuel?*

Key words
* fuel
* hydrocarbons
* oxidation
* complete combustion
* incomplete combustion
* greenhouse gas

Good King Wenceslas, 907–929 AD.

In science, a **fuel** is a substance which burns to release energy.

Here is the first verse from the well-known Christmas carol 'Good King Wenceslas'.

Good King Wenceslas looked out on the Feast of Stephen
When the snow lay round about, deep and crisp and even.
Brightly shone the moon that night, though the frost was cruel,
When a poor man came in sight, gathering winter fuel.

1 What sort of fuel was being gathered? What other sorts of fuels could they have used?
2 Which fuels do we use today?
3 Compare your list with other groups. How can we classify fuels? Decide on different ways of classifying fuels. Which method is the most useful?

The fuels we burn contain compounds consisting mainly of hydrogen and carbon – these fuels are called **hydrocarbons**. The main products of burning (combustion) are water and carbon dioxide. Other unwanted substances are also produced.

When elements burn in air or oxygen they produce oxides. When this happens, two hydrogen atoms in the fuel join up with one oxygen atom to produce water (H_2O), and one carbon atom joins up with two oxygen atoms to produce carbon dioxide (CO_2). The reaction of substances with oxygen is called **oxidation**.

The full word equation for the **complete combustion** of a fuel is:

hydrocarbon fuel + oxygen → carbon dioxide + water

4 Water could be called hydrogen oxide. Explain why this is.

The simplest hydrocarbon molecule is methane (natural gas). This is the gas used in domestic cookers, and also in the Bunsen burners you use in science experiments for heating.

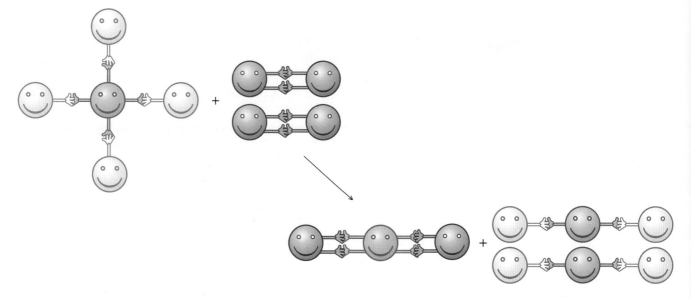

5 Copy and complete the word equation for the combustion of methane:

methane +   →

Incomplete combustion

Whenever the yellow Bunsen flame is used for heating, a layer of soot collects on the glassware. This is unburnt carbon. Water vapour is also produced. **Incomplete combustion** has occurred.

6 Write a word equation for burning methane in this way.

outer zone is a thin region of complete combustion

middle zone of incomplete combustion

inner zone of unburnt gas

air hole closed

Petrol does not burn completely in a car engine, and it produces carbon monoxide (CO) instead of carbon dioxide (CO_2). Carbon monoxide is a poisonous gas that can kill people. Faulty heaters may also burn their fuel incompletely, releasing deadly carbon monoxide.

7 Why is carbon monoxide produced when the supply of air is limited?

8 Water vapour is also produced when petrol burns. Write a word equation for the incomplete combustion of petrol.

Research

You can now buy carbon monoxide detectors in DIY stores. Explain why it would be advisable for a landlord to buy and fit carbon monoxide detectors. What advice do the manufacturers give to likely buyers of these detectors?

9 a) What effect does breathing in soot have on your lungs and trachea?

b) Carbon monoxide is breathed in by smokers. It attaches to red blood cells thereby preventing them from taking up oxygen. What harmful effect does this have on your body?

c) Carbon dioxide is called a **greenhouse gas**. What effect do these gases have on our climate?

Hydrogen as a fuel

Key word
* odourless

Hydrogen is used in fuel cells. Fuel cells use the energy from fuels to provide electrical energy. A fuel cell provides a continuous source of electrical energy, as long as the fuel and oxygen are constantly supplied. Fuel cells were an important feature of the Apollo space programme which landed people on the Moon.

Hydrogen has the following properties:

* colourless
* **odourless**
* very low density
* highly explosive when mixed with air.

This is the word equation for the reaction for the combustion of hydrogen.

hydrogen + oxygen → water

10 Which of the properties of hydrogen make it useful in fuel cells?

Research

Find out how scientists obtain the hydrogen to use in the fuel cells. What is the most abundant and easily available source of hydrogen?

Some fuel cells use methane instead of hydrogen. Methane has the following properties:

- colourless
- odourless
- low density
- moderately explosive when mixed with air.

11 Compare the use of hydrogen and methane as the fuel for these fuel cells. Copy and complete the table, using ticks or crosses where suitable.

Fuel	Possible combustion products			
	Carbon (soot)	Carbon monoxide	Carbon dioxide	Water vapour
methane				
hydrogen				

12 Why might conservationists and environmentalists prefer the use of hydrogen rather than methane in fuel cells?

Matches

Key word
* flammable

How do matches work?

These days you can buy two different types of match. Before the match was invented, making fire was both difficult and unreliable. Friction matches that can be struck on anything to light them were invented by the British chemist John Walker, in 1827. Safety matches were invented in 1855 by a Swede called Johan Lundstrom, and can only be struck on the side of the box.

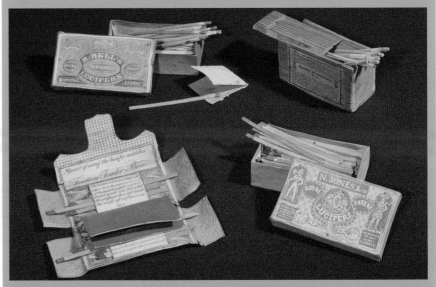

1 How do you light a safety match?
2 How do you light a friction match?

The safety aspect of Johan Lundstrom's matches comes from the separation of the **flammable** chemicals between the match head and the special striking surface on the side of the matchbox. The gritty material on the side of a matchbox is coated with red phosphorus. The match head contains potassium chlorate, sulphur and some red colouring. When the match head rubs against the box, friction ignites the mixture of phosphorus and potassium chlorate. The potassium chlorate contains lots of oxygen which supports the combustion, allowing it to burn enough to set fire to the wooden matchstick. The sulphur on the match head reacts with the oxygen provided and provides enough energy for the wooden match to light up. And there you go – instant fire!

The friction matches that you can light on any rough surface work on the same principle. The red phosphorus on the striking surface is replaced by phosphorus sulphide (of one form or another) in the match head. This decomposes and burns at the relatively low temperature generated by friction and sets fire to the rest of the match.

3 List all the chemicals named in the passage and classify them as either elements or compounds.
4 In the case of any compounds identified, name the elements it contains.
5 Fumes from burning matches are acidic. Can you suggest which of the elements named will burn to produce an acidic gas?
6 How did Johan Lundstrom adapt the original match to make it safer?
7 Name the products formed when phosphorus sulphide burns in a good supply of oxygen. Write a word equation for this reaction.

Word play

The chemicals in a match decompose during lighting. Can you think of other words or phrases that we might use instead?

'Decompose' is also used when we learn about recycling dead animals and plants. What other words could we use for this sort of decomposing?

DID YOU KNOW?

During 1888, workers at the Bryant and May match factory were on strike for better pay and conditions. The women were working 14 hours a day for a wage of less than 5 shillings (just 25 pence) a week. It was also discovered that the health of the women had been severely affected by the phosphorus that they used to make the matches. This caused yellowing of the skin, hair loss and phossy jaw, a form of bone cancer. The whole side of the face turned green and then black, discharging foul-smelling pus before the women finally died.

Campaigns continued against the use of yellow phosphorus. In 1891 the Salvation Army opened its own match factory in Old Ford, East London, using only harmless red phosphorus. The workers were soon producing six million boxes of matches a year.

Time to think

The combustion of a typical hydrocarbon, methane, depends on the amount of oxygen available. A group of pupils looked at the different products produced when methane was burnt in different amounts of oxygen. Here are their results.

Conditions	Reaction products with formulae
little air	soot (C), water vapour (H_2O)
more air	carbon monoxide (CO), water vapour (H_2O)
plenty of air	carbon dioxide (CO_2), water vapour (H_2O)

1 How would the pupils test for water vapour? What result would you expect?
2 What would they use to test for carbon dioxide? What result would you expect?
3 What evidence is there to suggest that methane is a hydrocarbon? Look at the reaction products to help you.
4 Write word equations for all three reactions, and check your ideas with another pupil.

Fireworks

Some fireworks contain fine powders of metals, such as magnesium metal. Magnesium is an element that is reactive with oxygen, especially when the powder is suddenly exposed to oxygen – the oxygen causes it to burn. Magnesium is the element that burns and gives off bright white lights in fireworks. You can create different colours of fireworks depending on what combination of other metals are used.

Creating firework colours is complicated, requiring considerable skill. Fireworks generally require an oxygen-producer, fuel, a binder (to keep everything where it needs to be), and a colour producer.

This table shows some of the chemicals used to produce the different colours displayed in fireworks.

Colour	Compound
red	strontium salts, lithium salts: lithium carbonate, Li_2CO_3 = red strontium carbonate, $SrCO_3$ = bright red
orange	calcium salts: calcium chloride, $CaCl_2$ calcium sulphate, $CaSO_4$
yellow	sodium compounds, for example sodium nitrate, $NaNO_3$
electric white	white-hot metal, such as magnesium or aluminium barium oxide, BaO
green	barium compounds: barium chloride, $BaCl_2$ = bright green
blue	copper compounds: copper(I) chloride, CuCl = turquoise blue

Suggest which compounds each of these fireworks might contain.

13 Write the word equation for the burning of magnesium.
14 Which combination of metal compounds would you use to produce purple?
15 Look at a periodic table and decide which groups the metals and the compounds in the table on page 272 belong to. Is there a pattern in terms of their colours?
16 Suggest three other salts that might be used instead of lithium carbonate to make a red firework.
17 Copy and complete this table. The first one has been done for you.

Compound	Formula	Number of elements	Name of elements	Number of atoms
lithium carbonate	Li_2CO_3	3	lithium carbon oxygen	6
copper chloride				
sodium nitrate				
strontium carbonate				

Key words
* phlogiston
* combustible
* caloric
* accurate

Burning ideas

Burning has been important to people ever since early humans worked out how to control fire. But HOW do things burn? This was a question that took centuries to answer, and until it could be answered chemistry could never make much progress. By the seventeenth century, scientists were beginning to realise that the burning of fuels, the reactions of metals in air and the breathing of animals all had something in common – they were all faster or slower versions of the same type of reaction.

Scientists observed that wood burns and turns to ashes when it is heated, while some metals become powders when they are heated. Some of these powders could be converted back into the metal by heating the metal powder with charcoal, but ashes cannot be converted back to wood.

An explanation was provided by Georg Stahl (1660–1734) and Johann Becher (1625–1682). They suggested that burning could be explained by the removal of a substance, and they called that substance **phlogiston**. Stahl developed this idea, which became known as the 'phlogiston theory,' and it was recognised as the scientific explanation for burning for around 100 years.

According to the phlogiston theory:

- metals and all other **combustible** substances contain a substance known as phlogiston, which is released into the air on burning, along with **caloric** (heat)
- substances lose mass when they burn because they lose phlogiston.

There were lots of problems with the theory, but it was better than no theory at all!

A theory helps scientists to explain observations, and it allows them to make predictions.

Enter Antoine Lavoisier!

Antoine Lavoisier was a French chemist who lived between 1743 and 1794. Like many other scientists of the day, Lavoisier was investigating burning. However, unlike them, he insisted on carrying out experiments involving **accurate** measurements. To help his work, Lavoisier developed a balance that could weigh to 0.0005 g, so that he could accurately measure the changes in mass that happened during his experiments.

He worked on the combustion of phosphorus and sulphur, and discovered that after burning, the mass of the material was greater than it had been at the start. This result does not fit with the phlogiston theory. If the elements had lost phlogiston, their mass would have decreased.

Using his highly sensitive scales Lavoisier showed that when he heated mercury oxide there was a loss in mass as during the reaction the mercury oxide released its oxygen. He also showed that when metals were heated in air they increase in mass. This increase was equal to the mass of oxygen taken from the air.

In another experiment, he heated charcoal with a number of metal oxides in closed containers, and discovered that the total mass of the container was the same both before and after heating.

1 Lavoisier designed a very accurate set of scales to measure the mass before and after each reaction. Explain why this was so important for his work.

Oxygen theory

As a result of this work, Lavoisier developed the theory that when substances burn in air they combine with oxygen from the air and form an oxide (a compound containing oxygen).

After sharing his ideas with another famous chemist, Joseph Priestley, Lavoisier went on to show that air was actually a mixture. By a series of careful experiments, Lavoisier showed that air was made up of several different components. From air he isolated the gases we now call oxygen, nitrogen and carbon dioxide. He also showed that carbon dioxide could be produced by burning charcoal in air. He accurately measured the proportion of oxygen in the air, and showed that oxygen was removed from the air during the process of burning.

Antoine Lavoisier.

Word play In the previous passage, what words could have been used instead of:

- converted back
- removal of a substance
- combustible substance?

Creative thinking Lavoisier

Imagine that you are a reporter who has just interviewed Lavoisier on his latest experiment that disproves the phlogiston theory. What headline would you use? What would be the opening sentence of your article?

EXTENSION Write a newspaper article explaining Lavoisier's investigation.

Evaluation Does the phlogiston or oxygen theory best explain how things burn?

Think about what takes place when a piece of magnesium ribbon burns in air.

1 Make a list of everything you might expect to see.

Method 1.   Method 2.

The teacher provided the class with two different balances. She suggested that the groups heating the magnesium in the tongs would need the more accurate balance.

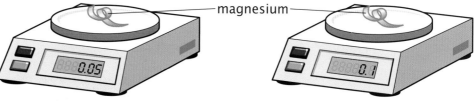

magnesium

Here are the results of their experiments:

Method 1	Group A	Group B	Group C	Group D
Mass of magnesium ribbon before burning (g)	0.05	1.0	0.04	0.03
Mass of ash after burning (g)	0.03	0.0	0.01	0.01

2 Look at the results for Method 1. What seems to happen to the mass of the magnesium after burning?

3 Which theory do these results appear to support?

4 Group A noticed that some of the ash produced in the reaction broke off and fell into the Bunsen flame. Group D said that they had difficulty scraping the ash off the tongs to be weighed. Suggest how these two observations might affect the reliability of the results for Groups A and D.

5 Can you suggest what might have happened in Group B's experiment?

Method 2	Group E	Group F	Group G	Group H
Mass of test tube, mineral wool and magnesium ribbon before burning (g)	15.50	16.60	15.92	14.30
Mass of test tube, mineral wool and contents after burning (g)	15.60	16.80	15.92	14.41

6 Look at the results for Method 2. What happens to the mass of the magnesium after burning?

7 Suggest what might have happened to Group G's experiment.

8 Which theory do these results appear to support?

9 Nita says that Method 2 is an improvement on Method 1 and provides more useful data. What do you think she means? Compare each method carefully and make a list of advantages for using Method 2.

10 Lavoisier insisted on taking accurate measurements. How did this lead to the phlogiston theory being disproved?

Nita suggested that if the masses of the reactants and products are measured carefully then the results will be more reliable. She suggested using this apparatus.

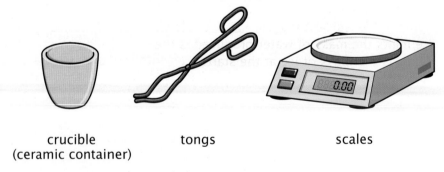

crucible
(ceramic container)   tongs   scales

11 a) Which piece of apparatus is missing?
   b) Think up a plan using this apparatus.
   c) Write down all the necessary measurements that you would take.
   d) What do you predict will happen using your method?
   e) Explain how your predicted results would help support the oxygen theory of burning.
   f) Get your plan checked before doing this investigation.

DID YOU KNOW? On 8th May 1794 Antoine Lavoisier was executed by guillotine. He pleaded for more time to finish a vital scientific experiment, but the judge replied, 'The republic has no need for scientists'. One of Lavoisier's friends said, 'It took only an instant to cut off that head, and another hundred years may not produce another like it.'

Time to think

Working as a group of three or four students, write out all the key words listed in this chapter so far on separate pieces of paper. Each member then writes out two more cards with a word that they found interesting in this chapter. Shuffle the cards. In turn, pick a card and explain to the rest of the group all you know about the word. Listen carefully to what each member says and correct or add to their ideas about the key word.

EXTENSION
Check through the cards again and come up with five questions that can be answered by the key words. Try these out on others in the group.

More burning ideas

Lavoisier suggested that the mass of the reactants will be the same as the mass of the products after a chemical change. This is the 'law of conservation of mass'. This law states that mass is neither created nor destroyed in a chemical change. When a reaction happens, the bonds holding the atoms together in the reactants break. The atoms are then rearranged into different substances by making new bonds.

The theory of conservation of mass also applies to physical changes, for example when ice melts the mass of water produced is the same as the mass of ice at the start.

1 Describe in simple steps how you would show that when sugar dissolves in water there is no change in mass. Compare your ideas with others in your group.

2 Write a word equation for this reaction.

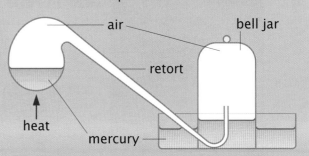

Apparatus used by Lavoisier (page 274) to measure mass changes when he heated mercury in air.

3 In the experiment which substances are easy to weigh and which are difficult? Explain why.

4 Which would be heavier, the mercury oxide or the mercury? Explain why.

5 How did this experiment support Lavoisier's oxygen theory.

→ *How are chemical reactions used to supply energy?*

Chemical reactions can be used to supply energy.

18 Look at the examples in these photographs and decide what forms of energy would be released. Which of the examples transfer chemical energy into electrical energy?

Rocket firework.

Batteries.

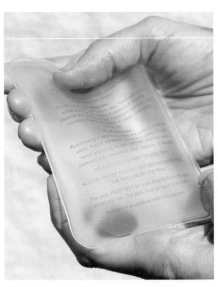

Gel handwarmer.

Dynamite.

In Chapter 5 you studied **displacement** reactions. Many of these reactions produce a rise in temperature. Reactions which produce a rise in temperature are known as **exothermic** reactions.

The Thermit reaction, an example of an exothermic reaction, is used to repair cracked railway lines by producing a supply of molten iron (see page 141).

In addition to large amounts of heat energy, the Thermit reaction also produces light energy. The word equation for the Thermit reaction is:

aluminium + iron oxide → aluminium oxide + iron

19 Why do you think this reaction is called a displacement reaction?

This reaction is also known as a **competition** reaction. Displacement or competition reactions take place because of the relative positions of the metals involved in the reactivity series. The metals that are high in the series (more reactive) displace those that are low (less reactive).

20 Which element do you think the two metals are competing over?
21 Which metal is higher up the reactivity series? What evidence supports your answer?
22 Where else in science have you learnt about competition?

Reasoning ## Reactivity

On the planet Zarg there are three metals: atium, bedium and posium. They all form oxides.

1 What are the names of the three common metal oxides on Zarg? Hot, finely powdered atium will remove oxygen from bedium oxide. It will not displace oxygen from posium oxide.

2 Which is the most reactive metal? Explain why you think this.

Enquiry ## Reactivity series

This table shows the results of mixing metals and salt solutions. Different combinations of metals and salt solutions were mixed and the maximum temperature change was recorded each time.

Salt solution Metal	zinc nitrate	copper nitrate	silver nitrate
magnesium	1°C	3°C	4°C
iron	0°C	2°C	3°C

1 What will pupils see when these displacement reactions take place?

2 Suggest the order of reactivity based on these results.

3 One of these metals does not react with the metal nitrate. Which one is it and how did you decide?

4 Write word equations for the reactions recorded in the table.

5 You are asked to include aluminium and tin as well as magnesium and iron in your investigation. You will be provided with suitable salt solutions – iron nitrate, tin nitrate aluminium nitrate. How many possible combinations could you investigate? Compare your ideas with others in your group. Note how other people have different ways of deciding this.

Comparing handwarmers

Camping shops sell hand warmers – these are small packages which help to warm your hands in winter. They are bags containing chemicals, and when the chemicals mix and react they produce heat. Similar packs can be used to heat food. These are exothermic processes.

These are the three different combinations that are used:

* the **crystallisation** of **supersaturated** sodium acetate solution
* dissolving calcium chloride in water
* the reaction of calcium oxide with water to produce calcium hydroxide. This is known as the slaking of lime (it is used for producing hot coffee in a canister).

Key words
* crystallisation
* supersaturated
* quicklime
* slaked lime

23 Classify these combinations as either physical or chemical changes. Give as many reasons as you can.

24 A saturated solution is one in which no more solute (solid) will dissolve in a solvent (liquid) at a given temperature. What do you think is meant by the term 'supersaturated'?

The chemist Joseph Black worked at the same time as Lavoisier. He noted that when calcium oxide was absorbing water, it swelled and gave out heat. Black thought that the calcium *oxide* appeared to be alive, and so he called it **quicklime**.

Calcium *hydroxide* was called **slaked lime** because calcium oxide reacts vigorously with water to form it. Quicklime seems to be thirsty for water.

In 1787 Lavoisier suggested that scientists should agree names for chemicals because of this habit that they had of making up unusual names.

Word play

The old-fashioned meaning of quick is alive. Slaked is an old-fashioned word for absorbing water. Can you suggest why calcium oxide was called quicklime and calcium hydroxide was called slaked lime?

→ *Generating electricity using metals*

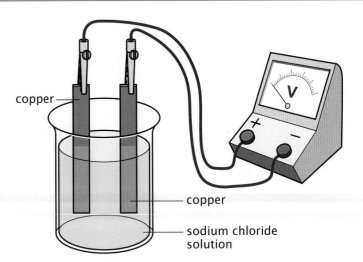

copper

copper

sodium chloride solution

Key words
* voltage
* electrolyte
* aqueous solutions
* electrodes

When two strips of the same metal (in this example, copper) are placed in a salt solution the voltmeter does not register any **voltage**. If one of the strips of copper is replaced with a different metal a reading registers on the voltmeter. The salt solution is called the **electrolyte** – any salt solution will work. The solvent in these solutions is water, and so the solutions are called **aqueous solutions**. An electrolyte is a chemical compound which conducts electricity and is split up by it. Strong acids and alkalis are also good electrolytes. The metal strips are the **electrodes**, which carry the electricity in and out of the electrolyte.

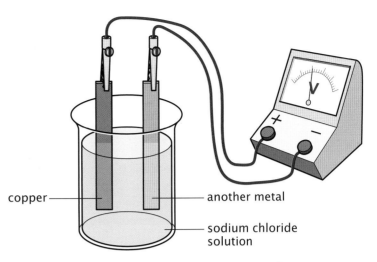

copper —
another metal
sodium chloride
solution

In this experiment, electricity has been generated.

Enquiry *Looking for patterns*

The experiment just described was repeated with a number of different pairs of metals, using sodium chloride solution as the electrolyte.

Electrode 1	Electrode 2	Voltage (V)
zinc	copper	1.1
iron	copper	0.78
lead	copper	0.47
magnesium	copper	2.71
magnesium	zinc	1.61
zinc	iron	0.32

1 What is the input (independent) variable?

2 What is the outcome (dependent) variable?

3 Which variable would you need to keep fixed?

4 Which pair of metals gives the highest voltage?

5 Put the metals used in descending order of reactivity.

6 What pattern do you notice in the voltage readings? Write down the relationship in your own words and then compare your answer with others. Do you agree? Select the best answer from your group and share this with the whole class.

7 What value for the voltage would you predict between:
a) iron and lead
b) magnesium and iron?
How did you decide this?

8 Why are metals used as electrodes?

9 Sometimes the non-metal carbon is used as an electrode. What property does carbon have that makes it a suitable electrode?

New electricity

In 1791, Luigi Galvani (1737–1798), an Italian anatomist, observed that a frog's legs violently contracted if a metal scalpel was touched to a certain leg nerve during dissection. In other experiments Galvani showed that contractions were produced if the frogs were placed on a metal plate with a brass hook on the nerve. These contractions were most obvious if two different metals were used. With non-conductors, the effects did not occur. He concluded that it was the muscles in the frog that contained the electricity.

Another scientist, Volta, disagreed with Galvani's conclusions. He had already developed very sensitive instruments for detecting electric charge (the electroscope), and did not detect any electric charge stored in animal tissue. Volta proved that when certain metals and chemicals come into contact they can produce an electrical current. He concluded that the contractions produced by Galvani depended on the presence of the direct contact between two different metals.

When Volta placed together several pairs of silver and zinc discs, separated by paper soaked in salt water, an electric current was produced. Volta had produced the first **battery**, which he called the voltaic pile.

Volta's work very quickly became known by other scientists, including William Nicholson and Anthony Carlisle, who went on to use these ideas to produce oxygen and hydrogen from the **electrolysis** of water.

Let's remind ourselves of how scientists go about their work.
1 Make observations or measurements
What observations did Galvani make?
2 Make up a cautious explanation, called a hypothesis, that fits with what you have observed
What was his hypothesis? What other conclusion could Galvani have reached about his work?
3 Use the hypothesis to make predictions
Imagine that you are Galvani. What prediction would you make if different muscle tissues were used?
4 Test those predictions by experiments or further observations, and modify/fine-tune the hypothesis in the light of your results
What further experiments did Galvani perform? Suggest further work that Galvani might have carried out to support his idea that the electricity was contained in the muscle tissue.
5 Check out the theory in other experiments
Volta repeated Galvani's experiments but with important improvements. What did Volta measure and how did this affect his conclusions? How did Volta use his electroscope?

1 Galvani noticed that non-metals did not produce the muscle twitching. Name some non-metals that he might have used.
2 Describe the key features of Volta's pile. What did Volta's pile develop into?
3 How did Volta's work help Nicholson and Carlisle?
4 Write a word equation for the electrolysis of water.

Word play Copy and complete the word puzzle below.

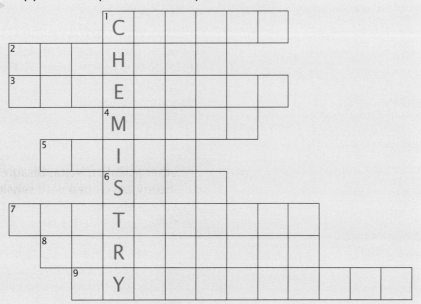

1 A non-metal that has some metallic properties.
2 The fuel from the gas tap.
3 Chemical that tests for CO_2.
4 A wooden stick with phosphorous on its end.
5 Formed when an element reacts with oxygen.
6 A metal compound.
7 A reaction that releases energy.
8 Explosives containing different powdered metal salts.
9 A fuel made from hydrogen and carbon.

EXTENSION
Now make your own word puzzle using the word COMPOUND.

→ *Using chemistry to make useful products*

Polymers

Chemists are continually making new substances. Half a million new chemicals have been developed since 1965 alone. Many of these have been different types of **plastics**. Plastics play a big part in our lives because they have special properties. Almost every product we buy, most of the food we eat, and many of the liquids we drink come covered in plastic.

Plastics are all manufactured materials called **polymers**. As well as the manufactured polymers there are some very important polymers which occur naturally in living organisms, such as proteins, starch, cellulose and DNA.

Key words
* plastics
* polymers
* synthesised
* monomers
* non-renewable
* biodegradeable
* renewable

25 What is the function of each of these important natural polymers?

All polymers are **synthesised** (made) by joining together thousands of small molecules called **monomers**. Each polymer is made from different monomers.

Monomer molecules	Polymer
nucleic acids	DNA
ethene (C_2H_4)	polyethene
propene (C_3H_6)	polypropene
glucose	starch
vinyl acetate	PVA

Word play

'Poly' means many. A *poly*mer is made from lots of smaller molecules bonded together.

   Make a list of words beginning with the prefix 'poly'. Write down their meanings

   'Mono' means one. Small molecules called *mono*mers join together to produce polymers.

   Make a list of words beginning with the prefix 'mono'. Write down their meanings.

26 Use the information in the text to construct a table of natural and synthetic polymers.

Natural polymers	Synthetic (manufactured) polymers
protein	polythene

Add to each column as many of your own examples as you can. The first one has been done for you. Compare your table with other pupils.

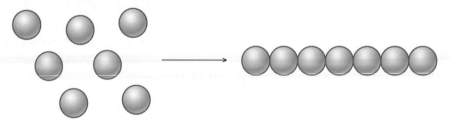

Monomers joining together to form a polymer.

27 Danny said that making a polymer is a bit like threading beads to make a necklace. Is this a useful model? Are there any other models that you could use to explain how polymers are made?

28 Copy and complete this table:

	Ethene	**Propene**
formula	C_2H_4	C_3H_6
total number of atoms in formula	6	
total number of elements in formula	2	
element or compound	compound	
atom or molecule	molecule	

The first manufactured plastic was made by Leo Hendrik Baekeland in 1907, and he called it Bakelite.

Radio with a Bakelite case.

Biodegradable plastics

Traditional plastics are manufactured from **non-renewable** resources – oil, coal and natural gas. Each year each person in the UK will use the energy equivalent of 3.5 tonnes of oil.

Packaging is the largest market for plastics, accounting for over a third of the consumption of raw plastic materials. Plastic packaging provides excellent protection for products. It is cheap to manufacture and seems to last forever. Lasting forever, however, is proving to be a major environmental problem. Plastics take a very long time to decompose.

In an attempt to solve this environmental problem scientists have been developing **biodegradable** plastics that are made from **renewable** resources, such as plants. The term biodegradable means that a substance can be broken down by the action of microbes, such as bacteria, and is therefore unlikely to remain for a long period of time in the environment. One type of biodegradable plastic has small amounts of starch added to the plastic, so that bacteria in the soil feed on the starch, causing the plastic to break down.

A biological reactor that converts a slurry of food waste into a biodegradable plastic has been developed by scientists in Hawaii. This provides a use for the large amount of food that more economically developed countries throw away every year. The greener packaging material created from recycling these items could be used to make disposable products such as bottles, or even pills that dissolve slowly to release drugs in the body.

29 What does 'biodegradable' mean?

30 A lot of plastic packaging is often unnecessary. Imagine that you are in charge of a newspaper campaign to persuade your local readers not to waste plastic. Prepare a leaflet and a full page advert to get your point of view across.

31 Why do you think 'greener packaging' is the name given to recycled materials?

Developing a starch-based biodegradable plastic

Type 1

Some biodegradable plastic bags are only partly biodegradable, and only 5–20% of the bag is starch. They consist of mainly non-biodegradable synthetic polymers, such as polyethene or polypropene. Under special conditions the starch degrades and the plastic falls apart into small particles, which will remain in the soil for many years although they are not visible.

Type 2

In other biodegradable plastics starch is used because it has similar properties to synthetic polymers. It is blended with synthetic polymers and contributes to the strength of the material. Some 50–80% starch can be used in these plastics. The starch part of the plastic can be degraded, but the rest of the bag material is not biodegradable.

Type 3

This plastic is completely biodegradable. All of it can be degraded biologically after use. It is made from pure starch.

EXTENSION

32 It has been suggested that biodegradable plastics are not as strong as non-biodegradable plastics. Design an investigation to test this.

33 Make a list of the properties of a plastic that make it suitable for producing carrier bags.

→ # Medicines

Key words
* clinical trials
* placebo

Medicines made from natural materials have been used for thousands of years. Many of them have been extracted from plants. The table shows some plants and their medicinal uses.

Plant extract	Used for
feverfew	migraine treatment
ginger	seasickness prevention
garlic	to lower blood pressure
Saint John's wort	antidepressant
ginseng	exercise performance enhancer
echinacea	immune system stimulant (upper respiratory infections)

With the onset of new and deadly diseases, scientists have to invent new drugs all the time. A drug has to be thoroughly tested before it can be used. This testing involves:

- millions of pounds in costs
- years of research
- the use of **clinical trials**.

What is a clinical trial?

Scientists have made great progress in discovering ways to prevent, screen for, and treat cancer. The key feature of these discoveries is the clinical trial – a carefully designed study for evaluating the drug. No new cancer treatment can be made available unless it has undergone careful testing through clinical trials to test that it is safe and effective.

How a clinical trial works

Each trial is designed to test a particular treatment on a specific type of cancer. The trial might be designed to test whether the new treatment makes people feel better, or if it shrinks the cancer growth or stops the cancer from spreading. Each clinical trial can take many years to organise and carry out. It involves several steps known as 'phases':

Phase 1
This first study evaluates the drug's safety and determines how best to give it to the patient, such as how much to give, how often, and by what means (i.e. injection, orally).

Phase 2
This next step continues to test the drug's safety and begins to evaluate how well patients respond to it.

Phase 3
This stage of the study expands the testing to include a larger number of patients and to compare the new drug with treatments already available to see if it produces better results. Cancer trials are different from the clinical trials of other drugs in that cancer patients are never given a **placebo** if a standard treatment is available. A placebo is a substitute that looks, feels and smells like the drug under review, but it has no real effect.

Phase 4
This final step takes place after the drug has received government approval outside the experimental setting. The purpose of this study is to monitor the drug for long-term effectiveness and side effects.

34 What is a placebo?
35 A scientist might explain a placebo as a 'control'. Why can it be a control in a clinical trial?

36 Why do you think that placebos are not used during cancer trials?

37 Use a table to summarise the main activities during each phase of a clinical trial for cancer.

38 During phase 2 of a clinical trial for a treatment for eczema the doctors noticed significant improvements to those patients receiving the trial cream. One consultant suggested that *all* the patients should be given the new cream. Another consultant wants phase 3 of the clinical trial to be done first, and suggests delaying giving the cream to all eczema patients. You have to make the decision. Discuss this dilemma in your groups. What do you decide?

Time to think

1 Make up a useful revision question for each of the words listed below. Test a partner to see if he or she knows the answer. Agree on the best question for each answer and make a loop game for the words.

- displacement
- oxidation
- exothermic
- synthesis
- reactants
- products
- molecules
- element
- compound

2 Look back through the chapter and write out the word equations for all the key chemical reactions that have been discussed. Annotate each word equation with the words from the list above. Produce a poster, concept map or set of cards to help with your revision.

3 Scientists are always looking to use chemical reactions in new and useful ways. Explain how scientists have used chemical reactions in the following examples;

- fuel cells
- batteries
- plastics.

Index